Verer b...♡ **W9-AQD-112**

Happer Birthday, Louise,

& Cariño siempre —

Bonnie Sue

The Gardener's Essential Companion

Proven Advice and Lively Information to Help You Garden Smarter, Not Harder

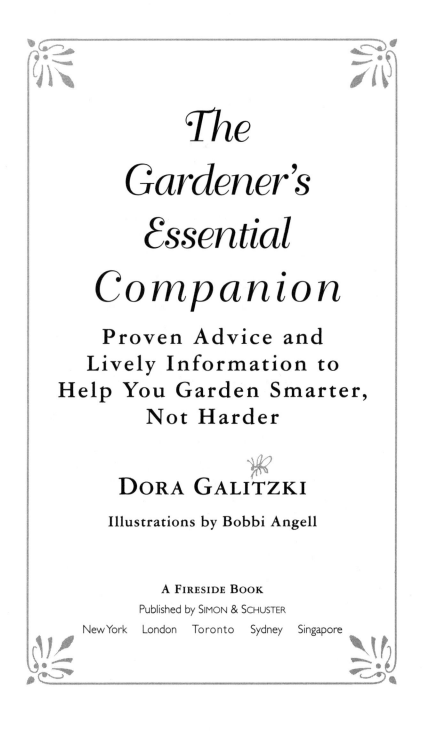

DORA GALITZKI

Illustrations by Bobbi Angell

A FIRESIDE BOOK

Published by SIMON & SCHUSTER

New York   London   Toronto   Sydney   Singapore

FIRESIDE
Rockefeller Center
1230 Avenue of the Americas
New York, NY 10020

FIRESIDE and colophon are registered trademarks
of Simon & Schuster, Inc.

Designed by Ruth Lee

Manufactured in the United States of America

1   3   5   7   9   10   8   6   4   2

Library of Congress Cataloging-in-Publication Data
Galitzki, Dora.
    The gardener's essential companion / proven advice and lively
    information to help you garden smarter, not harder / Dora Galitzki ;
    illustrations by Bobbi Angell.
        p.   cm.
    "A Fireside book."
    Includes index.
    1. Gardening—Miscellanea.   I. Title
    SB453 .G228 2000
    635—dc21   99-055316
        ISBN 0-684-86321-9

Contents

Contents

SECTION 3
Nature and the City

Acknowledgments

It's simple. I don't know everything. Sprinkled everywhere in this book, you will see the names of people throughout the horticultural world—at universities, cooperative extension services (the wonderful county-by-county state university–run offices dedicated to helping professionals and amateurs solve their horticultural questions), botanical gardens, government research facilities, growers, breeders, nurserymen, and seedsmen. To them, and to the plants they love, I am deeply indebted. Plants and people alike have been patient and willing to share their knowledge every time I have called on them.

These men and women, who devote their lives to learning more about plants, and to sharing that information, are too numerous to list individually, but whenever you read a name in one of the answers, please remember that he or she stopped work for a moment (more likely for a lot of moments) to help me. I thank them. And if you follow their advice, so will your plants.

A few people really have to be named here. The people at *The*

New York Times provided me with a place to write about horticulture and have frequently made my writing better. I am indebted to Barbara Graustark, editor of the Home/Style Department, who has given me the freedom to write as I wish; Martha Wilson, my immediate editor, who has taken turns at holding my hand and pushing me further; the staff at the copy desk, who must have struggled at times to make my writing fit the *Times*'s requirements for clarity, concision, and style; and Ann Raver, who started it all.

To the plant kingdom.
And to Jan.

Introduction

Gardening books mostly fall into one of two categories: the how-to's, filled with techniques, plant lists, and basic information, and the picture books, dedicated to some category of plants, like perennials, or to a meticulously designed garden that requires a crew of twenty.

Gardeners require both. The how-to's are necessary because no matter how much we learn on our own—and trial and error combined with interested observation does teach a lot—there is always more to learn: more plants and better ways to grow them. The picture books provide a valuable service when they introduce us to plants and combinations we haven't seen before. If only some of them showed a few Japanese beetle–damaged leaves, a bit of powdery mildew, and a couple of overgrown shrubs, they would provide a truer picture and lead to a bit less frustration with our own gardens. This book crosses boundaries. It covers cultural information at beginning and advanced levels and introduces a broader range of plants than you will typically find in your local garden center.

I hope you can use the book in three ways: to look up answers to specific problems and obtain the cultural information you need, to browse around and find new ideas for your indoor and outdoor gardening, and to take a bit of comfort in knowing that everyone else is facing the same problems, or worse ones, as you, that gardens should provide more pleasure than pain, and that attitude is everything.

Don't get me wrong. I love plants, gardens, and everything about them. It's just that, finally, I have decided the two best times of the year are the winter seed catalog time and the first killing frost in the fall, when I can finally put the garden to bed for another year. In between, I have to fight to make it work, just like you do.

What you are holding in your hands are answers to the most useful, most important, most interesting questions that I have addressed in *The New York Times* since I began writing my column in 1995. The human side of the equation seems to change faster than the plant side, and some people have moved on to other positions or have left academia for the full-time pleasures of their gardens. Inevitably, some phone numbers may have changed, and some companies may now be part of other companies. But plants, their joys and their problems, remain constant, and the horticultural information, updated as necessary, is accurate.

When Nature Goes Crazy

Ah, nature. Since a garden is an attempt to impose our human sense of order and beauty on nature, it is also the perfect place to discover what a ridiculous idea that really is. The infinite web that connects everything is broken at our own peril, and the unforeseen consequences of our actions add to the daily battles of the gardener. Bring in an interesting plant that is not native to the area, and you run the risk of another kudzu or bamboo running amok because its natural enemies are no longer around to keep it in check. Start a vegetable garden in the suburbs and discover just how many deer and woodchucks are still around.

It isn't that nature conspires against gardeners; it's just that we ignore how deeply entangled everything is with everything else. Control one problem in one place, and, like squeezing a balloon, another problem seems to pop up somewhere else.

Having gardened now for more than thirty years in one place or another, I am finally coming to peace with it all. I don't bank on winning the war through brute force and chemicals, and

I take pleasure from winning the small battles by being smarter than the pests, picking the right plants for the spot and helping nature work for me.

But always, there are two things going on in the garden. First, the dinner bell is always ringing for someone (although generally not for the gardener). And second, what the critters don't get, the weather might.

1

Animal Appetites

We would like to think that a garden is composed of magnificent plants in a pleasing arrangement, perhaps complemented by stone or brick, wood and water—the way they are in photographs in coffee table books. But they are not. Real gardens are composed of plants, of course, but also insects, viruses, mice, deer, and woodchucks. As beautiful as a plant may be, something would like to eat it, infect it, or curl its leaves up for shelter. Far from gentle Edens, gardens are small jungles, with battles happening everywhere, just out of sight. We see the results: chewed leaves, keeled-over tender transplants, stunted growth, gnawed stems, and trunks with neat patterns of holes.

But it's not all one-sided. Plants have their defenses, and every predator faces enemies. It is fair, or at least even-handed, in the larger scheme of nature, but to the gardener it sometimes feels like a very personal attack. Somehow it's all a little less overwhelming when you realize that every gardener faces a similar cast of characters.

Spruce Spider Mites

*When the needles on your spruce are flecked with a yellow-tan color
or completely turning brown, your spruce is being attacked by spruce
spider mites. Whether to treat them in spring or summer can be confusing.*

Mites are usually associated with hot and dry conditions, but
some, including southern red mites (which attack holly, azalea,
and rhododendron) and spruce spider mites (which attack spruce,
hemlock, pine, and arborvitae), are active in cool seasons.

Spruce spider mites feed on older needles and reproduce during spring and fall. They take the summer off. If left untreated,
they can cause serious injury.

Rayanne Lehman, an entomologist at the Pennsylvania Agriculture Department in Harrisburg, says that mite eggs spend the
winter at the base of needles and on the bark of branches. Eggs
can be controlled from late winter until the time the buds break
by using a dormant-season dilution (this will be listed on the
label) of a horticultural oil spray whenever the temperature is
above 50 degrees. Thorough coverage is necessary because the oil
works by smothering.

After bud break in the spring, take a spraying break. Very
young foliage should not be sprayed. Use a summer dilution if
more spraying is needed later in the season.

If you have a Colorado blue spruce, be aware that it is sensitive to dormant oil and may lose its blue-green color for two years
while new needles grow.

Mite populations should be checked every two weeks during
spring and fall by rapping three times on four branches spaced
evenly around the tree to drop mites onto white paper. Watch for
what look like dark, crawling pepper grains; if you see ten, take
action. But also keep an eye out for fast-moving, light tan

mites—predators that feed on the spruce spider mites. If the predator population rises and the spruce spider mite population decreases, treatment may not be necessary.

Destructive Woodpeckers?

Woodpeckers are beautiful birds, but hearing one hard at work in your yard or seeing the resulting holes is not one of the joys of nature; it is a cause for concern.

Woodpeckers and their cousins, the sapsuckers, drum on trees, posts, and sometimes houses for three reasons: food, shelter, and conversation. Sometimes they are busy for all three of these reasons. A male might be looking for a mate and warning other woodpeckers that this is his territory—sort of like that loud guy at the other end of the bar.

Following the age-old truth that if you're good at something, you should do it often, woodpeckers use their drilling skills to make cavities in trees rather than living in nests. Digging a big hole isn't much different from digging a small one; it just takes longer. The nice thing about nests is that they are built quietly.

Mostly, though, woodpeckers drill to eat, looking for insects that are living under the bark or in the wood. Sapsuckers are a bit more sophisticated. They drill a horizontal row of holes, which fill with sap. The sweet sap attracts insects, which become tangled in the stickiness and are then easy prey for the sapsucker.

Try to note which tree your woodpeckers are concentrating on for food or shelter. Nature doesn't make any dummies; woodpeckers pick on stressed trees that are infested with insects or have some other problem. It is unlikely that a woodpecker could kill a tree, since the holes it makes do not girdle the trunk, which would completely sever the vascular channels for water and food.

Any tree with that much interest for a woodpecker is already in trouble for other reasons.

Take the drumming as an alarm, and try to alleviate the problem. It isn't the woodpecker's fault, but the messenger is traditionally blamed for the message. In this case, the message is being delivered loud and clear.

Beetle Identification

Asian beetles, which have caused so much damage already in Brooklyn, are in danger of spreading throughout the New York area and beyond. But one bug that frequently causes alarm among homeowners is ³/₄ of an inch long and brown with a zigzag white stripe on its back. Seen them? Relax.

Most likely it's a western conifer seed bug, which likes to come indoors for the winter, moving from nearby needled evergreens. In the spring, it heads back out to feed on developing seeds and early flowers, creating a little excitement as it buzzes around trying to find an exit. It is just a nuisance.

Asian long-horned beetles, on the other hand, cause a great deal of harm. This recently discovered beetle kills trees. The key identifying characteristics are their black and white antennae, which can be more than twice the length of this 1¹/₂-inch beetle itself, and the black body with white spots.

If you suspect you have found an Asian long-horned beetle, immediately contact the New York State Department of Agriculture and Markets at (516) 288-1751 or (800) 554-4501, ext. 72087. If you live outside of New York, contact your state's Agriculture Department. It's a good idea to be on the lookout because so far, this insect has no natural enemies in the United States.

Tent Caterpillars

April not only brings spring; it also brings the tent-like cocoons that house the larvae of eastern tent caterpillars.

Among tree defoliators, only the gypsy moth can rival the eastern tent caterpillar. Although they prefer apple, crabapple, and wild cherry, eastern tent caterpillars also attack other popular deciduous trees, including ash, birch, maple, willow, oak, cherry, peach, and plum.

As the cocoons get larger and more obvious, and more ominous, gardeners begin striking back, but not always in the best ways. Burning them or dropping them into kerosene is a common method of control, but there are better approaches. Tent caterpillars can be controlled at several stages. Before they emerge in April, remove the distinctive egg masses, which are ³/₄ inch long and appear varnished black, encircling smaller twigs. After emergence, they gather at the branch crotches and begin to create their protective tents.

On rainy, cool days the caterpillars stay inside, so those are the best days for pulling the tents, occupants and all, into a bucket of soapy water, eliminating the problem of disposing of the contaminated kerosene. If you prefer, you can open the webs on inclement days and spray *Bacillus thuringiensis* (Bt), which attacks and kills young caterpillars. On days that they are out feeding, a drenching spray of insecticidal soap can provide acceptable control.

Advice on Applying Bt

I once told a reader that Bt, a product derived from the bacteria *Bacillus thuringiensis,* would be effective against eastern tent caterpillars if home owners drenched the caterpillars when they were out feeding or if they opened the tentlike nest and sprayed directly inside.

If caterpillar larvae were like baby birds and always had their heads turned up and their mouths open and waiting for food, this might actually work. Unfortunately, caterpillars are busy doing other caterpillar things inside their tents, and as a reader was kind enough to remind me, Bt has to be ingested. It does not work on contact the way insecticidal soap, horticultural oil, or most chemical insecticides do.

George Soares, the director of commercial development for international markets at Mycogen, a producer of Bt products, says that what we buy and use isn't actually the bacteria but rather a crystalline form of a protein that the bacteria produce. When it is sprayed on foliage and the caterpillars eat it, the crystals dissolve in the stomach and become toxic. The products are referred to as Bt, but the bacteria themselves remain at the factory, making more proteins.

Timing is important with Bt. It is most effective against the youngest caterpillars—those in the first two instars, or stages of life. Apply Bt as soon as there are young larvae actively feeding on the tree or shrub, which will be before the tents become large. Spray thoroughly, covering the top and bottom surfaces of leaves. But don't be surprised to see some caterpillars still on the branches two or three days later. Bt can take a few days to kill the caterpillars, but it prevents them from eating almost as soon as they ingest it.

When sprayed on foliage, Bt has a residual effect for up to one week, although bright sun can break it down and heavy rains can wash it off.

Summer Spraying

Using horticultural oil can be frustrating when the insects return after just a few weeks. Caution with chemicals is always appropriate, but the new fine horticultural oils can be applied more than once without burning the leaves on your shrubs.

As long as you follow label directions and use the summer dilution rate, 1 percent or 2 percent, rather than the dormant rate of 3 percent or 4 percent, your shrubs should not have a problem. Since horticultural oil kills by smothering and does not have any residual effect once it dries, you have to spray when the insects are in an active stage of life. That may mean two or three times during the season, but recent studies at the University of Maryland have shown little or no damage from up to four sprayings with the newer, highly refined oils.

Many people believe that applying oil in full sun risks damaging the leaves, but the opposite is true. Applying it on cloudy or humid days lengthens the time it takes the oil to dry, preventing leaf transpiration—the leaf's ability to transport nutrients—and increasing the possibility of damage.

Sap-Sucking Squirrels

Squirrels are always a little nuts, but occasionally they seem to go overboard. For no apparent reason, oaks are attacked, with dozens or hundreds of branch tips chewed off and tossed on the ground. But, as always, nature has a reason.

Tree sap is very nutritious, but the trees prefer to keep it inside, where it belongs. Hungry squirrels simply chew off a few inches of the terminal end of branches, suck the sap that oozes out, and drop the remaining twig. Sort of like piling empty crab legs on the plate.

Mark McDonnell, the director of the University of Connecti-

cut Bartlett Arboretum in Stamford, says this is primarily an
urban phenomenon, probably due to squirrel population density
and the limited spring food supply. In addition to oaks, maples
are often on the menu. It is unlikely that permanent damage will
result. Think of it as a very efficient pruning job.

One, Two, Three, Twitch!

*Bugs can be downright entertaining, if you forget that they some-
times damage your plants. Pine trees attract an especially interesting pest. In groups of twenty or thirty scattered around the tree,
green caterpillars with white heads suddenly quit chomping away
at the needles and, as if they were part of a single organism, twitch.
The whole tree seems to be moving, which is cute, until you remember
that they don't belong in your trees.*

From the time they hatch in mid-April and May, until they
molt in June or July, the larvae of the European pine sawfly hang
out together, eating the older needles on many species of pine, especially Scotch, mugho, and Swiss mountain. Unlike many
spring insects that feed on tender new growth, sawflies eat older
growth, and have finished by the time new needles expand, resulting in trees with bushy new growth on otherwise bare
branches. Sawflies cannot kill a tree, but they can weaken it.

The ³/₄-inch-long larvae can be identified by their black
heads, green body stripes, and eight pairs of yellow-green prolegs
attached to the abdomen. The twitching is the giveaway. When
they are disturbed, the group reacts together, turning both ends
up and holding on in the middle, looking for all the world like a
well-rehearsed conga line.

Sawflies can be controlled by several methods, depending on
your gardening philosophy. Hanging out in large groups may improve the individual's chances when it comes to most predators,

but it makes it easier for gardeners to pick them off branches and drown them in soapy water. Spraying with insecticidal soap is effective; read the label for dilution rates and directions. Chemical insecticides can also be used, but *Bacillus thuringiensis* (Bt), the natural gardener's favorite, is not effective because the larvae are not true caterpillars.

Clouds and Silver Linings

You have to hand it to Mother Nature. No matter what the weather, for every creature that suffers, another benefits. Consider these examples:

Mild periods during the winter make life easier for humans, but some insects have to draw unexpectedly on their internal supply of stored nutrients, making it harder for them to survive the rest of the winter.

Has the summer been too hot for you to move? Spruce spider mites also relax in hot weather and don't become active and start eating again until the cooler fall and spring. On the other hand, two-spotted spider mites (that is, spider mites with two spots each) go into overdrive when it gets above 85 degrees, being born, growing up, and starting families within a week.

During a wonderful spring, do you love to see all that lush new growth? Well, so do aphids and other sucking insects. After all, that new growth is nice and tender.

In periods of drought, plants conserve energy partly by cutting their defense budgets, producing fewer toxic chemicals that repel their natural enemies. They become more susceptible to insect attack, but better to suffer a little insect damage than to become a drought casualty.

Rainy summers also bring the good with the bad. Fungus

diseases spread quickly, but aphids and mites get washed away in heavy rains. Japanese beetles have trouble flying on rainy days, but well-irrigated lawns are a great place to lay eggs.

The left hand of Mother Nature gives the world wonderful gardens to enjoy, while the right hand is ringing the dinner bell.

Garden Buddies

Many gardeners want to take advantage of bugs that eat other bugs, and use one to protect their garden against another. Ladybugs in particular have a reputation for eating aphids in great numbers. One problem that holds many gardeners back is that the hired guns brought in for the job may not stay forever.

If we had the ability to see the take-no-prisoners warfare that goes on in our gardens, we would realize they are hardly little patches of Eden. That there are any leaves left at all by September reminds us that the bugs that eat also get eaten.

The various insects, bacteria, and fungi that dine on plants' enemies are grouped together under the term "beneficials," although they sure don't do it with any thought of helping the gardener out.

Whether bringing in mercenaries or encouraging home-grown critters, the principles are the same: try to create an environment where they can thrive. Michael Raupp, the chairman of the entomology department at the University of Maryland in College Park, says that two simple steps will turn any garden into a place ladybugs, lacewings, spiders, or big-eyed bugs would be pleased to call home.

First, quit dousing everything in sight with broad-spectrum insecticides. Spot treat instead, applying the right product (especially the less toxic horticultural oils and insecticidal soaps) only on badly infested plants. If damage is minimal, avoid spraying.

One-size-fits-all insecticides kill good bugs as well as bad. Spraying everything eliminates hiding places where beneficials can wait out the storm, perhaps finding someone else to eat in the meantime.

Second, increase the diversity of plants. At one stage in their life cycle, beneficials may eat your aphids, but at another stage they may need nectar or pollen. Biodiversity provides the good guys with a change of diet as prey populations decline.

Introducing beneficials into greenhouses has been successful, but there have not been enough controlled studies done outdoors to really know. But Raupp suggests you go ahead and buy the ladybugs. If they don't come back next year, at least you will avoid chemicals this year. Besides, even if they aren't in your garden, they're somewhere nearby, dining on the bad guys.

For a free copy of "Suppliers of Beneficial Organisms of North America," write to the California Environmental Protection Agency, Department of Pesticide Regulation, Environmental Monitoring and Pest Management, 1020 N Street, Room 161, Sacramento, CA 95814-5624.

Besieged Hemlock

Hemlocks with little clumps of white dots along their branches are hemlocks in trouble. Occasionally misdiagnosed as a fungus, these dots are really a particular insect's eggs. Indiscriminate spraying, no matter what with, won't do the job fully. Sometimes the white spots return just a couple of weeks later; sometimes they don't seem to go away at all. As always with gardening, it pays to know what you are dealing with and to have an effective plan for attacking the problem.

Hemlock wooly adelgid is a voracious pest that can kill hemlocks in a few years if it is not treated. Those white dots are a protective waxy substance the insect uses to protect itself and its eggs. If you were thorough in your spraying, the eggs and insects are most likely dead, but the waxy mass can persist for months.

There are two generations each year, so even though you should spray all parts of the tree with horticultural oil or insecticidal soap as soon as you see them, get into a regular schedule of spraying once sometime between April and late June and again in September to catch both generations when they are most vulnerable. Household soaps are lye based, and can damage young growth. Be sure to use insecticidal soap, which is fatty-acid based instead.

Maple Galls

Icicles on your sugar maple's leaves? Little green projections that eventually turn reddish occasionally show up, sticking straight up from the leaf surface. Some years there are more than others, but, few or many, they are so peculiar that they worry tree owners. Inevitably, gardeners are afraid that these are a sign of imminent danger.

These growths are not a disease or harmful. They are maple spindle galls, the equivalent of a condo with a restaurant on the ground floor. Several species of microscopic four-legged creatures called eriophyid mites feed on the leaf tissue. At the same time they inject into the leaf a growth-regulating substance. This chemical causes the leaf to grow the galls, making a home for the mite. Spindle galls may be as much as $1/2$ inch long and are very thin, like misshapen pencil leads. They stand straight up and turn from green to red to black over the season. Other shapes of galls, such as beadlike swellings or flat, felty patches, are caused by other species of gall mites on other kinds of maples, like silver, red, or Norway.

Mites that entomologists call special females begin the process. After the mite spends the winter under bark scales on the trunk or branch, it settles down on a nearby leaf and begins to feed. Once the gall is complete, the mite stays inside and may produce several generations over the summer.

By late summer, with the young mites refusing to move out and the summer's mess piling up, a new generation of special females leaves through an opening on the lower surface and looks for some peace and quiet under a bark scale. Once the rest of the mites discover that there's no one to cook and clean, they desert the galls and die. The galls become dark brown or black, looking like a summer rental on Labor Day.

Spittlebugs

Walk into the garden on a sunny morning and you might notice the sun shining off a white, frothy glob of something along the stems of some of your plants. Gone within a few days, it then returns.

When your garden looks as if someone has been drooling on the plants, spittlebug, a sucking insect, has announced its presence.

During the immature stage of the spittlebug's life, it feeds on plant sap and produces a frothy white mass along the stem or where the leaves join the stem. The spittlebug coats and surrounds itself with a drop of fluid made from undigested plant sap and a binding material produced by its abdominal glands.

The foam, which comes from mixing in air, much as an immature human does with a glass of milk and a straw, serves two purposes. It keeps the tender insect moist, and it provides protection by hiding a small insect in a large disguise. The coating makes the bugs hard to wash away, or even know exactly where they are or how many there are, since the frothy masses can run together.

Spittlebugs usually cause little real damage, except on pines and other conifers, where severe infestations can be trouble.

Using Nematodes

Few insects arouse our ire quicker than Japanese beetles. Gardening catalogs, especially "organic friendly" catalogs, promote nematodes as a natural control product for Japanese beetles. Biology at that specific a level isn't part of our schooling, so it is normal to wonder just how a tiny wormlike creature can catch, let alone eat, a flying beetle.

I'm tempted to say the early worm catches the . . .

Nematodes, tiny roundworms in the genera *Steinernema* and *Heterorhabditis,* are no more than $1/20$ of an inch long, but they are truly big-game hunters. Some species actively hunt for prey; others wait around to jump on a favorite pest as it passes by. The nematode enters its host through a body opening and releases bacteria with which it has a symbiotic relationship. The bacteria multiply and poison the host within two or three days.

Nematodes are used to control lawn pests during their larval stages, among them chafers, armyworms, and cutworms; various beetles; the borers that attack peach and dogwood trees; and the black vine weevils that attack rhododendron.

Although they may sound like the perfect gardening assistant, nematodes can be cranky. For one thing, they are fussy eaters, so you have to match the nematode to the pest. Knowing what pest you have is the key to buying and applying the right nematode at the right time. Some nematodes stay near the surface; others burrow down about 4 inches deep.

Because they live in the film of water between soil particles, nematodes will die if the soil gets too dry. They prefer soil temperatures of at least 75 degrees and are very sensitive to ultraviolet light.

To treat lawn problems, including Japanese beetle larvae, mix the nematodes with water according to the instructions, and apply them late or early in the day, when temperatures, drying winds, and light are reduced. Make sure that you put down at least ³/₄ inch water just before or after applying the nematodes so they can move through the soil.

If it sounds as if you have to be prepared to treat nematodes with the same care you would any other household pet, you do. They'll be out there after your garden and lawn pests just as long as you are willing to see to their needs.

Sources for nematodes include The Bug Store, 113 West Argonne Avenue, Kirkwood, MO 63122, (800) 455-2847, catalog; and Gardens Alive, 5100 Schenley Place, Lawrenceburg, IN 47025, (812) 537-8650, catalog.

Privet Problems

Old privet hedges can become quite a sight. Sparsely leaved branches and older dead or dying branches can turn the hedge into a pathetic sight. Sometimes it's a matter of poor maintenance—usually incorrect pruning. When that isn't the reason, it's time to look elsewhere.

My suspicion is that the hedge is being attacked by white prunicola scale, a small insect that also feeds on lilacs and ornamental cherries and plums. During mid-July, the insect is in its egg stage. Look carefully at the stems and branches, and you should see crusty, dirty gray-brown patches. The eggs provide protection, but when the insects hatch into the crawler stage, from late July to mid-August, they are vulnerable. Spraying them with horticultural oil (follow the label instructions carefully) should help.

Privet is most commonly sold in bundles of bare-root plants early in the spring. Ask your garden center to call you when they arrive.

Sticky Attack

Out wandering among your birch trees one morning, you discover a neat row of holes nearly girdling the trees. Small boys with swords? A coded message from the great beyond? No, it's those woodpecker relatives, sapsuckers.

Your birches are a busy place. The yellow-bellied sapsucker uses them not only for food but also for communicating with other birds in the surrounding area. But the sapsuckers aren't killing the trees, because those neat little rows of holes they drill, sometimes horizontal and sometimes vertical, do not cut off much of the supply of nutrients and water flowing up and down the tree's vascular system. When they rap for communication, they hold their beaks in a way that doesn't injure the tree. The cause of the decline may be birch borer or another problem, but the sapsucker's interest is just coincidence.

Sapsuckers especially like birch and apple trees, but they use more than 275 species of trees, shrubs, and even vines as a place to obtain a one-stop balanced diet. When they find a tree to their liking, they may return to it year after year. Unlike their woodpecker cousins, sapsuckers are not attracted to stressed trees and are not looking for insects under the bark. They simply find the soft inner bark and the sap nutritious, and when the holes fill, the sap attracts and traps insects. When the bird returns after doing whatever it is that birds do between meals, there is a bonus of a little extra protein.

It is possible to discourage the attack, depending on the size of the tree and your climbing ability. Sapsuckers are migratory birds, and they make their tree choices when they arrive, from late March through April. Individual trees can be covered with light plastic netting, although that is usually done only for commercial fruit and nut trees. The visual effect of a tall birch covered in net, swaying mysteriously in the evening breeze, may be somewhat disconcerting. Besides, the birds are beautiful and the damage isn't serious, so why not just relax and get out your binoculars?

Cicada Killers

August brings not just the height of summer but also an insect with a peculiar habit that can be very annoying. Using its large, powerful jaws it digs holes all about, especially in the dirt-filled spaces between patio stones and driveway paving blocks. They never, or almost never, attack people, but they can be destructive in their own way, causing a mess.

They are big, they are ugly, and they are threatening, but mostly they are harmless. These 1¼-inch wasps, called cicada killers, give their young a good start in life by burying a paralyzed cicada with each egg. The wasps are easily identifiable by their yellow abdominal markings, rust-colored head and thorax, and amber-yellow wings. Females can sting but normally have to be provoked. Males do not sting, but, as usual, are aggressive and territorial.

These wasps prefer bare soil, sandy areas, or lawns where they dig deep burrows 3 or 4 feet long, leaving small antechambers along the way for eggs. When the eggs hatch, the larvae feed on the cicada, spin a cocoon, and overwinter. The adults emerge in July and August, and repeat the cycle, annoying home owners and golfers (sand traps are a common nesting area).

Since they are around for only a month or so, live and let live is the best policy. If they have really outworn their welcome, a layer of metal window screening buried an inch or two below the surface between the rocks will discourage them, but they may just find another spot nearby.

Squirrel Invasion

For wildlife, squirrels are pretty entertaining. While these clowns are welcomed into the garden by many people, others resent their habit of digging up plants. Old gardener's recipes for keeping them away include sprinkling crushed pepper or mothballs around or in prized potted plants. Apparently squirrels don't read the old recipes, which rarely work for long. If they are driving you crazy, try to put yourself in their place to understand the problem.

The most likely explanation for a squirrel invasion is that either they are using your pots as a larder for burying nuts or they think they have. Squirrels are tough, stubborn, and smart, although they don't always remember where they put things.

Mothballs don't work, and you would have to put an awful lot of pepper down before any self-respecting squirrel would find it offensive. There is a possible home remedy, although it may be worse than the problem. A test by Paul Curtis of the Department of Natural Resources at Cornell University, in Ithaca, New York, showed that woodchucks stayed out of a cabbage patch when a strand of rope surrounding the garden was strung every 3 feet with cloth strips that were sprayed once a month with bobcat urine, hanging down around nose height.

It has to be a leap of faith, but since squirrels and woodchucks are both rodents, and both are the bane of gardeners, maybe it would also work on squirrels. Bobcat, fox, and other predator urine is rather pungent, and a terrace may be too close to an open window or a neighbor, but when gardeners fight squirrels or woodchucks, grasping at straws is an old tradition.

Bobcat urine is available from M&M Fur Company, Box 15, Bridgewater, SD 57319, (605) 729-2535. Fox urine is available from Turkey Creek Furs, 841 West 11th Street, Crete, NE 68333, (402) 826-2516.

Cicada Reminders

By midsummer of 1996, trees in the New York area and other places looked like they were under attack. Branch tips all over the trees were filled with browning leaves and every tree seemed to be dying. Thoughts of mysterious diseases occurred to passers-by, but then the destruction stopped.

The damage was done, but expect to see it again in 2013, the next time the seventeen-year cicadas are due to emerge in the Northeast. Fortunately, the damage is not fatal.

After spending their lives quietly underground, the nymphs emerged from the ground this summer, climbed into trees, and became adults. The males sang while the females deposited eggs in slits they made in the branch tips, where the wood was fresh and soft enough for them to cut into. This kills the branch tips. After a month or so, the eggs hatch, and the larvae drop to the ground and dig in for a new seventeen-year cycle. (They probably stay buried so long because they are embarrassed by the mess their mothers made.)

The Good Earthworm

Are you a friend of earthworms? Do you ever wonder whether they are doing someone, somewhere some good?

Earthworms help decompose plant material, improve the structure of the soil, and make nutrients more easily available to plants. Their tunnels, which may extend 3 to 4 feet down, improve drainage and help the movement of oxygen and carbon dioxide in the root zone. This soil aeration accelerates microbial action, which speeds the breakdown of pesticides.

By all means, stand up for earthworms.

Euonymus Scale

Scruffy, white scales on euonymus twigs and stems are a sign of trouble. The insect that forms the scales is susceptible to treatment with horticultural oil, but sometimes it seems as if the treatment doesn't work.

Euonymus scale is a miserable insect because it is both dangerous (to euonymus, pachysandra, ivy, and others) and well protected inside its hard cover. Since heavy infestations can kill euonymus, especially when repeated over several years, it is important to watch for the signs of scale: yellowing leaves that drop off, twigs that die back, and the tell-tale white or brown scale covers on stems and along leaf veins; or better yet, plant resistant varieties.

Scale insects should be treated with horticultural oil in early to mid-April, while they are waking up from overwintering inside their armor; in early June, while they are in the crawler stage; and in mid-July, when the season's second generation is out crawling. Use the oil only at these times, when the insect is vulnerable. Horticultural oil kills by smothering and has no residual effect.

It is difficult to tell when scale insects are really dead. No tiny bodies pile up at the base of the shrub, and the scale cover remains stubbornly attached long after the insect inside is history. Rub a scale or two with your thumbnail two weeks after spraying. If no liquid squeezes out, the insect inside has died and dried up.

A Crocus Mice Won't Eat

When a mouse is hungry during the winter, it looks undeground for a favorite treat—crocus.

Mice seem to love all crocus except *Crocus tommasinianus.*

Other crocus can be protected using a method found successful by Joe Eck and Wayne Winterrowd of North Hill Garden Design Associates in Readsboro, Vermont.

Fill an old plastic nursery container (2-gallon size or larger) with an equal mix of compost and sand until only 6 inches remains. Place the crocus corms so that they are only a corm-width apart, and finish filling with the mixture to the top of the container. Fold hardware cloth (a stiff wire mesh) tightly around the rim. Dig a hole deep enough so that the container is 2 inches below the surrounding soil level. Place the container in the hole; then fill it with soil until level. The crocus will come up through the wire mesh and will be protected against marauders. Winterrowd and Eck have found that planting crocus this deep slows their multiplication, so they do not have to be reset as frequently.

If you don't like the crocus where they are, it is easy to lift the can and replant it without disturbing the corms. It's also easy to create larger drifts by planting several containers in an area. If you don't want to go to the effort of planting in containers, try planting bulbs that mice, chipmunks, squirrels, and voles don't like: allium, *Anemone blanda,* chionodoxa, daffodils, fritillaria, leucojum, puschkinia, scilla, snowdrops, Spanish bluebells, and winter aconites. When planting these smaller bulbs, don't skimp on numbers, and plant them as soon as you can. Planting depth differs for many of these bulbs, so be sure to check the package.

Sad Glads

Gladiolas are an old-fashioned favorite in cottage gardens, but they can have problems. One common set of symptoms you may see are stems that turn brown, leaaves tinged with silver, and a lack of flowering.

Those glads are showing all the classic signs of thrips, one of their most serious pests. Thrips are tiny insects (the adult females are about $^1/_{16}$ inch long), and they hide themselves inside the flower bud and leaf sheaths, where insecticides can't get to them. Thrips are very selective about their hosts, so it is unlikely that they came from somewhere else in the garden. If you bought new corms last year, they are probably the culprits.

Thrips can be beaten at their own game. They overwinter under the scales of the corms, so when you dig them up to bring them inside for winter storage, you are also protecting the thrips.

You have two options, each with an excellent chance of solving the problem. You can store the corms between 35 and 40 degrees (but don't freeze them) for at least four months during the winter. This is fine for the corms but kills the thrips. Or before planting in the spring, you can soak the corms for ten minutes in water at 115 degrees, which also kills thrips.

In research done at the University of Florida Agricultural Research and Education Center in Bradenton, soaking the corms reduced the number of flower spikes. But since uncontrolled thrips will eventually infest all of your gladioli and kill them, that may be a small price to pay.

A Tale About Scale

Privet hedges may protect your privacy, but sometimes they need their own protection. Dead or dying branches with white patches, especially near the base, often look like they are infected with a fungus.

It's not a fungus; it's white prunicola scale (*Pseudaulacaspis prunicola*). Privet, lilacs, and ornamental plums and cherries are the reluctant hosts for this insect.

White prunicola scale prefers the trunks and larger branches, not the tender new growth. Once it finds a branch it likes, it stays put. The soft-bodied insect would be an easy target for predators, but each produces a hard scale for protection. Within this cover, it simply sits there and sucks the juice out of the plant. It's a boring life but an effective survival strategy.

What you're seeing are huge numbers of bright white covers of maturing males, which eventually molt to a winged stage and fly off to find a mate. The females' covers are less obvious; they're larger and rounder but more subtle—sort of a mousy gray. As with at least one other species I can think of, the females stay home, and the males get to travel.

There are three generations each year. The females that overwinter on the branches lay eggs in the spring. When those insects mature, they mate and lay eggs in midsummer, giving birth to the second generation. Those young insects mate and lay eggs in late summer.

The key to their control is to get at them when they are most vulnerable: the females before the eggs hatch and the young insects during their crawler stage, after they leave the mother's cover and strike out on their own, but before they can produce their own protective scales.

September is a prime time for controlling them by spraying with horticultural oil (following the label instructions for summer dilution rate or growing season rate).

Fall Webworm

Recently I have been seeing ailanthus trees with what appear to be gauzy bags full of worms. Any leaf unfortunate enough to be inside the bag has been eaten down to the quick. Week by week the bags enlarge, engulfing more and more leaves, and appear to threaten the tree itself.

Common tiger moths lay their eggs in late summer on the undersides of leaves of more than a hundred species of trees, especially trees that are along roadsides or in other open locations. The larvae, aptly named fall webworms, spin webs enclosing both themselves and their food supply, the leaves. The larvae go through several stages of their life cycle within the webs, leaving only when they are ready to pupate into adults. They leave by crawling down the trunk or by the more dramatic route of lowering themselves down a single strand of web, like bungee jumping on a small scale.

Webworm infestations may be ugly but aren't dangerous, and there is no need to treat the problem. Unlike tent caterpillars, which emerge in the spring and can weaken a tree by defoliation, fall webworm emerges when the leaves have just about finished food production and are getting ready to drop anyway. Webworm populations fluctuate for a variety of reasons and you may see more in some years, but they balance out over the long haul.

Sowbugs

Moving houseplants back inside after a long summer out of doors usually means lifting pots and finding a zillion little armadillo-like bugs underneath. Between watching them run away or curl up into a little ball, you have to wonder what they have been up to under there.

Sowbugs, or pillbugs, are commonly found in the moist shelter under pots, but they have no interest in eating your houseplants because their jaws are too weak. Their under-pot diet consists of molds, fungi, blue-green algae, and any decaying matter—stuff that you don't particularly want under your pots anyway.

By the way, sowbugs are not insects; they are crustaceans, with eleven pairs of legs, and are distantly related to lobsters.

Hemlock Wooly Adelgid

Insects and diseases are usually pretty specific about which plant species they attack. A neighborhood hemlock is infested with something that looks like a wooly aphid, and they appear to migrate into your yard, settling on some of your shrubs. The issue is whether or not to take action.

Your dogwoods and hydrangea are in no danger, but your neighborhood's hemlocks are in a life-and-death struggle. Hemlock wooly adelgid (not an aphid) is very host specific, attacking only hemlocks.

Mark McClure, chief scientist at the Connecticut Agricultural Experiment Station in Windsor, says he does not know of any insect pest that would attack both hemlocks and dogwoods or hydrangea. The adelgid excretes a waxy mass with the appearance of cotton or wool fluff, about the size of a tightly wound cotton swab, as a way of both protecting and raising the humidity level around itself and its eggs. This material is dry and light, and can be dislodged, letting wind or animals carry it about, with some of it coming to rest in your garden.

The hemlock wooly adelgid is voracious in large populations. Left untreated, healthy hemlocks will be killed in four to six years, and trees in poor condition can die in just one or two.

Hemlock adelgid can be treated with horticultural oil or insecticidal soap any time the weather remains above freezing, usually between April and late October. Since there are two generations each year, McClure recommends a thorough drenching of all parts of the tree in April and then in late June, or in the fall and again in mid-May.

Ladybug, Ladybug

It's really too bad that Alfred Hitchcock is dead. If you open your door these days to a swarm of lady beetles trying to come inside, he might be the first person you think of. No matter that this is the one insect no one jumps from, the one people entice onto a fingertip and coo over, the bunny rabbit of the insect world.

The multicolored Asian lady beetle (*Harmonia axyridis*) has clearly established itself in this country after many attempts by the U.S. Department of Agriculture to introduce it for aphid control on crops and ornamental plants. Up to $3/8$ inch long, it is red, orange, or yellow-orange with spots ranging from none to nineteen or twenty (which can make it look nearly black). Like other lady beetles, it preys on aphids, scale insects, and psyllids.

Populations of all living things wax and wane, a function of food supply, environmental pressures, and predator populations. In this case, predators have not yet caught up with the new immigrants. In fact, over the last few years, this species has had more waxing than a bowling alley, and hundreds are showing up looking for winter shelter at windows or doors, from the Deep South on north and as far west as Michigan.

But they don't bite and have finished feeding for the year. They spend the winter under rock outcroppings, shingles, clapboards, in window frames, outside in leaf litter, or inside, up near the ceiling. Those that can't find shelter will die in the first heavy frost; those that make it into the house will die too, because the heat and dryness will dessicate them. Meantime, vacuum or sweep them up and release them outside, or recaulk your windows and seal your air-conditioner vents. The minor annoyance is a small price for the great service they provide to garden and crops.

At War with Voles

Voles. They tunnel in your garden and gnaw at the roots of vegetables and foundation plants alike. Probably among the cures that haven't worked for you is placing mousetraps baited with apples, peanut butter, and even small pieces of Juicy Fruit gum in their holes. Now that many gardeners are trying to keep to organic principles, it would be nice to have a simple way to deal with these voracious pests.

Not that you really care what *kind* of voles you have, but if you are seeing their runs—the surface mounding that is a result of tunneling—you have meadow voles. Pine voles, which tunnel deeper and attack roots, are harder to catch, but for trapping either kind, apples, cunning, and patience are the keys. Paul Curtis, extension wildlife specialist at Cornell University, said home remedies don't work, nor do the grain-based poisons on the market because voles don't like grain as much as they like nearly everything else in your garden.

Two traps will work. Harpoon-style traps are buried upside down over a section of the tunnel that you first flatten. When the vole tries to clear the tunnel, he springs the trap. Mousetrap-style traps are baited with food and left near exit holes. Apples are Curtis's favorite bait, but voles are easily frightened, so the trap should be made cozy by protecting it with a tent made of a folded piece of a roofing shingle. (Leave enough room overhead for the trap to spring.) An upside-down shoe box with a $1^1/2$-inch hole on each side and a rock for a weight will also work and has the added benefit of keeping most other animals out.

Voles prefer mulched plants, so clearing down to bare ground may discourage them from eating specific plants. And don't confuse voles with moles. Voles eat plants and have typical rodent front teeth like squirrels, short tails, and tiny ears. Moles eat insects, their teeth are sharply pointed, and they have enlarged claws on heavy front paws, perfect for digging.

Under certain circumstances shotguns are considered organic, but I'm not so sure about Juicy Fruit.

Saying Goodbye to Gnats

Water a ficus tree and sometimes a small cloud of tiny brown bugs takes off from the soil and hovers around until the flood of water goes down, whereupon they simply disappear. It's as if they were patiently waiting to keep their feet from getting wet. Whether you are good with houseplants or not, this sort of thing can be disconcerting.

That little cloud of bugs is most likely fungus gnats. It should bring the pride associated with ownership of a miniature ecosystem, but many people prefer to own plants without the associated wildlife. The weak flying adults are slender, long-legged, with long antennae, clear wings, and dark brown or black bodies, about $1/8$ inch long. Altogether it is a very stylish pest, and one that does little damage.

Over a three-week life cycle, eggs become larvae, which form pupae, then adults. Adult fungus gnats get around, usually coming into the house on other plants or through windows. They lay eggs in the rich, damp soils that are inevitably home to decaying plant material and microscopic communities of algae and fungi.

The larvae dine on these entrees and occasionally on the fine root hairs of the plant.

To see if fungus gnats are the problem, place the cut side of a raw potato on the soil for 3 to 4 days. When you pick it up, if larvae are present, you will see them on the soil under the potato, or see their tunnels in it. Unless the population is large, they are simply a nuisance. Repotting in sterile soil and not keeping the soil too wet—and keeping the house a bit cool—can help. High infestations can be controlled during the larval stage with the product Knock-Out Gnats, a strain of *Bacillus thuringiensis* (Bt), bacteria that produce a substance that is toxic when ingested by the larvae. Since pupae and adults are not affected, more than one application is necessary. As with any other control product, read the label and don't be tempted to improvise on the instructions. It is available from Gardens Alive, 5100 Schenley Place, Lawrenceburg, IN 47025, (812) 537-8650.

Adult populations can be monitored, and reduced, with Sticky Traps, yellow 3- by 5-inch cards covered with a sticky material and laid horizontally across the pot. Yellow seems to attract gnats. The traps are available through Gardens Alive and Gardener's Supply Company, 128 Intervale Road, Burlington, VT 05401, (802) 863-1700.

2

Diseases

Bacteria, fungi, and viruses are standing by, ready to lower your gardening morale. Whatever the larger members of the animal kingdom don't eat, these guys will infect.

Symptoms? Practically everything seems to cause either splotches (red, brown, yellow, black, white, or multicolored halos; your choice), brown margins (those dying leaf edges that can also be the result of too little or too much watering), or drooping (unless it's from being too hot or too dry). Figuring out what caused the symptom is difficult, especially when you get a short description through the mail. Occasionally people send in samples—dead leaves, cankerous twigs. Just a little something to infect my own plants, thank you.

Diseases are no more fun for plants than they are for people. And in the same way that many people are looking to natural herbs instead of prescription drugs, many gardeners are trying to cut down on their reliance on powerful, synthetic chemicals, both for feeding and for curing their plants. As it is with humans, sometimes the natural cures work, and sometimes they don't.

You won't see a lot of advice on using chemicals, but sometimes they are still the best way to go, using natural and organic chemicals first, synthetic and inorganic second. Mostly, though, there are three other possibilities offered: use disease-resistant plants to avoid problems in the first place; apply better cultural practices to raise plants that are in great condition and have the best odds of fighting their enemies on their own; or give up, throw the plant out, and start over. Frequently the little guys win, and your gardening experience will be calmer if you remind yourself of that occasionally.

Sycamore Problems

Spring comes and all the trees in the neighborhood leaf out. Except your sycamore. Just a few tiny leaves, sitting there looking pathetic. After a while you get nervous, wondering if this is a sign of the latest blight.

Just wait—the leaves will probably start falling off pretty soon. But don't panic; it has happened before, and it will happen again. Sycamores, with their contrasting patterns of gray, brown, and creamy white bark, look like trees dressed up in forest camouflage. Unfortunately, they can't hide from sycamore anthracnose, a fungus disease that can defoliate a large tree if the early spring has been cool and damp. The fungi, which overwinter in cankers (areas of dead bark tissue) formed on twigs and branches, produce spores that are carried to leaves and buds by spring moisture. Infected leaves expand to only about 2 inches before the twigs are girdled by cankers, causing the leaves to wilt and die by early June. By early July, however, the sycamore will have put out a second set of leaves from dormant buds, drawing on extra food reserves stored the previous year. These new leaves may get some blotches, but they will survive and produce all the food the tree needs.

Generally anthracnose does not require treatment, because the overall amount of leaf and twig dieback isn't life threatening and has no long-term effect on the tree's health. Several bad years in a row could cause enough branch dieback to disfigure the tree seriously, but variations in weather and fungi populations usually combine to limit the problem.

London plane trees, a hybrid of American sycamore and oriental plane, are quite similar looking to American sycamores, but are more resistant to anthracnose and are a better choice when planting.

Ideal Fungus Conditions

When there is a cool, wet spring, I'm always willing to predict a banner year for peach leaf curl, the fungus that overwinters in the buds and on the twigs of peaches and nectarines and attacks new growth. As the new leaves unfold, the infestation gives them a seersucker appearance as they pucker and curl, changing from green to yellow to reddish. As the infection gets worse, the leaves take on a white, powdery appearance, deteriorate, and fall. Young fruit that becomes infected also falls. In a severe case, the tree may become defoliated.

A second flush of leaves appears in the early summer, and these leaves are unaffected. A home owner may think he has won, but wind and water have already spread the fungus, and the twigs and buds are infected. If the next spring is also cool and wet, the symptoms will reappear. If the weather isn't right, it will simply wait for a better year.

Peach leaf curl can be managed with a single application of a fungicide registered for this use. It can be applied only in the fall, after the leaves have dropped, or in the spring, before the buds begin to swell.

Blossom End Rot

Tomatoes are undoubtedly the most comonly grown vegetable (actually a fruit, but why quibble?). They should be simple to grow, but suddenly you spot those sunken, brown, leathery spots on the bottom end.

Remember how your mother made you drink milk daily because the calcium helped build strong bones? Well, it (calcium, not milk) builds strong cell walls in tomatoes too. Calcium in the soil gets carried throughout the plant as part of the transpiration stream—the flow of water and nutrients that moves up through the roots and eventually evaporates through the leaves. Under normal circumstances, enough calcium gets into the developing fruit, resulting in a healthy tomato. A calcium deficiency causes weak cell walls, which can collapse, causing blossom end rot. The damage always begins opposite the stem, at the blossom end, because that is the farthest point from the flow of water and calcium.

Some tomato varieties are more susceptible, especially the longer plum types, but none is completely resistant. On all varieties, damage is more common in the early fruit, so don't go ripping up the plants in frustration.

To prevent, or at least minimize, blossom end rot, make sure that the soil pH is close to 7, the neutral point. This ensures a soluble form of calcium in the soil for the roots to take up. It is most important, however, to prevent an uneven moisture supply, which is the major cause. Alternating dry and wet periods, even if the droughts are mild, can disrupt calcium delivery and start cell breakdown. Tomatoes should be mulched to conserve soil moisture and should be watered as often as your mother made you drink your milk.

Raspberry Problems

A raspberry patch can be torture in more ways than one. After a few productive years you have a few where the berries begin normally, approach the time they should ripen, and then just shrivel up and die. As conscientious as you are, cutting down old stems and draping the new ones on strung wires, things continue to go wrong. But you haven't really done anything wrong, and the problem is curable.

On a cool, rainy day, while you were in the house, thinking about the delicious fruit beginning to set as the flowers faded and died, the fungus *Botrytis cinerea* was cozying up to those dying petals and digging in to wait. As the berries started to ripen and soften, and as you began to decide between having the raspberries on cereal or over ice cream, the fungus was sending out spores, infecting other berries, and dashing your hopes as it covered the fruit with a fuzzy gray mold. (If there's a better hobby than gardening, I sure don't know what it is.)

Botrytis attacks different parts of dozens of common ornamentals, fruits, and vegetables, and the symptoms can vary widely. On many vegetables, including peppers, tomatoes, and lettuce, and on ornamentals such as dogwood and pansies, it shows up as leaf spots. On chrysanthemums, snapdragons, and roses, it causes stem cankers. Flower buds, including those on peonies, dahlias, and zinnias, are attacked, while the fruits of strawberries, grapes, and raspberries are targets. Some plants, including geranium, peony, and hydrangea, may be attacked in more than one place.

Good air circulation, which helps wet leaves, stems, and flowers dry quickly, is your best preventive. Trellis the raspberries, and prune them so that each foot of planted row has only three fruiting canes. Because botrytis overwinters on dead tissue, clean up any fallen leaves and other debris in the fall.

It may be too late to save this year's crop, but with gardening, there's always next year.

Banner Year for Black Spot

Rainy summers seem to bring more black spot on roses than dry ones, even though rain and many fungi just don't go together.

In gardening, weather giveth and weather taketh away. Summer's prime examples are black spot and powdery mildew, both diseases caused by fungi. Rain, which beachgoers hate and gardeners love, keeps powdery mildew under control while it provides an ideal environment for black spot on roses. Leaves that have black spot will have ¹/₂-inch black spots surrounded by a fringe on the upper surface. Part or all of the leaf turns yellow and eventually falls. Another sign is raised purple-red blotches on this year's canes.

Abundant summer rain exacerbates these conditions. Most fungi require free water—real drops sitting on the leaves and stems—in order to attack plants or to germinate from spores. The fungus that causes powdery mildew is an exception, preferring high humidity without the water. But the fungus that causes black spot likes water so much it even creates two kinds of spores: one that travels by air and one by water. In the spring, newly expanding leaves and young

Rose

canes can be infected by a breeze or splashing water that carries the spores that overwintered on or near the plant.

Black spot can be controlled or reduced by eliminating the favorite places the spores overwinter. Clean up fallen leaves, prune out infected canes, and put mulch around the roses after the ground freezes. Mulch provides a pleasant environment for predator bacteria and fungi, which eat the spores. Choosing resistant roses is always wise, but there are many strains of the fungus, and it mutates frequently. The rose that is resistant today may be delicious tomorrow.

Cedar-Apple Rust

Crabapples are highly prized trees for flowers, fruit, and fall color. Many have good immunity to disease, but in the right circumstances you may find leaves with yellow-orange spots, rimmed in red on top and a hairy swelling underneath.

This is cedar-apple rust, and unless you live in a commercial apple-producing area it is more unsightly than it is dangerous.

Outside of the pictures in magazines, diseases and insects are part of gardening, and it is important to moderate the passion for perfection, because you can't always win.

The fungus that causes cedar-apple rust lives a compulsively nomadic life, traveling by wind back and forth between apples, including crabapple, and some junipers. In the Northeast, the eastern red cedar (*Juniperus virginiana;* actually a juniper, not a cedar) is a common host, as is common juniper (*J. communis*). Other rust fungi prefer amelanchier or hawthorn or quince, but each always returns to a juniper host.

Both hosts are necessary for the fungus to survive, so the key to control is to remove one of them. Since you have the apple family host, all you need to do is to convince all of your neighbors within half a mile that they should let you cut down their red cedars.

If for some reason you think this is impractical, when choosing crabapples look for selections that are resistant, like 'Naragansett,' 'Royalty,' and 'Snowdrift.' Check with your local county cooperative extension office for a complete list of resistant crabapples and junipers.

Mimosa Wilt

Yesterday your mimosa (*Albizia julibrissin,* also commonly called silk tree) was full of wispy pink and pale yellow flowers held above fernlike leaves. This morning it is completely wilted, hanging like a flag without a breeze.

Here is the bad news: the tree is going to die, and you can do nothing about it. Take some small comfort that it is not your fault.

The first epidemic of mimosa wilt occurred in North Carolina more than fifty years ago, and the disease is widespread. The mimosa that is cold-hardy to Zone 6, *A. julibrissin* f. *rosea,* is rarely planted anymore because of mimosa wilt. Young trees are not affected, and it can take years before an apparently healthy tree dies, after unsuspecting home owners have built a patio around it and sat in its dappled shade, imagining the tropics.

The culprit, *Fusarium oxysporum pernicosum,* is a fungus that penetrates the roots and travels through the vascular system. It lodges in pits and end walls, begins to multiply, and forms a colony, which sends new spores into more vessels. Like cholesterol, the fungus gradually restricts fluid flow. When an adult tree has a greater need for water—during a hot summer, for example, when it is in full bloom—some branches, a side of the tree, or even the entire tree can wilt overnight, depending on how much of the vascular system has been invaded. Less dramatically (but not less fatally), leaves may turn yellow or shrivel and drop without wilting. Some trees live for a year or more. Some die in a single season.

You may be tempted to replace the mimosa with one of the seedlings that commonly sprout up nearby. But the fungus can live in the soil for a long time and travel far on waterborne soil particles. Seeds can become infected even while still on the tree.

So far, the search for a resistant mimosa has been unsuccessful. My advice is to find a different tree for that suddenly empty spot.

Hollyhock Revival

I grew up during one of the "alley" phases for hollyhocks—between the period when everyone had them in the front yard for a cottage garden look and the years when no one grew them because they were tired of looking at hollyhock rust.

Hollyhocks

This popular biennial is back in the front yard now, with many gardeners recalling the wonderful flowers of their youth but repressing the memories of blotchy leaves with orange-brown warty pustules on the undersides.

If you have hollyhocks, you have hollyhock rust. The rust is caused by one of the best-prepared fungi you'll ever battle. It has everything on its side: its windborne spores can travel a mile, it grows on common mallow (a widespread weed known as cheeses), its spores can survive the winter on any tiny piece of infected debris that you miss in your fall cleanup, and its spores cling to the surface of new seeds, infecting your hollyhock as soon as it sprouts.

It is possible to devote your summer to fungicide treatments, but why would you want to? The hollyhocks will flower, just as they did for your grandparents. Enjoy them: look at the flowers, not at the leaves.

Unwanted Guests

One landscaper, two sod lawns, right next to each other, just a few weeks apart. Both of you water every day, as instructed, but your stories are different. The neighbor, of course, has smooth sailing while you have mushrooms popping up everywhere. You don't think you're watering too much, but something is clearly wrong here.

Don't blame the landscaper, don't envy the neighbor's greener grass, and don't worry about the mushrooms. Mushroom spores are everywhere, looking for a good home. Yours may have come in with the sod, they may have already been present in your soil, or they may have been lucky enough to float in while the bare soil was waiting for the sod to arrive.

How they arrived isn't important, and they pose no threat to the grass. Since your landscaper probably told you to water often enough to keep the sod moist until it knits together and extends its roots into the soil below, the spores have found what they were looking for: a dark, damp environment. Once the sod is really in and you cut back watering to a more normal pace (about 1 inch a week during summer droughts and none during spring and fall when there is adequate rain), the mushrooms will not be a problem.

You can tell when the sod is knit into the soil by lifting a corner of a strip. If it doesn't lift easily, the roots have begun to grow into the soil, and it is safe to reduce watering.

In the meantime you can remove the mushrooms as they

sprout. Depending on your mood you can hand-pick them, kick them off, or practice your golf swing.

Beyond the Common Lilac

High humidity and hot days provide the kind of environment that fungi write home about. But late summer does not have to mean powdery mildew on lilacs if you consider an alternative to common lilac hybrids, which are so white with mildew by late summer they look as if they had been dusted with flour.

Syringa patula 'Miss Kim' not only is resistant to mildew but is a terrific lilac. The panicles are more delicate and subtle than those of the common lilac. As buds, the fragrant flowers are purple, fading to an icy blue-white before falling. Dark green leaves with wavy edges have a beautiful burgundy tone in autumn, providing an impressive shrub even without flowers.

'Miss Kim' was named by Elwyn M. Meader in 1954, when he was a lilac specialist at the University of New Hampshire. He named the plant not for Misses Hunter or Novak, but for all the Miss Kims in Korea, where it was discovered and where Kim is a common name.

If you are serious about lilacs and are willing to have a twiggy, somewhat messy-looking shrub, *S. microphylla,* the little-leaf lilac, offers a bonus of a second, although lighter, flowering in late summer. The flowers are pale lilac and can be very sweet scented, and the shrub grows slowly to 6 feet, wider than it is tall. *S. microphylla* 'Superba,' more commonly available, has pale pink flowers that develop from deep rose buds.

Two nurseries that carry both lilacs are Oliver Nurseries, 1159 Bronson Road, Fairfield, CT 06430, (203) 259-5609, and Twombly Nursery, 163 Barn Hill Road, Monroe, CT 06468, (203) 261-2133.

Resistant Phlox

Some summers phlox is a mildew magnet. Pulling them from their bed is one answer, but understanding what's going on leads to a better way of preventing the problem in the future.

Most fungus diseases are at their worst in rainy weather, so gardeners are constantly amazed and frustrated to find that distinctive powdery white coating when there hasn't been a cloud in the sky. You may have to live with some powdery mildew, but you shouldn't lose sleep worrying that it will spread across the garden. Powdery mildew on phlox does not spread to roses or lilacs, and vice versa, because each of these plants is attacked by a different member of this fungus family.

It's a large family, full of near and distant relations, but all of them grow and reproduce similarly. Give them dry leaves, high humidity, and cool nights, and they are keen to release spores. Actual water on the leaves, however, inhibits their reproduction, but a hard rain or spray from your hose can physically move the fungus onto fresh, uninfected leaves. And just to make things especially complicated, as water on the leaves begins to dry and just a very thin film remains, the fungi use it as a sort of amusement park water slide to travel to other leaves. You have to admire a fungus like that.

If you don't want to commit yourself to a regimen of regular preventive spraying with ultrafine horticultural oil, help fight powdery mildew by making sure your phlox are in full sun and have good air circulation. A few varieties are more or less resistant, but growers say two are the best: 'David' (white) and 'Robert Poore' (magenta). Remember, though, that resistance does not mean complete immunity.

Sources for phlox include Niche Gardens, 1111 Dawson Road, Chapel Hill, NC 27516, (919) 967-0078, catalog; and

Busse Gardens, 5873 Oliver Avenue, S.W., Cokato, MN 55321, (320) 286-2654, catalog.

Decaying Trees

Money doesn't grow on trees, but sometimes mushrooms do. One common type is half-moon shaped, purplish-brown with white edges. They are hard and shiny on top but dull underneath. What's important is where they grow.

Mushrooms or other fleshy fungi coming from the side of your tree, not necessarily from the base, can be signs of hazardous decay. Of course, not everything growing on the tree is dangerous. Small, hard lichens are there just as a convenient place to live.

The fungi to be concerned about are fleshy and sizable, may resemble single shelves or clusters of shelves, and range from white to hot orange to red to purple to brown. These are the fruiting bodies of fungi that invade an open wound and decay the wood. The visible portions usually form after considerable decay has occurred beneath the bark.

Examine fungi growing at the base of trees. If they are coming out of the wood, they are probably indicators of decay. Those growing out of the ground may or may not signal a problem.

Diseased trees can collapse before they die, and the fungi may be the only obvious sign of trouble. You should have a qualified arborist evaluate the potential for the tree's collapse. Arborists who are certified by the International Society of Arboriculture or a state chapter of the society are qualified to diagnose these problems. Your local county cooperative extension office has a list of certified arborists serving your area.

Daylilies

When the leaves coming up from the base of daylilies (Hemerocallis) *turn the color of dried parchment, drought is the natural suspicion. But when the same thing occurs during a summer of adequate rains, the discoloration begins to look like a natural part of the growth cycle. Think again.*

Gregory Piatrowski, curator of the Arnold A. Stout Daylily Collection at the New York Botanical Garden, says that some daylilies are more susceptible than others to fungus diseases that cause the foliage to streak yellow-brown before or after flowering. He removes leaves if only a few are affected. If the entire plant looks bad, don't be afraid to cut the foliage back to the ground after it finishes flowering. A second flush of leaves will grow in a few weeks and renew the fresh look, although the daylily won't flower again this season.

While you're out there slashing and cutting, look for signs that the daylilies need to be divided. Check around the base of the plants. If there are little hummocks of soil pushed up at the base or if roots are being exposed at the surface, the clump should be divided. After flowering is ideal, as is the spring, when the new foliage has just appeared.

Since drought stress also contributes to the browning, daylilies are very dependent on regular watering. They are shallow rooted and are usually planted in groups or with other plants, so there is strong competition for water and nutrients. Sometimes we lose interest after they finish flowering and forget to keep watering them. Shame on us.

Blue Mold on Bulbs

Luckily for gardeners, things are often not as serious as they appear. For example, once in a while bulbs that come by mail order show up with a blue, powdery mold on them.

Wipe the mold off with a damp paper towel and plant the bulbs. This penicillium mold, a cousin several times removed from the mold that makes the famous antibiotic, is a surface mold and is not a serious problem. Bulbs contain moisture, and keeping them in a closed package allows a buildup of humidity, which encourages the mold.

It Isn't Talcum

While dry weather reduces most fungi, which need a film of moisture for their spores to grow, powdery mildew fungi prefer humid conditions but hate rain. Powdery mildew is one of the crosses that gardeners have to bear. What's most amazing, and frustrating, is that even late in dry summers zinnias can get a good case of it.

Plants with powdery mildew look like losers in a flour fight. The group of related fungi that cause it have a healthy, if indiscriminate, appetite, attacking lilac, tulip tree, monarda, phlox, aster, cosmos, dahlia, verbena, zinnia, roses, dogwood, cucumber, squash, pumpkins, and other trees, shrubs, annuals, perennials, and vegetables. Fungi might look alike to us, but each has its preferred hosts.

Beginning in summer, they are most likely found on the undersides of lower leaves, among crowded plants with poor air circulation. Warm days and cool nights encourage growth. Late in the season the mildews grow rapidly, becoming obvious. The spores overwinter on fallen leaves and in bud scales of trees and shrubs. Cleaning up fallen leaves is an important chore, but some spores will remain in the bud scales. Potassium bicarbonate products have been registered for use on powdery mildew, and are worth looking for.

Most experienced gardeners look for resistant plant varieties; they pay attention to spacing to improve air circulation among the plants; and they toss out plants that are severely affected or don't bother treating it, except, perhaps, on plants that are up front, where the flocked-white leaves drive them crazy.

Bearding the Bad Tulip

I know people who resist planting tulips because they have heard that certain tulips with "broken colors" are infected with a virus that does them no harm but can be spread to oriental and Asiatic lilies. They worry that monochromatic, bicolor, parrot, and even Rembrandt tulips may not be safe. With dozens of oriental lilies planted nearby, it is an understandable concern. They even extend their worrying to tiger lilies, and avoid planting them near tulips. But, really, no special precautions are necessary.

Tulips—every size, shape, and color combination—are safe to plant with any and all lilies, and late fall is a good time to be outside planting both.

A family of viruses, some of which could infect members of the lily family, originally caused those fascinating "broken" colors in Rembrandt tulips (colors, by the way, that Rembrandt wouldn't have been caught dead using). But the bulbs now on

Tulips

the market with those colors and patterns are simply cultivars bred to look like virus-infected Rembrandts.

For about ten years, every tulip has undergone thorough inspections, including one by U.S. Agriculture Department inspectors stationed in Holland (and paid by the Dutch growers). Those wonderful spring displays in the Dutch fields not only delight tourists, but also reveal any infected bulbs, which are quickly destroyed.

Even if a Dutch grower should be blinded by the spring riot of color in his fields, and the Dutch and American inspectors should mistakenly allow an infected bulb to end up in your garden, chances are your lilies wouldn't even notice. The virus is transported by aphids, which are generally not active in the spring when tulips bloom. Since lilies don't bloom until summer, it would be quite the aphid who could manage to visit both while keeping the virus alive for the time in between.

Fallen Angels

I once received a letter that a reader's angel-wing begonias had developed a powdery white mold that spread rapidly from plant to plant, causing the leaves to drop off. She believed it traveled airborne since she found it in her turtle's tank. First she assumed it was something coming off her damp brick walls. After trimming some of the plants down and removing the infected leaves, it still spread.

I don't know anything about turtles, but you can rest assured that whatever is in the tank is not the powdery mildew fungus the begonias have. This fungus, or actually family of fungi, is stubbornly unlike most others. Instead of using a film of water to start growing, these spores like humid air but dry leaves.

You haven't quite gone far enough for a cure. Angel-wing

begonias, named after the shape of their leaves, are cane begonias, sending up bamboo-like canes. Examine the canes for discolored areas, and prune back below them while removing any infected leaves. In a serious case you may have to cut the canes back as much as halfway. Even if you have to remove all the leaves, come spring it will have healthy new growth.

It's always better to prevent diseases than to fight them. Keep angel-wing begonias healthy by using a well-drained potting medium, letting them become fairly dry between waterings, and finding a spot with bright light but not direct sun. Pots crowded together can trap air and humidity, providing ideal conditions for powdery mildew. Keep it from getting started by providing good air circulation around the plants, increasing the space between pots, and using a small fan to move the air. Try to moderate temperature swings; warm days and cool nights spur powdery mildew growth.

Sources for angel-wing and other begonias include Kartuz Greenhouses, 1408 Sunset Drive, Vista, CA 92083, (760) 941-3613, catalog; and Logee's Greenhouses, 141 North Street, Danielson, CT 06239, (888) 330-8038, catalog.

As for the damp brick walls, that has to be between you and the landlord.

3

Weather and Other Problems

Droughts and ice storms, blazing summer heat and unexpected frosts all take their toll in the garden. Sometimes we can ameliorate the effects with easy steps—watering during droughts, throwing row covers on vegetables and seedlings before a frosty night—but sometimes there's nothing we can do. The longer I garden, the more I realize that most years are "unusual" in one weather regard or another and that a normal year is most un-normal. And even if things are just fine in my own garden, somewhere else in the country everything is going to hell in a handbasket. There have been days when I've opened a letter from one person complaining about the drought and a letter from another wondering what problems all the rain will cause.

Come summer heat or winter cold, too much rain or too much drought, gardeners are trying to beat them all: to grow what doesn't naturally grow in their area, to start it early or harvest it late. We're all alike—we can't get enough of that great gardening punishment.

Working the Soil

Many seed package instructions tell you to plant the seeds as soon as the soil can be worked. Last frosts have dates, but no gardening calendar tells you when the soil is ready or why you shouldn't start too soon.

Avoid getting out there too early and stomping around the garden, turning beds over and trying to force the return of spring. Walking on wet soil or working it with spade or fork will compact it, making it difficult for air and water to reach plant roots. Once the soil is damaged, it can take years for microbial action to reestablish the structure of small clumps gardeners refer to as good tilth.

There is no easy date to give because soils and microclimates differ so much. Try taking a handful of soil and squeezing it. If it stays together, it is still too wet. When it begins to crumble into smaller pieces, it's ready.

Maple Decline

When mature trees begin dying in older neighborhoods, people take notice. After a period of sidewalk renewal efforts in Westchester County some time ago, several maples died and numerous others had less than leafy boughs in the following years, leaving tall trees without their typical heavy leaf cover. At first glance the trees seemed to be suffering from some disease, but officials blamed the sidewalk work. Many residents of the neighborhood were in disbelief and were certain they would be left with mere stumps because the government wouldn't listen to them.

It's always news to find out that a public official might actually be right. Maple roots are very shallow and are easily affected by nearby construction, especially if the trees are between the sidewalk and the street. Since air and water are unavailable under the street, most roots grow toward the sidewalk and lawn. If they are cut during the work or if heavy machinery compacts the soil above them, they can easily be damaged and even die. The result is maple decline, an environmental condition with the symptoms one reader described: reduced twig and foliage growth and dying branches, beginning high in the crown. Early fall color is another sign of decline.

How a tree reacts to the injury depends on how healthy and vigorous it was to begin with and how early the decline is diagnosed. Compaction, moisture stress, low soil fertility, and exposure to road salt in the winter all play a part in the tree's health. Given a typical urban or suburban environment, having its feet cut out from under it could very well be the last straw.

Keep the trees well watered, fertilize in spring or fall (not both), but don't expect the trees to recover fully if the symptoms are that advanced.

Those Blooming Trees

Some springs, the trees are more productive than others, with species like black locust and catalpas blooming their heads off. But the reasons go back to the previous year.

The same combination of a long, cold winter and a cool, rainy spring that we all complained about deserves the credit. Dr. Tom Whitlow, an assistant professor of horticultural physiology at Cornell University, said that at least two factors contributed to the unusual display: lots of flower buds and little time.

The typical weather pattern in the Northeast includes a midwinter thaw. A few days of temperatures in the 50s followed by a rapid drop below freezing can kill buds on trees during their winter rest. When winter gets cold and stays cold, we don't have the rapid up and down temperature cycle that is more typical. When winter ends, the long period of wet, cool weather usually provides a good growing season. With fewer buds lost than normal, more are able to become flowers.

Normally trees flower over a period of time, with some buds opening earlier than others. When cool weather delays the early buds, the tree's period of bloom is compressed into a shorter time. Some species are delayed, so their bloom periods overlap, giving us a colorful recompense for an otherwise forgettable spring.

Tough Time for Tomatoes

Don't take it personally if your tomatoes aren't setting fruit. Like everything else, they have a hard time in the heat. Temperatures of 95 degrees or higher kill pollen, and as a result tomato flowers, which are self-pollinating, may fail to become fruit. But just wait. When the temperatures drop, tomatoes will start forming again.

Hot, dry weather followed by a rainy period will also cause some fruit to crack, especially in varieties like 'Better Boy,' 'Sweet 100,' and 'Ponderosa.' Two that are less prone to cracking are 'Mountain Spring' and 'Mountain Supreme.'

Leaf Scorch

Leaf scorch is ugly but rarely fatal. The reactions to leaves with crispy, brown edges on Norway maple, dogwood, linden, horse chestnut, and Japanese maple, or leaves that wilt, yellow, and drop off on London plane, tend to take one of two forms: reach for the fertilizer or reach for the chain saw. Both approaches to these drought-stress problems are wrong.

Trees without leaves in late August certainly look dead, but by midsummer the leaves have done their basic job, providing enough carbohydrates (stored in the root structure) for the tree to survive the coming winter and put out new leaves next spring. It may be bald, but it's not dead.

Given a summer drought and an otherwise healthy tree, scorch is a symptom of a physical problem, not a nutrient deficiency. The exact relationship between a tree's nutritional status and its ability to withstand water stress is not clear, but there are good reasons for not fertilizing. In dry soil, dry fertilizer is unlikely to benefit any plants because moisture is needed to release the nutrients from the fertilizer and move the nutrients through the soil and for absorption by the roots. Liquid fertilizers might have more success in getting into the tree, but soluble fertilizers applied to dry soils can injure the roots.

Don't take drought stress too lightly. It's hard on trees, and too many years in a row can kill them. Young trees may suffer bark cracking. Additionally, stressed trees are more susceptible to insect and disease attack. You should continue to water unless your community has restrictions. Three inches of mulch helps conserve rainfall or water that you apply. Make sure the tree receives adequate water during the next spring growing season.

Drought Symptoms

Wooly caterpillars are suspected of predicting how early or severe the winter will be, and they may be right. But people also think that early fall color, especially in sugar maples, does the same.

When you see sugar maples begin to color six weeks early, don't start airing out your sweaters. Fall comes early enough each year, but premature coloration, especially in sugar maple and littleleaf lindens, are signs of summer drought, not a change of seasons. Many tree species enter dormancy earlier than they should as a result of water stress. Scorched brown leaf edges on sugar, red, and Norway maples may also be signs of drought stress.

Dr. Nina Bassuk, professor of horticulture at Cornell University's Urban Horticulture Institute in Ithaca, New York, says that sugar maples that show early color year after year are inevitably falling into sugar maple decline, a syndrome that results in the death of large branches after several years.

Curbside trees, in the city or the suburbs, face a series of environmental stresses, including compacted soil, restrictions on where their roots can grow, desiccation from deicing salts, branch amputation by utility companies, and assaults by wayward lawn mowers. Trees that face these assaults become easy targets for insects and disease; repeated drought stress alone can cause decline and death.

Drought's Consequences

Don't be surprised if a current drought comes back to haunt us the following year.

Wounds to the living bark of trees and shrubs take much longer to heal when they are water stressed, allowing the fungi that cause canker diseases to invade before the tree can defend itself. Cankers are visible symptoms of localized diseases or physical damage caused by lightning, animals, or people to the living bark of a tree, says Dr. George Hudler, professor of plant pathology at Cornell University in Ithaca, New York.

Most of these canker-causing fungi produce their spores in late summer or fall, so they are out and about looking for a home. One obvious residence is the wound created by pruning. So, other than for safety, save your pruning chores until late winter.

Might as Well Be Spring

Cherries blooming in winter? It's always good for a moment on the TV news when nature does something out of the ordinary. But if unusual weather produces a few cherry blossoms, should we expect that spring will be flowerless? Not really.

A mini–heat wave one year sent news cameramen to the Tidal Basin in Washington to photograph, among the 3,700 cherry trees, the 20 or so that were in bloom. On one hand everyone was ready to blame El Niño, and on the other, we worried about a spring without cherry blossoms. But if the cameras had been there the year before, or if they show up next year, they could get the same pictures. On a reasonably warm day in early winter, El Niño or no Niño, blossoms on one particular variety of flowering cherry will pop out.

Robert DeFeo, the National Park Service horticulturist who tracks Washington's cherry trees, says that individual flower buds on that variety, *Prunus subhirtella* 'Autumnalis,' seem to have some leeway in their chilling requirement—the period of cold necessary before flower buds can be induced to open. The variety name 'Autumnalis' reflects its sporadic late fall and early winter flowering during warm spells, although the tree reserves enough buds to provide a spring show too. Maybe the early ones are scouts, checking the world out.

So don't worry. Ornamental flowering cherries will bloom when they should. Washington, D.C.'s Cherry Blossom Festival takes place in late March to early April, and the National Park Service tries to coordinates it to the peak bloom. To track the progress on the Internet, go to the Park Service's cherry page: www.nps.gov/nacc/cherry.

Protecting Against Salt

A winter of heavy snows means a winter of extra salt for the roads. And for plants that are nearby.

Salt used to deice roads and sidewalks can cause injury during winter thaws and in the spring. Salt spray kicked up by passing cars (or ocean spray carried inland by storms) collects on exposed buds and twigs. When the temperature approaches freezing, osmotic pressure, caused by the presence of salt on one side of cell membranes, draws water out, resulting in desiccation. Terminal buds may die, promoting growth in buds lower down the stem. Repetition over several winters can result in the familiar "witches' brooms"—unsightly masses of twig growth that prevent proper growth from continuing and weaken the tree.

Salt mixed with snow and plowed up onto nearby landscape plants finds its way into the soil when the snow melts. It causes damage when plants break dormancy in the spring and need to take up water and nutrients. Salt absorbs water, and large concentrations in the soil can result in what is called chemical drought conditions, even though there appears to be plenty of moisture. Chloride ions are taken up by the roots and accumulate in the growing leaves, causing scorch along the edges, smaller-than-normal leaf size, twig dieback, and brown needles on evergreens, especially eastern white pine.

If there isn't significant rainfall in early spring, prevent salt injury by flushing the area around plants with water as soon as the soil thaws, before any signs of growth appear. Waiting until growth is apparent is too late; the chloride ions will already have accumulated in the new leaves.

When choosing new trees or shrubs for sites that may be exposed to salt, remember that some plants are more salt tolerant (for example, Austrian pine, bayberry, Callery pear, fragrant sumac, gingko, gray dogwood, honey locust, Japanese black pine, larch, London plane, Russian olive). Most others are intolerant. A local county cooperative extension office can provide a more complete list.

Flood Damage in Trees

Low-lying areas have an unfortunate tendency to flood once spring comes and the snows melt. If you live with this situation, it has probably occurred to you that your trees and shrubs may not like it any better than you do.

Anyone who has ever watered a houseplant to death is likely to view a flooded yard with alarm. Melting 5-foot snow piles can cause waterlogged soil now and threaten more damage as streams overrun their banks later on.

In nature, however, nothing is either simple or obvious. Flooded soil can cause oxygen deficiencies that kill roots, but it can also cause roots to shut down, preventing the uptake of water and nutrients. Strangely, flooded plants can actually die of thirst.

But season and species make a difference too. Some plants can survive several weeks of flooding when dormant, but die after only a few days if it occurs during the growing season.

Given the same conditions, some species are adapted to survive much longer than others. Among the trees and shrubs tolerant to flooding are deciduous holly, some red maples, green ash, bald cypress, pin oak, tupelo, osage orange, black alder, red osier dogwood, river birch, sweet gum, silver maple, pussy willow, and weeping willow. Most other trees and shrubs need air in their root zone and should not be planted where flooding is likely. Among these are American beech, European white birch, crabapple, flowering dogwood, eastern hemlock, saucer magnolia, sugar maple, eastern white pine, tulip tree, and yew.

Frozen Soil Test

Advice for preparing a perennial bed for the winter usually includes the line "mulch once the ground is frozen." But they never tell you how to figure out just when that might be.

It's not hard. Well, the soil is hard, of course, but determining that it is frozen really isn't. According to Steven Bodin, director of the soils laboratory at the University of Massachusetts in Amherst, if you can't dig into it with a spade, it's frozen enough. And it doesn't have to be frozen to any specific depth before laying down the mulch.

In the fall, the most compulsive gardeners can insert a soil thermometer a couple of inches deep somewhere in the garden. When it reads 32 degrees, it's time to mulch. Since the thermometer will be frozen in for the winter, don't spend a lot on it.

Bulbs and Cold Weather

Every winter is likely to have warm spells. When they last long enough, bulbs begin peeking out to take a look-see. Some gardeners want to rush out and protect them somehow.

No need; the bulbs have it all figured out. Bulbs are just coming out of dormancy, and the cell fluid has a high concentration of sugars and salts, which act just like antifreeze. By the time the cell has a normal balance of water to sugars and salts, the season will have changed, and the danger of freezing will be past. And those little leaves benefit by being close to the soil, which is warmer than the air, and radiates a bit of heat—not much heat, but it doesn't take much to make a difference when you're only a couple of inches tall.

Crocuses, winter aconite, and snowdrops, of course, are supposed to be early, reminding us that spring is coming. Some early daffodils have buds showing, and other bulbs are coming up to take a look around and are well prepared for late winter's tricks.

4

Sometimes It's the Plant's Fault

No matter how carefully a garden is planned and planted, occasionally it seems as if plants have their own mysterious agendas. Understanding their responses to the pressures of their genes and environment and trying to see their behavior in terms of a struggle to survive long enough to reproduce sometimes adds a new appreciation for the stubbornly independent quality that plants can have, and sometimes just piles on another level of frustration for the gardener trying to tame them.

I'm often asked how to make a plant do something out of its nature in order to make it fit or function better in a garden. Mostly you can't. Gardening, like politics, is the art of compromise. Gardeners have desires, but plants can be obstinate. A plant's response to the world is the result of hundreds of thousands of small genetic changes, little trial-and-error experiments, over hundreds of millennia. Those experiments that succeeded were rewarded with the next best thing to immortality: surviving long enough to reproduce. Experiments that failed could mean the end of a species. With that much at stake, it's no wonder that a plant's self-interest takes precedence.

So there we are, trying to breed flower colors that a species' natural pollinator can't see, coaxing apple trees into bearing enough fruit to break their branches, and complaining about immature plants that won't flower and are spoiling the look of that corner of the garden.

Those Old Conifer Blues

What's in a name? 'Blue Rug' junipers, which should be both blue-green and rug-like (low growing), occasionally turn dark green. If you have one, there are a couple of possible reasons.

It's a question of light. Dr. Kim Tripp, Vice President of Horticulture at the New York Botanical Garden, says that ground cover junipers, including your 'Blue Rug' juniper, are full sun plants.

Some evergreens are not just satisfied to produce food through photosynthesis; they also make a protective blue, waxy substance. But to do the whole job, food and protective covering, requires a lot of light—six to eight hours each day of uninterrupted full sun. If they are already in full sun, Tripp says, they may be younger plants, which typically show less blue than mature ones. If so, they just need a few more years to start showing off their color.

Some evergreens change color in the winter and then change back in the spring. That happens when the cold causes a chemical change that is reflected in the coloration. Siberian carpet cypress (green to plum) and some eastern arborvitae (bright green to dull yellowish-green) are two examples of this change. Spring warmth brings back the normal color, sort of the same effect that it has on people.

'Blue Rug' juniper, along with some other cultivars, includ-

ing 'Blue Chip' and 'Saddle River,' hold their blue color during
the winter, while others, such as 'Blue Horizons' and 'Prince of
Wales,' turn purply bronze. The eighty or so cultivars of ground
cover junipers are hard to tell apart, and Tripp says that what is
labeled 'Blue Rug' frequently turns out to be something else. If
you have one that turns, enjoy it. Just because we call them evergreens doesn't mean they think of themselves that way.

Growing Cilantro

*Growing cilantro (also called Chinese parsley), whether from seed
or from purchased seedlings, can be a frustrating annual event.
Everything goes well for a very short period, and then the plants
stop producing foliage, the cilantro, and start producing seeds,
which are the spice coriander. You want one and not the other, but
the plants don't offer a choice. Maybe you should learn to use more
coriander in your cooking.*

Because that's what cilantro does. There are two distinct
stages in the life of the annual *Coriandrum sativum.* After germi-
nating, it begins to grow the leaves we call cilantro. But less than
two months later, it stops producing these leaves and uses all its
energy to send up a flowering stalk. The fruit formed from the
clusters of flowers is called coriander.

You can increase your foliage harvest by picking when the
leaves are smaller—every two weeks if the plants are fertilized
after each harvest. You may get five or six harvests this way before
the plant becomes totally frustrated and dies. Or you can look for
cultivars like 'Long Standing,' 'Slow Bolt,' or 'Santo,' which are a
bit slower to flower.

Cilantro is considered a cool weather crop; when the summer
heat starts, it grows and flowers even faster. You can take advantage of that by continuing to sow seeds every week or so during

the summer and just pull the plants up once they are ready for harvest. And when you are thinning seedlings, wait until the first true leaves grow. You can eat the thinned-out seedlings too.

Fascinating Fasciation

Fantail willows, sold for decoration, are unlike any plants you normally come across. Their branches have a flat, ribbon-like stem that doesn't seem like anything nature would do on her own. But it is.

In many plants, something happens that causes the normal growth pattern to change from round stems to ones that may be wide and flat, bunched into ribs, or forming unusual crests. This trait is called fasciation, and the most common garden plant showing this is crested cockscomb, *Celosia argentea* var. *cristata,* whose wide head is twisted into a velvety, convoluted crest.

Cells at the growing tip normally follow one another, lengthening the shoot. In fasciation, some cells may take an abrupt turn and line up in a row. Each cell on the line then acts as a growing point, convincing new cells to follow it, thus changing a round shoot into a ribbon composed of growing points along the entire width. Two ribbons may grow and twist about each other, forming a crest, if the central part of the stem, where the growth should have taken place, dies. In other cases, many individual stems will begin to grow and fuse together, forming a bundle of shoots.

The causes of fasciation are not well understood, but several factors appear to be involved, including heredity, environment, and damage to the growing point by insects or disease. Some plants with a predisposition to fasciation are grown for ornamental uses, including Japanese fantail willow, brain cactus, and cockscomb celosia.

Have you ever bought those large strawberries that end in a

wedge rather than a point? They are a delicious example of fasciation.

Up Where the Sun Shines

Campsis radicans, *also called trumpet vine or simply campsis, is very popular with gardeners, but demands a great deal of patience. I have heard the same tale a thousand times—it grows well, seems to like the soil, water, sun, and fertilizer, but it never blooms. Invariably the plant is five years old or younger and has covered just about everything in its path, but the wonderful yellow flowers its owners expected are nowhere to be seen.*

    Many people become frustrated enough, and mad enough, to even threaten to yank it out if it doesn't do what they expect, when they expect it. As if you could threaten a plant. The one thing they don't want to do is exactly what I recommend.

Trumpet Creeper

Wait right there. Campsis like some other vines, including wisteria, climbing hydrangea, and English ivy, has a long juvenile stage when it isn't interested in boys or reproduction—only in growing up big and strong. Five years is not unusual, but it will flower—when it's ready.

You may have the plant in an ideal spot, but these growing stages are genetically determined, the result of a vine's lifestyle. In the wild, vines start life in the shade of other plants, so they devote all their energy to growing large enough to climb into the sunlight, up to where the pollinators can find them, high enough that wind-blown seeds can really travel. Until you get big enough, there's not much reason to make seed, and if you're not ready for seed, why make flowers?

Pluots, Apriums . . .

Pluots, a plum-apricot cross, are beginning to show up in mail-order gardening catalogs, and people are wondering if they can grow them in the Northeast. Pluots?

While I still struggle to remember if the Santa Rosa plum is the red one or the blue one, the rest of the world has apparently decided that it needs more kinds of fruit. After fifteen years of breeding, enter the patented pluot, more plum than apricot, which looks like a plum, tastes more like an apricot; and the aprium, more apricot than plum, which looks like an apricot and tastes like both. Plumcots are half and half, and peachcots are in development. Actually, I think I need a plain cot.

It isn't just fruit trees. Jostaberries, a cross between a black currant and a gooseberry, and trazel, a hybrid of Turkish and European filberts, are also out there. Even less well known is the hican, a shagbark hickory and pecan cross.

It may sound as if the geneticists are just doing things to

keep busy, but there are other, better reasons. New hybrids are always bred with the intent to improve some characteristics. Many
are more disease resistant, taste better, store longer, or have longer
harvest periods.

The plum crosses generally grow anywhere 'Santa Rosa'
plums grow. They are hardy in zones 6 through 9, but the early
blooming characteristic inherited from the apricot means a late
frost may kill the flowers, resulting in a year without fruit.

It's a good idea to have that 'Santa Rosa,' because pluots require a pollinator. Apriums, on the other hand, are self-fruitful.

Mail order sources include Sonoma Antique Apple Nursery,
4395 Westside Road, Healdsburg, CA 95448, (707) 433-6420,
catalog; and Stark Brothers, P.O. Box 10, Louisiana, MO 63353,
(800) 478-2759, catalog.

Tomato Intentions

*Tomatoes are always described on the tags as determinate or indeter-
minate, but I have yet to see a tag that explains what that is or
why I should care.*

Just remember that a determinate tomato plant has determined just how large it wants to be, while an indeterminate one
isn't sure. Determinate tomatoes are more confined in their
branching pattern. Each branch ends in a flower cluster and stops
right there. Consequently these tomatoes bear most of their fruit
at nearly the same time. Indeterminate tomatoes grow more like
vines. They continue to grow and branch, producing flowers
along the way. Although there is a period of heavy harvest, they
continue to drag on for a longer period. They should be supported in some way—caged or tied to a trellis or stake—or they
will sprawl around the garden, getting mixed in with everything
else. Containment is more than an aesthetic consideration. A

jumble of leaves and tomatoes on the ground reduces air circulation, increasing the possibility of fungus diseases. There are also semideterminate varieties—plants that can almost make up their minds.

Japanese Maples

Some of those striking Japanese maple cultivars that have red leaves become a little less striking and a whole lot greener by midsummer. If yours is like that, it may not be the right cultivar.

Most Japanese maple cultivars begin red in spring, change to green in the summer, and then have rich orange-red fall color. The Japanese, for whom the appreciation of nature is a national ritual, take joy in the changes that mark passage through the year.

Some Japanese maple cultivars, however, stay red all summer, assuming they are in full sun for at least half the day, although they appreciate partial shade from the late afternoon sun. But even with these trees, the seasons are reflected in color changes. The bright reds of spring can become dark, almost black-reds, during summer, and then a brilliant red-orange in autumn.

Two lace-leaf Japanese maples, with deeply incised leaves, 'Inaba Shidare' (also sold as 'Red Select,' but that sounds more like a tomato) and 'Tamukeyama,' are especially notable. 'Bloodgood' and 'Moonfire' are dark red during the summer and crimson in the fall. 'Fireglow' is a bit brighter in color than 'Bloodgood' and does well in hot, humid areas.

A word of caution when buying Japanese maples: seedlings, even from named cultivars, may not grow up with the same characteristics as the parent, no matter how good the neighborhood. Grafted trees, where a piece of the parent is grown onto another root stock, do remain true.

Sources for these maples include Mountain Maples, 54561 Registered Guest Road, Box 1329, Laytonville, CA 95454-1329, (707) 984-6522, catalog, and Twombly Nursery, 163 Barn Hill Road, Monroe, CT 06468, (203) 261-2133, catalog.

June Drop

No one with apple trees can fail to notice the difference between the number of blossoms and the number of apples. Increasing the yield may not be a possibility.

From the first flower bud opening until picking time, a lot happens that reduces the potential yield. In the end, if 5 to 15 percent of the flowers become ripe fruit, it should be considered a good crop.

Unpollinated flowers are the first cause of lost fruit. A late frost can damage buds, and strong winds can dry the stigmas in open flowers, making them unable to receive pollen. Trees that cross-pollinate, like apple trees, need bees to bring pollen from another apple variety. That may be a problem if bees are decimated by a combination of a hard winter and an increase in parasitic mites.

Flowers that are poorly pollinated may also set fruit, but the fruit eventually will be dropped. Trees that require cross-pollination may accidentally pollinate their own flowers in a wind-driven fit of confusion. Bees that concentrate on a single tree effectively self-pollinate the blossoms.

And sometimes bees, normally experts at their work, may not cover the pistils with enough pollen. In all of these cases, the resulting fruit that sets will have too few seeds or seeds that are not viable, and the tree will drop them.

Finally, some fruit drop is self-protection. A natural thinning, the phenomenon called June drop, can occur from late May

Apple

into July. Fruit begins to enlarge and then, for no apparent reason, falls. If it all grew, the competition for nutrients would prevent any fruit from reaching full size, and the weight would break the branches, so the tree sacrifices quantity for quality. After the June drop, thin out any remaining weak or small fruit by hand until the fruit is sufficiently spaced for optimum ripening. Apples and pears should have 6 to 8 inches between the fruit; peaches, 4 to 6 inches; and plums, 2 to 3 inches.

And summer is still ahead. Some fruit will be lost to insects, birds, and neighborhood children. And some disease may yet wipe out the entire crop. Happy harvest.

Dwindling Peaches

Peaches, too, suffer from the same problems as apples and June drop. Readers often try to blame their squirrels, or themselves, for poor crops. Sometimes better gardening techniques can increase your crop. This is especially true if you have one of those peach trees that only

Peaches

ends up with four or five peaches that reach maturity. Generally it isn't the things that people try—more fertilizer or throwing nets around the tree. Usually it is simpler. And usually it isn't the squirrels. Whom you might owe an apology.

This is the nature of the beast, although your harvest can be improved.

A mature tree will produce about 500 peaches from its 30,000 blossoms—about 1 in 60. That ratio sounds as if there is a natural conspiracy, and there is—sort of. Fruit may fail to mature for several reasons. Win Cowgill, a county agricultural agent with Rutgers Cooperative Extension in New Jersey, said that cloudy weather forces fruit trees to make choices: use the limited sunlight to produce more leaves for photosynthesis or to produce fruit. Leaves win. Another reason is that, if pollination isn't complete, the seed inside may not be viable. And finally, there's June drop.

To get the most from your tree don't overfeed it (nitrogen

promotes foliage growth, not fruit), keep the ground weed free out to the drip line (the distance that the branches extend from the trunk), thin the small peaches to provide 4 to 6 inches between fruit, and prune every March or early April, while the tree is still dormant, to promote vigorous new growth. Prune older branches, since peaches fruit on one-year-old wood. Of course, the easiest way to increase your production is to buy more trees.

Invasion of the Bamboos

Bamboos can appear out of nowhere and proliferate at an amazing rate, ready to take over your yard. They grow with such speed and aggression that people worry about having them march up to the house and dig right through the foundation.

Out-of-control bamboos, and at least one bamboo look-alike, are a common problem in the Northeast. A probable invader is the weed *Polygonum japonicum,* formerly *P. cuspidatum* and commonly known as Japanese knotweed or Mexican bamboo.

Bamboo or weed, all of them spread like . . . well, like weeds, through underground rhizomes branching from the parent plant. If the main stand of plants is outside your yard, cutting down what you have in your yard will not kill them because they continue to receive and store food made by the plants on the other side of the fence.

This polygonum is a noxious weed, and uncontrolled bamboo can be just as invasive. These plants are the Bruce Willis of the plant kingdom: they die hard, and there's always a sequel next year.

Of course a lot of people grow ornamental bamboo in their landscapes, but even ornamental bamboo needs to be controlled. Michael Bartholomew, a consumer horticulturist in Albany County, New York, and editor of the *American Bamboo Society Newsletter,* suggests rhizome-resistant barriers for control.

The barrier, a thick (16 mil) polypropylene, should be placed across the path of the invasion. Dig a trench at least 24 inches deep, and install the barrier tipped at an angle back toward your property. Leave 1 to 2 inches of the material above ground. As new rhizomes invade each year, they will follow the contour of the barrier, angling up and above ground, so you can cut them off. As for those plants already in your yard, you will have to cut them down repeatedly or carefully spray them with a systemic herbicide to kill them.

House foundations with good, smooth walls will not be damaged by bamboo, but if the foundation has cracks, the rhizomes can get in and enlarge them.

A list of suppliers that sell bamboo and related items, including barrier material, is available from the American Bamboo Society, P.O. Box 215, Slingerlands, NY 12159-0215. Barrier material is also available from New England Bamboo, P.O. Box 358, Rockport, MA 01966, (978) 546-3581.

Patience with Perennials

If you are disappointed with the perennials you planted at the start of the growing season, don't worry. The first year is for settling in, not for performance. Like puppies, plants change as they grow. Height and spread, numbers of flowers, and other characteristics of the mature plant take time to develop. Wait at least another full year to judge them.

A Ficus Mystery

Ficus benjamina, *a popular small tree grown as a houseplant, can be attacked by scale insects, but finding those pinhead-sized, wax-colored bumps on the underside of the leaves shouldn't lead to panic.*

First, it's not a problem. What you see is not a scale insect but a waxy glandular spot found on ficus, although the number and location of spots is not the same on all species. (Insects are poor at organization; you'll never find them arranged in the same way on every leaf. This is a clue that the problem is caused by something other than insects.)

But the question remains, what is it? C. C. Berg, a ficus expert at the University of Bergen Botanical Institute in Norway, confirms that these waxy spots are characteristic of ficus, but that their function is unknown. One theory is that the spots emit a substance that attracts fig wasps, which pollinate the plant.

Nature is rarely frivolous, so I'm sure they do have a function. But the figs aren't talking.

Variable Beets

Organic beet growers will swear that their beets are vastly superior to those found in supermarkets, and they are probably right. But once in a great while a few of your home-grown beets may look a little strange. They ought to be globe-shaped, but a few are cylindrical.

You can blame the grower or the seed company, but either way it isn't your fault (or the beet's). Probably your beet is an open-pollinated variety—one that is pollinated randomly—rather than a hybrid, where the choice of parents is controlled by the grower. With open pollination, some genetic diversity always shows up. If the field of globe-shaped beets is within 3,000 feet of a field of cylindrical ones, cross-fertilization can occur. As with humans, some offspring will resemble Mom; others will look more like Dad.

The other possibility is rare, but a packaging mix-up can happen as seed companies turn millions of seeds from thousands of vegetable and flower varieties into small packages. When you think of the number of seeds involved every year, how small they are, and how similar many of them appear, the odds are against perfection.

You may prefer the look of globe-shaped pickled beets in a glass jar, but I'll bet the cylindrical ones are tasty too, and easier to cut into uniform slices.

Pepper Problems

Pepper plants can look as lush and healthy as can be, but then the flowers just drop off and they refuse to bear any peppers. You might assume it has something to do with whether or not the bees have been around pollinating, but that's not it.

Peppers self-pollinate, and the wind takes care of that, so the parasitic mites and other problems that have been reducing bee populations isn't the answer. Most likely it is a pollination problem of another sort. High heat—90-degree days and nights that never seem to cool off—renders the pollen grains sterile. Stress from lack of rainfall also kills pollen. If the flowers aren't pollinated, they shrivel up and fall off without setting fruit, and you are left with a hole in your harvest.

A slightly different problem—that of peppers' forming fruit that falls off while still small—is frequently due to shade. Peppers need direct sun and lots of it—at least seven hours a day. Sometimes we don't realize that a clear view when looking straight up isn't enough for a vegetable plot. Nearby buildings and trees may cast shadows in the morning or afternoon, reducing the amount of direct sun, sometimes to levels below the plant's needs. Remember that something as big as a pepper takes a lot of energy to produce, and energy means lots of sun.

Fertilizing peppers in the spring is important, as with most other vegetables. But because peppers have shallow roots, nitrogen moves out of reach as it leaches downward in the soil, and peppers need fertilizing more often than other vegetables. In addition to the spring compost or top dressing of granular fertilizer, apply a soluble fertilizer when the flowers first appear and then every three weeks until the peppers begin to form.

Don't be clever (or lazy) and think that a stronger fertilizer will reduce the need for frequent applications. Fertilizers with a high nitrogen content encourage foliage at the expense of fruit, and terrific foliage is not the reason to grow peppers.

The Color of a Firethorn's Flame

Your mother's firethorn (pyracantha) has loads of bright red berries, so you buy one. But yours turns out to have orange berries, and they don't look the way you want. So you set out to change them.

Fertilizers or soil amendments won't help any more than you could eat your way from brown eyes to blue. Berry color, like so many other plant and animal characteristics, is determined by genetics. Your mother's firethorn will always be red, and yours will always be orange—except, of course, when the two main enemies of pyracantha, fireblight and apple scab, blacken the berries and leaves.

Pyracantha could be seen more often in the landscape as an informal hedge, in foundation plantings, or as espaliers since it offers spectacular clusters of red, orange, or even yellow fruit, which persist well into winter, and has narrow, glossy, dark green leaves. Unfortunately, its vulnerability to disease and poor winter

Pyracantha

hardiness have limited its usefulness—until recently, that is.

Two cultivars introduced through the breeding program directed by Dr. Elwin Orton, research professor at Rutgers University, New Brunswick, New Jersey, offer a high degree of resistance to the two diseases, as well as improved hardiness. 'Fiery Cascade,' a low-growing pyracantha at 3 to 4 feet tall and 5 feet wide, can handle winter temperatures as low as zero. It produces a large number of berries that are orange in late summer but turn bright red in the fall. 'Rutgers,' the other variety, has orange berries and grows 4½ feet tall and 5 to 6 feet wide. 'Rutgers' is even hardier, surviving to -5 degrees. Both might suit places in the garden where taller pyracantha won't work.

Sources for these two cultivars include Appalachian Gardens, Box 82, Waynesboro, PA 17268, (717) 762-4312, catalog; and Forrestfarm, 990 Tetherow Road, Williams, OR 97544, (541) 846-7269, catalog.

Bark Shedding

Sycamores are beautiful, stately trees, but they have an interesting characteristic—they shed large plates of bark every year. Some years more than others. Much more.

As far as the tree is concerned, nothing's wrong, nothing to fret about. Last year drought, this year rain—over the course of a lifetime in one place, everything balances out.

To be able to shed bark safely, trees must first form barrier zones to protect against pests. Since growing anything, including barriers, takes water, your tree will most likely shed very little bark when there is low rainfall. During a year with greater amounts of rain, more bark is shed, thus providing you with a little more raking exercise than you had before. It all averages out.

The unasked question, though, is more interesting. Why do sycamore, London plane, and many conifers shed bark plates in the first place? Under the protective outer bark lies another layer of protection, the phellogen. In some species, like ash, old and new segments of phellogen become attached through intertwined fibers, resulting in a characteristic furrowed appearance. In species that shed, these layers are not interconnected, and the bark plates easily fall as the new ones develop.

Classifying Annuals

Annuals, whether seeds or seedlings, are usually labeled as hardy, half-hardy, *or* tender.

The botanist's definition of an annual is a plant that not only dies at the end of the growing season but is supposed to. That is, true annuals germinate, grow, flower, produce seed, and die in a single growing season even if you remember to water and fertilize them.

Those terms, *hardy, half-hardy,* and *tender,* are cultural terms that reflect the plants' tolerance to cold. Hardy annuals, like cleome, annual poppies, sweet alyssum, bachelor's buttons, and love-in-a-mist, will survive a light frost and can be sown directly in the garden while the forsythia is in flower.

Tender annuals, such as heliotrope, datura, lantana, Madagascar periwinkle, gomphrena, and zinnia, cannot be planted until warm weather settles in for good and the soil is well warmed. In the Northeast there isn't time for them to be sown directly outside and still put on a long summer display, so they are either sown indoors weeks earlier or purchased as young plants.

Tender annuals resent anything other than the high-summer sauna, coming into their own as everything else in the garden, including the gardener, begins to droop.

Half-hardy annuals, and some tender perennials that are treated as annuals because they cannot survive the winter in the Northeast, like petunia, snapdragon, nicotiana, marigolds, and verbena, fall in between. They can withstand the cool, wet weather of spring, but cannot be planted until all danger of frost is past. *Half-hardy* is a British term and has more importance in England, where springs tend to be very cool and wet. For the Northeast United States, it is generally safe to treat half-hardy annuals the same way as tender ones.

Late-Blooming Cosmos

Your tallest, strongest cosmos occasionally fail to bloom on time. They'll dwarf their blooming brothers, but they just stand there, blind. It rarely happens to other annuals, but it does happen to your friend's cosmos, too, so it isn't likely to have anything to do with your care or the soil. After all, most of them are doing just fine.

Two cosmos characteristics are combining to add a little frustration to your day.

First, your cosmos, probably *Cosmos bipinnatus,* the cosmos usually planted for its tall, graceful stalks of ferny foliage and lovely flowers in white, pink, and shades of magenta, is not a controlled, uniform hybrid. It is an open-pollinated plant, that is, pollinated naturally—in this case by bees. Open pollination leads to a genetically diverse population, which will always contain a small number of blind plants—those that never flower. While breeders always work toward reducing the number of blind cosmos, the genes are just a result of a diverse population. Some of your cosmos, however, may yet burst into flower. Dr. Allan Armitage, professor of horticulture at the University of Georgia in Athens, says that cosmos are classified as short-day plants, which initiate flower production when the day length is shorter than a critical amount. For cosmos, the critical length is about 14 hours. Once this is started, of course, the flowers put their clocks away and get on with the business of blooming.

Cosmos

Plants that were started late and were not mature enough to initiate flowers in the spring, when days were shorter, may not be able to do so during the long days of summer. But as we slip into the shorter days of fall, some of those nonbloomers will respond by starting to flower. Since they didn't flower before and all their energy went into growing thick, tall stems, you'll have to look up to see them.

Flowerless Vines

You garden like crazy, with great fruits and vegetables, and loads of various flowers, but you and morning glories just don't seem to be made for each other.

One possible reason your morning glories (*Ipomoea purpurea*) didn't bloom is that they didn't get a good night's sleep. Like many other plants, morning glories contain a clock—a chemical system for measuring how long the night is.

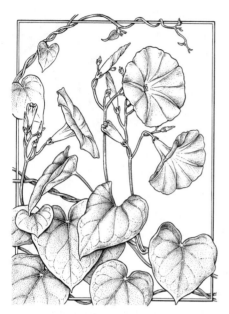

Morning Glory

Morning glories and several other plants—poinsettia, chrysanthemum, and kalanchoe, among them—will flower only when they have a minimum number of hours of continuous dark. The critical night length for a plant depends on a variety of factors, including the latitude at which it is growing, temperature, and moisture levels.

The key for any plant that needs a minimum dark period is that its nights are not interrupted before the right number of hours has passed. Interruptions do not have to be very long or very bright to affect a plant's timing system. Terrace or porch lights, incandescent street lights, even a few minutes of light barely bright enough to read by can delay or prevent flowering in plants that require a long, continuous dark period.

The chemical mechanism that controls a plant's response to short or long nights is complex, but the logic is simple. Plants use this timing mechanism, called photoperiodism, to trigger flowering as well as other seasonal events. For example, to ensure their survival, some species must form dormant winter buds; others must begin storing food in tubers, bulbs, or thick storage roots; and still others must have time to develop frost-hardy cell walls.

While the sun is consistent from year to year in its timing, the plants never counted on Thomas Edison.

Needle Drop

Nothing panics a gardener like a summer of low rainfall. Every-thing looks peaked, and crisped, even your white pine. Suddenly you notice that many of the interior needles are turning yellow, then brown and dropping.

Premature fall color and leaf drop on some deciduous trees as a result of drought stress has made us more conscious of all of our trees and shrubs, even the conifers. Most likely there is nothing wrong with your white pine; you are just seeing the normal needle cycle.

Evergreens are "ever green" not because they don't lose leaves or needles, but because they don't lose all of them each year. Some new needles grow every spring, and some older, interior ones die every fall, but the plant is never bare because each needle lasts for more than one growing season. For example, white pine needles grown in the spring of 2000 will remain on the tree all winter, and finally fall in October of 2001.

Each year the needles that persist hide the ones that die. Some needles may turn yellow and brown and drop early due to drought stress, but most of what you're seeing is normal. Lush growing seasons are often followed by excessive needle drop.

Here is the typical needle life of some common conifers:

- Hemlock: three or more growing seasons
- White pine: two or more growing seasons
- Scrub or Jersey pine: two to four growing seasons
- Scots pine: three or more growing seasons
- Fir and Douglas fir: five to seven growing seasons
- Norway spruce: 7 or more growing seasons
- Yews: 3 to 5 or more growing seasons

On the commonly planted arborvitae, the interior leaves turn yellow and then red-brown, and the entire branchlet drops at the end of the second growing season. And just to keep it confusing, the deciduous conifers bald cypress and dawn redwood have an orange-brown to red-brown color change, larch turns yellow, and all three drop all of their leaves every year.

Fall Color in a Nutshell

Somehow most of us get through school without learning what makes the sky blue or the leaves red. Or maybe we prefer forgetting because the mystery is more satisfying than the science.

Two classes of chemicals, carotenoids (yellow and orange pigments) and anthocyanins (reds and blues), cause fall color. When temperatures drop in the fall, the leaves stop making chlorophyll, the green pigment, and the carotenoids, which are there all the time, show through.

Anthocyanins form as food production declines during dry weather, with sunny, warm days and cool, frost-free nights. Different proportions of the chemicals combine with the cell environment to create the color effects we see, from brilliant red and yellow to subtle purple and apricot.

The sky is blue because . . . oh, sorry, out of room.

Unexpected Flowers

Fall comes; some cold hits. Enough to make us bundle up but not exactly winter. Yet here and there we notice a splash of color—a tree is blooming. At least, a few flowers have opened. Two things come to mind. One is why the tree flowers when it hasn't had a cold period, which is usually a necessity. The other is what happens when the real winter hits.

Nature has a variety of ways to cause flowering. Some plants require cold, others need a large drop from day to night temperatures, and some respond to long days.

Many trees and shrubs are induced to flower by a combination of factors that cause them to stop growing and go into dormancy. Sometimes drought, sudden cold, or other environmental stress can put a plant into a temporary state called eco-dormancy. When the stress is relieved, a few buds may break into flower, a phenomenon called stress flowering. This is especially common in rhododendron, flowering quince, forsythia, lilac, Callery pear, and apple.

Drought, heat, and late frost can confuse a number of trees. When these are followed by rains and cooler weather, the stress is relieved, and the trees celebrate by flowering. There is no danger to the plant; it will go into dormancy when winter actually starts. The buds that broke early will not flower in the spring, but their numbers are usually so small that you wouldn't even notice the difference.

Dioecious Plants

Moving into a new house with existing landscaping can set you up for some disappointments. For example, a yard may come with big, healthy hollies, but they don't produce the berries you want. As always, nature has her requirements.

The overwhelming number of flowering plants produce both male and female parts within the same flower, so that every plant will produce the same flowers and fruit. But in some plants—not many, but more than one might think—individuals are either male or female. In these plants, called dioecious (pronounced die-EE-shus), both sexes have flowers, frequently small and inconspicuous. Pollen passes from male to female flowers by wind or insects. When pollinated, the female plants produce fruit, while the male plants hand out cigars. If the fruit adds to our enjoyment of the plant, as with hollies, the occasional male is necessary in the neighborhood. If the fruit is a distraction, as with ginkgoes, where the fruit smells like the streets of Paris three weeks into a garbage haulers' strike, it is important to not have both sexes.

The evolutionary pressures behind dioecious plants are unknown, but there are some interesting trends. Dioecy is more common in plants that tend to be large and that are native to the tropics and isolated islands.

Given that tall trees from tropical islands rarely show up in northeastern gardens, there are a surprising number of common temperate-zone trees and shrubs that are dioecious and that require a gardener to plan a bit before using them. Hollies, katsura tree, yew, juniper, bayberry, fringe tree, Osage orange, poplar, sumac, willow, and ailanthus are all dioecious. Having fruit may or may not be important, depending on the plant and how it is used in the landscape, but when fruit is desired, both male and female are required.

Sex can be determined by looking at the flower parts, although the differences are small, vary between species, and may not be obvious. If the plant is not in flower when you want to buy it, look at the labels.

Winged Wahoo Fall Color

A hedge that not only provides privacy but also shows bright red fall color fills both functional and ornamental needs. Euonymus alatus is often planted for these reasons, but sometimes fails to deliver on the color, being very blah instead of bright. Since some plants are pH sensitive, people wonder if acidifying the soil will help.

Euonymus color does not react to soil pH the way *Hydrangea macrophylla* does. Its distinctive corky-winged branches give this shrub one of my favorite common names, Winged Wahoo, and brilliant fall reds give it another—Burning Bush. Since yours appears to have its fire put out, I have to assume that the variety planted is unfortunately not one of the more colorful ones.

If brighter is better, try some of the cultivars that have been selected for color: 'Nordine' (red with orange tones), 'October Glory' (brilliant magenta-red), or 'Rudy Haag' (pinkish-red). Each has vibrant fall color and is more compact than the straight species, growing from 4 to 8 feet tall, depending on the cultivar.

The straight species, *E. alatus,* is variable in its fall color, ranging from a soft peachy rose with hints of yellow through bright pinks and dark rosy reds. The fact that it is adaptable to a range of soil pH and propagates so easily from seed has allowed it to escape from cultivation and become invasive in woods and prairies in parts of the East and Midwest.

"Bleeding" Trees

Late winter or early spring may be pruning time for many shrubs and trees, but working on particular trees at that time will just lead to a run of watery sap.

A. Maple, birch, and dogwood are considered the prime "bleeders" of the tree world and are best pruned when they are in full leaf. As metabolic activity begins to increase in late winter, fluid pressure also begins to build and the sap starts moving up the tree. Like a shaken soda bottle, everything looks normal from the outside, but there is no such thing as a gentle opening. Once the pruning cuts are made, sap will flow. Don't bother to try to seal the wound, the sap will come right through. The wound will eventually heal itself.

Bleeding is not harmful for the tree, which has plenty of sap. The sap flow looks bad, and it can make a mess on cars parked below, but it poses no real danger. After all, the sap from your maple tree is just a less purified form of the syrup you put on pancakes.

Red Edges on Leaves

Red edges on leaves that are normally green can cause quite a surprise, and more than a little worry.

Common in jades, Christmas cactus, and New Year's revelers, the color is usually caused by having too much of a good thing: in the plants' case, carbohydrates. If the plant is happy in its situation—plenty of sun, well-drained growing medium, enough water, a comfy pot—it was able to make more food during the active growing period than it needs when cooler temperatures and shorter days slow it down. Unused carbohydrates are stored in the leaves and are important for producing the red pigment anthocyanin. You may notice it more in the leaves on the window side of the plant because they get colder than those on the interior side and use food at a slower rate.

But stress caused by exposure to too much cold can create a carbohydrate imbalance, which also produces anthocyanin. If the leaves appear healthy and turgid, the plant is simply beaming with joy. If they are shrunken and wrinkled, the red is a distress signal.

Section Two

Better Gardens from Better Gardeners

Better gardens come only when gardeners get better, and there are two significant ways to improve both. The first is to learn the techniques and cultural conditions that individual plants need (the soil, air, water, nutrients, sun, and climate) and the techniques (planting, pruning, propagating, pest control, and the rest) to be happier and stronger and to learn to do gardening tasks more efficiently. I am a firm believer that the amount of pleasure drops as the number of blisters rises. There is enough hard work in gardening as it is; no need to add more.

The second way to improve is to wander further afield in the plant kingdom. Get away from house builders' idea of landscaping, even away from your friends' and neighbors' ideas. There are probably a couple of hundred thousand plant species on the planet, and tens of thousands more cultivars and varieties. Obviously not all of them will thrive where you live, and many more are, shall we say, less attractive than others. But there is a whole slew of plants, available at local nurseries and through the mail, that are a lot more interesting than lawn, tea roses, and arborvitae. And if you garden for food, the range of fruits and vegetables, both brand new and heirloom, has never been larger.

Once the balance changes and there are more successes than failures, more joy and interest, many people begin collecting, going deeper with their involvement. Not much offers more satisfaction to more people than new knowledge combined with a place to use it.

5

Doing It Better

Practice may make perfect, but it helps to know what to practice. The rapid explosion of gardening as a hobby, plus an equally rapid explosion in the numbers and kinds of plants that homeowners are trying to grow, means an ever-expanding need for information.

The vast majority of questions that come to *The New York Times* are how-to questions. Nothing is simple or obvious to someone who doesn't know the answer. These questions cover a lot of territory, and I have even tried to expand that in the answers, being a bit more thorough than the immediate question. The questions and answers cover introductory techniques and basic terms as well as more advanced cultural information.

Rather than rely on the "it always works for me" school of gardening, I check and double-check the latest scientific research being done at universities and the best techniques that knowledgeable professionals use. Interestingly, I find that most of the university and professional people are also home gardeners, so much of the science has been tested in backyards, where it really counts.

Topsoil versus Loam

Topsoil. Gardeners may quibble over the exact interpretation of what topsoil should look or feel like, but all will agree that it is the best, the soil you want for your beds. Most expect it to be rich in humus and wonderful to the touch. Instead, it sometimes shows up on the back of a truck as slimy, poor quality dirt.

The "top" in *topsoil* refers to location, not quality. Topsoil is the uppermost layer, but the big question is, uppermost from where? Usually topsoil is preferred by gardeners because the upper 6 to 8 inches are likely to contain more decayed organic material. Unfortunately, some topsoil could be richer in heavy metals, spilled oil, pesticides, or other unwanted by-products of our industrial age. Testing for contaminants can be expensive, but if you are planning to use it for growing vegetables, you should contact your local county cooperative extension office for advice.

Loam, on the other hand, is a textural classification. Technically, loam is soil with 7 to 27 percent clay, 28 to 50 percent silt (particles that are larger than clay particles and smaller than sand grains), and less than 52 percent sand. Depending on the proportions, it can be called loam, sandy loam, sandy clay loam, clay loam, silty clay loam, or silt loam. Notice that none of this has anything to do with nutritive value. Expect to add amendments like fertilizer and compost or aged manure, which also improve texture.

There are no agreed-on quality standards for topsoil, so ask for loamy soil. Since loam can vary so widely, it is best to see and touch it before buying it. Gently rub a moistened handful between your fingers and use the Goldilocks criteria: not too much clay (sticky and slippery), not too much sand (gritty), loam should be just right—moderately smooth and firm enough to roll into firm rods.

Rotating Crops

When spring comes and it's time to lay out the vegetable garden, most people simply do what they did last year—put the tomatoes where the tomatoes have always been and the beets right where the beets belong. You may want to shake things up a little.

Imagine how comforting it is for bacteria or fungi to arise from a deep winter, stretch, and burrow up to the surface to find their breakfast tomato waiting right where it was last season. Rotating your plantings is a simple thing that helps ensure healthier plants.

Many diseases specialize in the plants or plant families that they attack. Since disease organisms overwinter or leave their offspring in the nearby soil, plants can suffer the same problems season after season. Crop rotation breaks the chain by depriving these organisms of an easy living.

Complicated charts showing how long to wait before planting something in the same place bring back the horror of high school algebra story problems, and many of us prefer to lose the tomatoes rather than figure it all out. Dr. Stephen Reiners, an assistant professor of horticulture at Cornell University's Geneva Research Station, says that three years between replantings will break the cycle of most diseases as long as you avoid replacing one vegetable with another in the same family. Peppers, potatoes, and eggplants, for example, are in the nightshade family, so substituting any of them for tomatoes, another relative, provides an acceptable diet variation for the bad guys. Reiners suggests planting vegetables 8 to 10 feet from last year's site just to be safe.

Aloe Propagation

Some plants come and go, but others are handed down from mother to daughter as valued members of the family. Aloe is a prime example. Some family stories have them around since the early twentieth century or before. The best way to hand them on again is through cuttings.

Whether your aloe is really on Social Security or whether it's a younger plant from a previous cutting that your mother never mentioned, the procedure is just the same.

If the aloe is bushy, with multiple stems, cut a piece of a stem about 6 inches long, and remove the lower leaves, ignoring the runny sap. If it has a single stem, cut off a 6-inch piece of a leaf. Lay the cutting on its side to dry overnight. Mix and prewet a growing medium of one-quarter peat, one-quarter houseplant potting soil, one-quarter fine sand, and one-quarter perlite. Use a small pot, so the mixture will dry out easily and quickly between waterings. Put the cutting into the mixture deep enough so it is stable and won't fall over, water thoroughly, and place the pot in very bright light, but not direct sun, while it roots. To help avoid rotting, do not place a plastic bag over the pot. Let the growing mixture dry out, and then wait another day before watering again.

New growth and resistance when the plant is gently tugged are sure signs that the rooting has been successful and the aloe is ready to be handed down again.

Dividing Grasses

Miscanthus, like many ornamental grasses, is typically cut back in the fall. But the right time to divide older clumps depends on how they grow, not just on when it's convenient for you.

Ornamental grasses are either warm-season growers, like Miscanthus and many native North American species, including Indian grass (*Sorghastrum nutans*), little blue stem and big blue stem, and fountain grass (Pennisetum), or cool-season growers, such as the ornamental fescues and some feather-reed grasses, including *Calamagrostis* 'Karl Foerster.'

When grasses begin to die out in the center, it's probably time to divide. Getting popped out of the ground and whacked into pieces can be traumatic, so it's best if the dividing takes place while the grasses have time to grow and recover before winter. Cool-season grasses grow in early spring and again in the fall, so they can be divided at either time. Warm-season grasses, however, don't grow in the late fall, so they should be divided only in the early spring, within the first month after they begin to grow. Your miscanthus should be divided before late April.

You might want to consider not cutting them back in the fall. Left standing, grasses provide winter interest through color and texture and become a flexible, changing armature for snow sculpture. Try cutting back in late spring, before the new growth is tall enough to interfere with a close-to-the-crown clipping.

Rick Darke, former curator of plants at Longwood Gardens in Kennett Square, Pennsylvania, has written *The Color Encyclopedia of Ornamental Grasses: Sedges, Rushes, Restios, Cat-tails, and Selected Bamboos* (Timber Press, 1999), a book illustrating and describing a wide variety of ornamental grasses. It includes a wealth of cultural information as well as how to use ornamental grasses in garden design.

So Many Spruce, So Little Time

Time pressures face us in gardening, just as they do in the rest of our lives. We would like to do garden tasks when we're supposed to, but it is tempting to alter the calendar. For example, to stimulate dormant buds to produce growth that "fills in" the tree, spruce and fir should be sheared back in very late spring or early summer, a fairly short window of time. But since the terminal buds form the previous season, doing them during the winter is tempting.

There is more to a spruce (or any other plant) than meets the eye. Because the terminal buds form the previous year, pruning schedules must take account of the tree's internal chemistry.

Wayne Cahilly, the manager of arboreta and grounds at the New York Botanical Garden in the Bronx, says that pruning the new growth after it has lengthened but before the needles have begun to expand from the twig removes the terminal growing points and stops their production of growth-regulator chemicals. These chemicals suppress growth in lateral or side buds, so reducing the supply limits their growth, helping the tree to fill in.

Removing the terminal buds during the winter would allow the lateral buds to grow unchecked in the spring because no growth regulators would be present. Each lateral bud would try to take over as the new terminal. The result would be internal chaos and a tree with a decidedly ragged look. Plan a shearing party, and get friends to help. Timing is important.

Getting Peace Lilies to Bloom

Peace lilies, with their lovely white blooms, come into our homes in full bloom and great expectation, and then let us down. There they sit, healthy but stubborn.

Spathiphyllum, the peace lily, is a tropical plant that normally blooms in the late spring or early summer. There isn't a day of the year when you can't find one for sale in bloom, and yet, try as we might, many never seem to bloom again. Frustrating, but there is a reason, and maybe an answer.

Growers defy the seasons by spraying spathiphyllum with a

growth regulator. Like clockwork, the plant blooms ten weeks later and gets shipped to market. But that may be the last bloom that plant will ever produce because few homes can provide the right conditions.

Roy Bennett, production manager at Florico Foliage in Apopka, Florida, offers a suggestion: since spathiphyllum goes through a rest period before blooming in nature, move yours away from the window for a month into a cooler spot with lower light, where the soil temperature can drop 10 degrees at night. Then put it back into bright light without direct sun—and hope for the best. And keep repeating to yourself, "Peace lilies really are lovely foliage plants."

Willows Will Root

Over the last dozen years or so, many cut flower arrangements you have seen on display or for sale might have included light, reddish-brown, very twisted (almost arthritic) jointed willow twigs. If you change the water regularly and pay close attention, you may find that the twigs begin to grow roots and put out delicate, thin, spring green leaves. Placed in water by themselves after the flowers die and are thrown out, the twigs continue to grow leaves and put out roots. They can even be kept, if you have the right spot.

The Japanese fantail willow (*Salix udensis* 'Sekka'), with its fused twigs, is a staple in museum floral displays and spring flower shows and at sizable florists. As you have seen, the twigs will root. Pot them up in a well-drained medium, and keep it very moist, but don't drown them; let the delicate roots adapt to the change from water to potting medium. Keep it in a cool room in a north window, covered with a plastic bag to raise the humidity. After a week or two, remove the bag and begin reducing the water, keeping in mind that willows don't like to be completely dry. Don't be surprised if the leaves wilt; the plant will probably survive. Willows are not houseplants. This one can grow 10 feet tall and wide, so transplant it in May to a nice, moist site in the garden.

There are a large number of unusual willows, with a whole range of twig and catkin color, including the purplish-black stems and catkins of *Salix melanostachys* and the rosy catkins of *S. gracilistyla*. Sources include Heronswood Nursery, 7530 288th Northeast, Kingston, WA 98346, (360) 297-4172, catalog; and Forestfarm, 990 Tetherow Road, Williams, OR 97544, (541) 846-7269, catalog.

Staking Trees, with Care

Whether or not to stake newly planted trees is a dilemma for many homeowners. They see their town staking everything in sight, yet their own landscaper tells them not to bother. What nobody tells them are the reasons.

For trees that come with burlap-covered root balls or are grown in containers and can stand upright by themselves when planted, staking can do more harm than good. Tree growth research now recognizes that nature expends no more energy than necessary, said A. William Graham, an arboreal consultant at the Morris Arboretum of the University of Pennsylvania in Philadelphia.

Trees that regularly move in the wind respond to that stress by growing thicker, better tapered, and stronger trunks. Supporting them so that the trees can't move reduces their impetus to grow strong, resulting in trees that may be too weak to withstand storms. Graham advises staking only when a newly planted tree can't stand straight by itself.

If a tree must be staked, never tie the stake directly to the trunk. Preventing light from striking one side of the trunk causes uneven growth around the trunk. When the stake is removed, the tree will bend away from the side the stake was on rather than grow straight up.

If staking is necessary, use only one stake, so that the tree is supported but still flexible. Use broad, smooth material that can give as the tree grows, like inch-wide lengths of an inner tube or plastic webbing. Hose-covered wire, often used in the past, is no longer recommended. The wire doesn't give, and the hose doesn't relieve the pressure. Attach the material to the stake using wire through grommets, so the wire does not circle the tree. And remove the stake as soon as its job is done—usually in eight to twelve months.

Disappearing Tulips

Complaints about tulips are legion. Not against the flowers, but about the display getting punier every year until they finally just peter out altogether.

For contradictory information and confusing recommendations, there's nothing like asking for advice on bulbs. To straighten this out, I asked Dr. August De Hertogh, a professor of horticulture at North Carolina State University in Raleigh and an authority on bulbs, who says that tulips are considered "annual replacement bulbs." And the fact that many people don't realize that is one key to understanding their disappearing act.

Within each tulip bulb are the beginnings of several daughter bulbs. Food energy is devoted not to the survival of the mother bulb but to producing a flower and to growing these daughters. After flowering, the mother bulb is exhausted, dies, and gives up its reserves to its daughter bulbs—but not equally. One or more of the daughters becomes strong enough to flower the following year, as the new mother or mothers.

Anything that interferes with food production in the original mother bulb damages the chances that a healthy, full-sized daughter will form, ending the display we look forward to each spring. Instead of a flower, a weak daughter may put up just a single leaf.

Once the floral display is over, many people make the mistake of either cutting the foliage off before it dies down naturally or trying it up in neat bundles, as many people do with narcissus. Without foliage exposed to the sun, there can be no photosynthesis, no food production, and no healthy daughter bulbs for next year.

Tulips and other geophytes (the proper term for bulbs, corms, rhizomes, and tubers) have two essential needs: they must be planted in well-drained sites to keep from rotting, and they need water and nutrients while their roots are actively growing, in fall and spring. Fertilizer should be applied in October and in the spring after the shoots emerge, about six weeks before flowering. It is also important that the bulbs get adequate water at these times; though there isn't much to look at, there is a lot of action below the surface.

Spring Lawn Ritual

Spring means different things to different people. To you, it means daffodils and fresh green leaves, but to the guys at your local garden center, it means selling you 50-pound bags of lime for your lawn.

Liming is important, but only if your lawn needs it. The right pH, or acid-alkali balance, keeps nutrients and minerals available to plants and makes the environment amenable to beneficial microorganisms.

Most plants, including grass, are accepting of a pH range between 6 and 7 (7 is neutral). If the pH is lower than this, phosphorus, calcium, and magnesium aren't soluble; if it's higher than this iron, zinc, copper, and boron can't be taken up.

Soil that is too acid, the most common problem, needs lime; soil that is too alkaline needs sulfur.

The key is to find out where your soil pH is. Garden centers sell simple pH test kits, and the county cooperative extension office can have a sample tested for a small fee. The kits contain simple instructions, and the cooperative extension test results will advise you how much lime you may need to add based on the results and type of soil.

It isn't necessary to delve deeply into the mysteries of pH in order to lime your lawn or garden. True, applying liming is actually chemistry, but unlike chemistry in school, you don't have to understand what's happening in order to do it right. Just follow the simple instructions.

And also unlike school, an exact answer isn't necessary (in other words, you don't have to hit a pH of 6.8 on the dot). After all, plants are more flexible than high school science teachers.

Lime takes months to change the pH, so don't expect instant changes. Test the soil each spring until it is in the ballpark, then every other year to keep it right.

Liming Plants

Lime, of course, is also recommended regularly every spring for baby's breath. But has anyone explained why?

Adding lime prevents plants from absorbing aluminum, manganese, and iron—metals that are toxic when taken up in large quantities. Lime raises the pH of the soil, making it more alkaline. In alkaline conditions, these metals form compounds that are insoluble in water, so they cannot be taken up by roots.

The amount of the metals that has to be absorbed to be toxic is different for different species. Those that are affected at low levels, such as red valerian (*Centranthus ruber*), clematis, lilac, and baby's breath, need an application of lime whenever a soil test shows the pH to be too acidic, because in acid soils the metals can be absorbed. Liming is also recommended for vegetables in the crucifer family, including cabbage, cauliflower, and broccoli, but for a different reason. A higher pH protects them from club root, a soil-borne fungus.

The Crabgrass Encounter

Crabgrass. The very word can give you nightmares. Your spring ritual probably goes something like this: early April sees you applying a preemergent block. Spring and early summer have you keeping the height of your lawn at the correct 2^1/$_2$ to 3 inches. Summer comes in to the sight of you pulling the crabgrass out by the fistful. The answer is to really prevent germination.

Crabgrass seeds begin to germinate when the forsythia petals begin to fall. Forsythia serves as the indicator that moisture and soil temperature conditions are right for crabgrass seeds to wake up ready and raring to go. They are wonderfully outfitted by nature to compete, and once established are a match for most lawns and gardeners. Timing is critical, and the time to beat crabgrass is before it can fight back.

Since crabgrass is an annual, there are no older, stronger plants to worry about, just the new kids. Unfair? Perhaps, but we're talking about crabgrass here, and no holds barred is the best policy. The best defense, of course, is a dense, healthy lawn that doesn't give crabgrass room to grow.

Understanding a bit about preemergent herbicides will help you avoid the more common reasons for failure. Preemergents mix with the soil and water to form a chemical barrier in the first inch of soil, where crabgrass seeds overwinter. Timing, temperature, rainfall, and the amount of seeds produced the previous year all have an effect on success.

Too much rain can move the herbicide down in the soil, below the seeds, or it can dilute the concentration to the point where it is ineffective. Warm temperatures can cause any chemical to volatilize, going off into the air as a gas as you lay it down, and also encourages microbial action that decomposes the herbicide.

I hate to say it, but if last year was a celebration of crabgrass in your lawn, there will be plenty of seeds waiting for this year, making control even more difficult.

Open Before Planting

Trees and shrubs purchased in containers or balled and bound in burlap or burlap-like plastic require preparation before planting. Roots that touch container walls turn and begin to grow in circles. Pulling some of them away from the root ball with a hand cultivator helps them grow into the surrounding soil and become established. If they continue to grow in circles, the roots never move into the soil to establish themselves and may become so densely packed that they cannot take up water and nutrients.

Burlap weakens and disintegrates in the ground within a relatively short time, allowing roots to grow into the surrounding soil. Make sure that the burlap is untied at the top, and that it is opened and folded back.

Plastic is used because it is long lasting and tougher than burlap in transport and handling. Unfortunately, it is tougher in the ground also and is about as biodegradable as a brick. Plastic wrappings must be removed completely, or they form an effective barrier to root growth. Not removing them can result in the death of the tree or shrub. Death may take as little as a few months, or may take years. The stress symptoms are hard to identify until the dead body is exhumed and the plastic shines in the sunlight, as good as the day it was planted.

Too Many Seedlings

When your hellebores have hundreds of seedlings popping up at their bases you try to pot up some or move them to other parts of the garden. But it is impossible to move each one and you may be afraid of injuring the mother plant by digging too deep and too close. If you just leave them there, so many so close together, you worry that they will crowd out each other and take nutrition away from the mother plant.

From early spring through the end of May is the best time to move those seedlings. Richard Lighty, the former director of the Mt. Cuba Center for the Study of Piedmont Flora in Greenville, Delaware, suggests using a dandelion weeder or a kitchen fork to loosen the soil gently with a jiggling motion and then lift and tease out the roots of the individual seedlings, letting them come apart at their own speed. Avoid using trowels or other large tools, which may disturb the mother plant if you go too close.

Hellebore

Transplant the seedlings, which are probably two to three years old, into a shady area, where drainage is good. Water them in well, and watch for drought stress over the summer. Don't try transplanting if it is hot, because they could become stressed before the roots recover and begin to transpire.

Helleborus foetidus and *H. orientalis* seed prolifically. Practice a little birth control by deadheading flowers before they produce seed. That is the easiest way to reduce your transplanting work later.

And don't worry about the seedlings' starving out the mother. Large, mature plants nearly always win the contest for food and water. The maternal instinct is way down on the list of plant characteristics.

Plant Slow for Long Life

When you think of the devastating effect on a landscape of the early death of a mature tree, it pays to remember that when planting trees, speed sometimes kills.

Being strangled by its own roots is one common cause of decline and eventual death in a transplanted tree. Symptoms of decline (early fall color, more branches dying back every year) won't show for about ten years, and trees may linger on another ten before they die.

Container-grown trees are especially susceptible to root girdling. Roots hit the container wall and begin to encircle the root ball. But for all trees, container grown or not, root girdling occurs this way: If the root flare—the transition point between roots and trunk—is below the soil surface, roots may circle the trunk above the flare. Eventually, as both root and trunk thicken, the flow of sap stops, killing the tree.

Before planting, examine the root ball. Any roots at the edge that are larger in diameter than half a pencil's width should be worked free and spread out before planting. Balled and burlapped trees sometimes come with soil pushed up over the flare. Remove soil until the flare is visible, then plant with the flare an inch or two higher than the garden soil level because the root ball eventually sinks down a bit as it settles.

Girdling can also occur when a root reaches clay or compacted soil at the edge of its hole and turns back, taking the path of least resistance. Dig holes three times as wide as the root ball and rough up the hole's walls so the roots can more easily enter the surrounding soil. Dig your hole just deep enough so that the top of the root ball is at the same level as the garden soil.

A tree's strangling itself may sound like suicide, but really it's murder.

Wandering Lilacs

The most interesting cure for two-year-old lilacs that haven't bloomed was a nursery that instructed the homeowner to move them, as they enjoy that kind of treatment. Once moved, they bloomed, but not again the following year. The thought occurred to their owner that perhaps they should be moved yet again.

If lilacs really enjoyed being moved, they would grow feet, not roots. Roger Coggeshall, who specializes in lilacs as the owner of Syringa Plus in West Boxford, Massachusetts (*Syringa* is the botanical name for lilac), said that transplant shock frequently induces lilacs to set flower buds for the next spring.

There are two likely reasons your lilacs have not continued to bloom. First, lilacs need full sun—at least eight hours each day. And, second, lilacs can take six or seven years to bloom. What you did was to terrify them into blooming. Assuming they are now in full sun, just be patient.

Coggeshall says lilacs can be transplanted successfully anytime after flowering, but fall is the best time, right up to Thanksgiving.

Pruning Forsythia

Forsythia pruning can be controversial. People who typically prune out about ¹/₃ of the old canes every year are aghast when told by their nurseryman that they should never be pruned at all.

What he probably meant to say was that they should never be pruned into tight little balls or overly manicured hedges. The glory of forsythia is in its airy, arching habit. Pruned right, it is a tracery of see-through golden wands; pruned wrong, it becomes a screaming neon mass, suitable for a Las Vegas casino.

Forsythia

Prune every two or three years right after the bloom, removing the oldest canes down to the ground. Light, new wands will sprout from the base, and the following year they will begin to have side branches. Do your pruning thoughtfully. The object is not a massacre, it's to retain the height and spread you want with a balanced, open appearance.

Left unpruned, some forsythia branches will arch over until they touch the ground. When one does, it will form new roots where it meets the ground, beginning new plants and spreading wherever they can.

Raising Happy Blueberries

Lots of people try growing blueberries, but few succeed. They assume it's their fault, but with blueberries, you never know.

Blueberries can punish you. Given the wrong circumstances, they will raise your hopes without ever producing enough to make buying a box of cereal worthwhile.

They thrive in sunny sites and require lots of water throughout the growing season, but they must have a well-drained sandy loam soil high in organic matter.

Unlike most other plants, blueberries need an acid environment. The soil pH must be 3.8 to 5.2. Amend the soil with sulfur to lower the pH. Blueberries do better if they are mulched, preferably with aged wood chips, which help keep the pH down.

They need a little ammonium sulfate each year as established plants, but not when planting. Give plants 1 ounce per year of age, but no more than 8 ounces. Split the dosage, applying half in May when they flower and half four weeks later. Too little is better than too much.

Blueberries lack root hairs (baldberries?) and make up for this by associating with a fungus that gathers moisture and nutrients in exchange for carbohydrates and a place to live. The fungus also has to be happy, one of the reasons that the blueberry is fussy about its location.

Wood Chips for Mulch

More and more communities are providing huge piles of wood chips for their residents to use. The newer chips may look better in the garden, but knowledgeable gardeners head only for the decomposed chips. The differences can be significant.

Many communities make chips of storm-damaged tree limbs and other wood refuse, and let residents use them. Many wood product companies sell wood and bark chips by the bag. The benefits of mulching shrubs and trees in both summer and winter are well known to gardeners: moisture retention, weed control, winter protection against freezing and thawing. Less known are the possible dangers associated with improper mulching. Fresh wood chips make a great garden path, but for mulching, they need to be partially composted.

High in carbon but low in nitrogen, wood chips attract bacteria, which use the carbon as a food source. To find the nitrogen needed for reproduction, the bacteria move down through the wood chips into the soil, where they take nitrogen that the plants need. Fertilizing before putting the chips down or mixing the two together does not help. Dr. Frank Gouin, professor of horticulture at the University of Maryland, said the fertilizer leaches into the soil and the bacteria travel after it, going as deep as 2 inches. Since the bacteria are better competitors than the plants, the plants go hungry while the bacteria use the nitrogen.

Compost wood chips three to four months, in piles 3 to 4 feet high and wide. They need to be kept watered and turned every week or two. Improperly composted or sour mulch can be toxic to plants. Don't use it if it smells like ammonia, vinegar, or sulfur. The fungi that grow in the pile break down the wood and release nitrogen as they do so. When you mulch with this compost, the bacteria get a balanced diet and leave your plants' supply alone.

You may want to think twice about mulching young perennials with wood chips anyway. Gouin notes that wood chips, especially from hardwoods, leave manganese behind as they decompose. In sufficient quantity, manganese can inhibit plant growth.

Moving Houseplants Outside

Once those glorious spring days arrive, everyone is in a rush to move both themselves and their houseplants outside. But it isn't the days that count.

Pay attention to the temperatures at night, not just during the day. Tropical and subtropical houseplants, having neither warm blood nor warm sweaters, resent temperatures below 50 degrees. And resentment usually involves a lackluster, wilted plant.

Houseplants

Mild, sunny early spring days have a way of turning into cold nights.

If the object is to get rid of them and finally reclaim the floor space, wait until the night temperatures are steadily in the 50s. Earlier in the spring, plants can be moved outside when the day warms up and inside again in the evening, assuming the size of the plants matches the strength of one's back. Unfortunately, the back strength to plant weight ratio changes each year, usually in the wrong direction.

Remember that in nature, plants don't travel much and haven't developed the ability to adapt to change quickly. Being moved from a cushy indoor life to an outdoors of strong sunlight, drying winds, and fluctuating temperatures takes getting used to gradually. A sudden change from the living room window to the harsh light outdoors is likely to result in sunburned, scorched leaves.

Move plants first into shady, protected areas. Gradually, over two or three weeks, move them into less shady, more open locations. This acclimation period allows them to withstand these new stresses. Most houseplants prefer to be in bright light but not in direct sun. After all, if they needed full sun, they wouldn't be very good houseplants. Hibiscus, oleander, citrus, rosemary, croton, and yucca are exceptions, and love the sun after they have been acclimated.

Bringing Houseplants Inside

What goes out has to come in. Moving houseplants in either direction can be confusing.

It's not a particular date that's important: it's the night temperature. Most houseplants are tamed tropicals, able to survive the warm, dry conditions that are our idea of comfort. To avoid the shock of a drastic difference in temperature and humidity, all of them must be inside before your heat goes on.

Most need to be inside before the night temperature drops to 50 degrees but a few can stay out until it regularly approaches 40 degrees. These hardier ones include bay laurel, bougainvillea, cacti, calamondin orange, camellia, clivia, ivies, jade, Norfolk Island pine, rosemary, scented geraniums, and oleander. But several plants, like cymbidium orchids, and Christmas and Thanksgiving cactus, depend on cooler temperatures to start their flower bud formation.

There is still enough time to acclimate the plants properly and get the house ready for them by washing your windows (not to reflect on your housekeeping, but clean windows let in a lot more light). If possible, while the plants are still outdoors, move them into shade one to two weeks ahead to prepare them for the drop in light in the house. As you bring the plants indoors soak the pots up to their rims in a sink full of water to force free-loading insects, especially sowbugs, slugs, and millipedes, up to the surface where you can make them pay the price of their audacity.

It's best to leave repotting until just before the new growing season begins. Moving to larger pots means more growing medium, which holds more water. With lower light levels and shorter days, overwatering is more dangerous than being a little pot bound for the winter.

And quit fertilizing. They worked hard at growing all summer, so give them a rest until they start growing again in late winter.

Plants Too Have Edema

Like people, plants can respond to changes in the weather in unforeseen ways. That brand-new hanging basket of ivy geranium you bought may suddenly develop strange brown eruptions on the undersides.

Before you rush off to make some poor salesclerk miserable, take a closer look. If these are small white, tan, or brown wartlike or corky swellings, the problem is probably edema, an environmental problem, not a disease.

If two or three 90-degree days are followed by cool weather, the soil ends up warmer than the air. Under these conditions, the roots take up water faster than the leaves can eliminate it. With more water coming in than going out, some cells swell and can burst. Reduce watering (without letting them die of thirst) and wait for warmer days. Chances are good that the plant will recover.

Foliar Fertilizers

Garden centers and catalogs often sell foliar fertilizers. Just spray the leaves with liquid nutrients and, supposedly, you never have to apply fertilizers to the soil.

In the category Greatest Thing Since Sliced Bread, Horticulture Division, the hands-down winner would appear to be foliar feeding products that claim to help increase growth and disease resistance with a simple spray. If only it were so.

Plant leaves are designed for transpiration—allowing oxygen and carbon dioxide to pass in and out—but not much else. Some nutrients can be absorbed in small amounts, and foliar spraying can be valuable for quickly correcting deficiencies in micronutrients, like boron, iron, or manganese, which are needed in extremely small quantities. But leaves can't absorb the larger quantities of the major nutrients (nitrogen, phosphorus, and potassium) that plants need, so applying them through the soil is the best method.

It is harder to get a plant to change its feeding habits than a teenager, so why try? Let the roots do what they are built for, absorbing nutrients, and let the leaves do what they were developed for, collecting sunshine and making food.

Window Boxes

Everyone wants pansies, one of the best-selling annuals every year. Even window box gardeners try them, but often find that they grow too tall and fall over, looking pretty pathetic.

When the summer hits, some plants thrive and others dive. It is a good rule of thumb that annuals that grow well in cooler weather and look great in spring react to heat by growing lanky, reducing flower size and number, and looking bedraggled.

Martha Washington geranium, felicia, nemesia, osteosper-mum, stock, and sweet William are a few of the other annuals that won't look good in high summer either.

Try redecorating when the early bloomers have had it. Substitute plants like the great new heat- and humidity-loving petunias (especially for those who think they hate petunias). These summer-lovers for window boxes in full sun are called Supertunias or Surfinias and the smaller-flowered Millifloras. Don't forget 'Homestead Purple' verbena.

The many striking cultivars of coleus are a good choice for partially shaded boxes. Don't keep thinking of the same old stuff—many smaller houseplants can be used in interesting foliage combinations. Just remember not to mix plants that have different light and moisture requirements.

Epsom Salts

There are a lot of gardeners out there who swear by a dose of Epsom salts for their tomatoes and peppers as soon as the first blossoms appear.

Like many other old gardeners' tales, this one has a kernel of truth covered with a patina of exaggeration.

Epsom salts, which are hydrated magnesium sulfate crystals, provide two nutrients that are needed in small quantities: sulfur, which is found in several proteins, and magnesium, which is a central component of the chlorophyl molecule that makes plants green and produces food.

I could not find a plant nutritionist armed with anything more than anecdotal evidence that any plant other than spinach can be doused with Epsom salts (1 or 2 teaspoons in 1 gallon of water) to darken the foliage if it suffering from a magnesium deficiency. But if the garden soil is fertile and the pH is 6.5 to 7.0, slightly acid to neutral, there is probably enough magnesium present in a form already available to the plants. The most common advice was to keep the pH at the right level by using dolomitic lime, which also releases magnesium into the soil.

Gardening being what it is—highly personal and variable, subject to strange quirks and unknown forces of nature—there is no doubt that many experienced gardeners will swear by their Epsom salts treatments for tomatoes and peppers (roses too, I have heard). But then, I have a friend, a great gardener, who would rather be caught dead than without his vile-smelling infusion of stinging nettles—sort of a foliar pick-me-up for tired plants, he says.

If you want to try Epsom salts, apply the solution when the plants are using a lot of nutrients—for example, when the first tomatoes are 1 inch in diameter and new flowers are open, ready to set fruit.

The oldest gardening-related use of Epsom salts, however, is still the best: about a cup dissolved in a hot bath after a long day.

Sources for Epsom salts include most local drug stores.

Beating the Bolt

Growing lettuce is essential for most vegetable gardeners. But as soon as the heat of summer arrives, the lettuce just stretches and gets bitter, a process called bolting.

When lettuce gets ready to bolt, it takes a quick look over its shoulder (heads must have shoulders, right?), fills its leaves with bitter sap, which discourages browsers, sends up a flower stalk, makes seed, and dies. It's all pretty dramatic but not much good for a midsummer salad.

Two different varieties may be sitting next to each other in the garden with the same soil, sun, and water and same days and nights, but suddenly one takes off and the other doesn't. As they say (although usually not about lettuce), the devil is in the details—in this case, genetic details.

Every variety of lettuce comes complete with an internal clock, and as it grows it counts the hours of daylight each day. When the total on the clock matches the number specified by its genes, it bolts. However, about halfway through the required hours of daylight, it begins to get anxious. From then until its scheduled wakeup alarm, stress from too much heat or longer days will speed up its metabolism and trigger the seed production process early.

Since lettuce should be planted in succession, a few seeds each week, to keep your harvest at a constant level, you can make changes to help your crop as summer comes. Reduce the stresses by providing a little shade (interplant among taller crops) and enough water (heat increases evaporation loss), but the clock still ticks. Your best bet is to start planting varieties that come with slower clocks, listed in catalogs as slow to bolt, summer varieties, or heat tolerant. 'Simpson Elite,' 'Sierra,' 'Buttercrunch,' 'Medallion,' and 'Red Sails' are all worth looking for.

Sources for a wide variety of lettuce include Johnny's Selected Seeds, 1 Foss Hill Road, Albion, ME 04910, (207) 437-4301, catalog; and the Cook's Garden, P.O. Box 5010, Hodges, SC 29653-5010, (800) 457-9703, catalog.

Rampant Ivy

Having mature trees in your yard is a constant source of joy. Whether conifers or deciduous, trees can provide both structure and backdrop for any kind of garden. But trees are a responsibility, too. When ivy begins to cover the trunk, working its way upward, it may be beautiful but you have to think about its effects on the tree.

One of the drawbacks to immobility is being subject to the indignities and dangers of more aggressive neighbors. We may enjoy the aged look, but the tree finds itself bark to rootlet with a fierce competitor for food and water.

Ivy doesn't stop with the trunk. As it grows among the branches and into the crown, it shades out leaves or needles, traps ice and snow, and adds tremendous weight, making the branches more vulnerable to damage from winds and winter storms. But the real problem is underground, where the ivy's dense, shallow root mat takes up most of the water before the tree can get any.

Cutting the ivy at the base will kill what's on the tree, but not necessarily the ability to re-sprout, and it doesn't solve the other problems. It won't just fall off on its own accord, and stripping it requires some care. If you yank it from below, it may break off just out of reach, or it may pull away with large sections of the outer bark. That won't kill the tree, but it does make the tree more vulnerable to other pests until it heals. If the ivy extends beyond your reach, call a qualified arborist to do it for you.

Dying Dill

If you run an active kitchen, every summer you probably have window boxes full of herbs—basil, parsley, chives, dill. But what you may find is that everything thrives except the dill, and then, of course, your salmon pays the price. This is not only frustrating, but also a cause of some embarrassment to anyone who considers herself a good cook and a good gardener. There is something you can do about it.

Make your salmon before the hot weather hits; then switch to lobster. The true destiny of dill is to produce seed, not sauce. Were we more classically educated, we would take a clue from its botanical name, *Anethum,* the Latinization of the Greek *Athenon,* from *ano* ("upward") and *theo* ("I run"). As the cool weather and

Dill

lengthening days of spring give way to the heat of summer, dill, along with cilantro and chervil, suddenly hear their biological clocks ticking loud and clear. Time to grow tall and reproduce, then die.

Dr. Arthur Tucker, a research professor specializing in herbs at Delaware State University in Dover, said you can lengthen your season by planting early, as soon as the night temperatures stay above 25 degrees. Seed directly or transplant young potted plants, keeping as much growing medium around the roots as possible, because dill resents being transplanted bare root. Seed again in the early fall for a few more weeks of fresh dill; it will even withstand light frost. The compact selections 'Fernleaf' and 'Bouquet' are ideal for pot or window box culture.

Propagating Bay Laurel

Bay laurel (Laurus nobilis), *which is magnificent when full grown, is something to be shared. But if you have tried making cuttings, you know that it isn't so easy.*

There are plants that take root at the drop of a hat, and then there's bay. It can drive you crazy.

Make sure you give yourself the best chance. Start with a bay stem that is half-hard—neither still growing nor hardened enough as to snap when broken. The right stem will have lost its youthful gloss and will have some middle-aged stiffness reminiscent of the morning after a rumba contest. In both spring and fall, bay grows, rests for a month, and grows again. During the rest periods, around June and September, the new growth begins to harden and will reach the desired half-hard state.

Cut a piece 4 to 6 inches long using a sharp knife. Keeping at least four leaves and the growing tip, strip the leaves from the lower half by running your thumb and index finger down the stem. Scrape a short, small area on opposite sides of the lower stem to expose the white underlayer. This makes it easier for the cutting to absorb water and encourages root production.

Bay Laurel

Thomas DeBaggio, who has been propagating and growing herbs commercially for more than twenty years at DeBaggio Herbs in Arlington, Virginia, says he has found a method that will increase the home gardener's success rate from less than 15 percent to 70 percent. Instead of starting the cuttings directly in a growing mixture, start them in water. Change the water every day to keep bacterial growth down and provide enough aeration. The cuttings won't grow roots, but in about two months they will develop ugly wartlike nodes below the water level. Then move them into a growing medium until roots develop, in about a month.

For the growing medium, DeBaggio uses a mixture of one part perlite and one part ProMix BX (available in many garden centers). This mix contains sphagnum peat, perlite, and vermiculite, but similar mixtures will work as well, as long as they hold water yet drain well, and support the cutting yet are loose enough to be well aerated. Insert the cutting deep enough that the lower remaining leaves are just above the growing medium. The cuttings need bright light (but not direct sun) for about fourteen hours a day. They don't need to be covered with plastic bags to provide humidity.

Don't give up until the cuttings either root or turn brown and shrivel. Sometimes bay can seem to take forever.

Drainage for Houseplants

Among the many things gardeners like to fight about is how to obtain the best drainage in their houseplant pots. The typical debate is between pot shards and pebbles, and how deep to make the layer.

One single shard, please, and put the pebbles back in the driveway. Even the one-shard recommendation is just to make the traditionalists feel better about hiding the evidence when they break a clay pot. And the only drainage help the shard provides is to help keep the soil from draining all over the windowsill before it has a chance to settle in.

Drainage is controlled by the structure of the potting soil or growing medium itself. The small particles of soil attract and hold on to water. When more water is added than the soil can retain, the excess drains.

It is reasonable to think that the larger pebbles or shards will help the pot drain faster, because there is so much more air space between pieces, but they can drain only the excess water that the soil gives up. They cannot reach up and suck water away from the soil particles.

About the only thing the pebbles do accomplish is a negative: they reduce the amount of growing room for the roots. If the potting medium doesn't drain well on its own, don't depend on pebbles to bail you out.

Pruning Rhododendrons

Pruning rhododendrons doesn't have to be too complicated. When yours get to be too large for the garden, cut them back. But the buds for those fire-engine red blossoms seem to appear as soon as the blossoms wane, and you hate to cut them off.

It's difficult emotionally to cut off any of next year's flowers, but if you continue to avoid pruning, you'll end up even more devastated. In fact, you could end up having to cut the rhododendrons to the ground and start all over again.

Overgrown rhododendrons require imagination as well as pruning. Dr. Richard Lighty, former director of the Mt. Cuba Center for the Study of Piedmont Flora in Greenville, Delaware, advises that you try to visualize what the shrub should look like. Reach that goal by critically selecting strong, outer branches that, when pruned back, will expose smaller, inner branches that are in the right position to fill in, forming the right size and shape. Once exposed to light, those inner branches will begin to grow.

As the flowers fade, trim no more than 15 to 20 inches from the strong branches. Prune where the strong branch is near the tip of an inner branch that has a whorl of glossy leaves surrounding the scale-

Rhododendron

covered buds, your signal that the branch is healthy. If they are still too big, reprune in two years.

To make sure the plant has stored enough food so that it can easily handle pruning, fertilize it in late fall the year before you intend to prune. If you fertilize after pruning, it will respond by putting out long, leggy growth.

Although it is better to stay on top of your regular pruning chores, if necessary rhododendrons can be cut down to 12 to 15 inches from the ground. They have buds at their base that will generally send up new shoots. But there won't be any flowers for two or three years.

Poppy Propagation

Increasing your population of poppies quickly and easily is a contradiction. If you have really great ones, like those that are white with burgundy edges, you can't count on seeds because seeds often don't grow up to look like their parents. Yet having to divide the plants would take too long.

If you really want a field of oriental poppies, you can try taking root cuttings. It's fussy work and not always reliable (make twice as many as you want plants), but it's still the best way to increase your poppy population rapidly.

After the leaves have yellowed, the roots have accumulated enough carbohydrates to take the plant through dormancy. Winter is the usual time for most plants to go dormant, but poppies do it in midsummer. Dig up the plants, cut off a piece of a healthy, fleshy root about the thickness of a pencil, and then cut it into 2-inch pieces. It is very important that you know top from bottom. One method is to make a square cut on the upper end, nearest the poppy's crown, and an angled cut on the other end. Unless you do that, one end of the piece will look pretty much the same as the other, but shoots will grow from the upper end, roots from the lower. Planting upside down just about guarantees failure.

Let the root pieces sit overnight to callus, and then plant each one vertically, with the upper end just at the surface, in a small pot containing a well-drained, soilless medium. Keep them moist and in bright light, moving to direct sun after the new shoots have formed leaves—with luck in about five weeks.

Ideally, they should spend the winter in a cold frame and should be planted out as soon as the soil is workable in the spring, but you can put them in the ground in the fall, mulch well, and hope that a bad winter doesn't heave them out. They take time to settle in, so don't expect flowers the first summer.

Root cuttings really work: the proof is the dandelion that keeps coming back no matter how many times you pull (most of) it up.

Lawn-Mowing Dangers

Lawn mowing generates a lot more questions than you would think possible for something that straightforward. One common question is whether or not dull blades really tear the grass tops and allow diseases to enter through the rough edges. Since the grass is being cut open anyway, why should dull or sharp be an issue?

Mowing a lawn is not exactly like giving a haircut. Cutting living tissue is stressful under the best conditions, and using a dull blade adds insult to injury, especially on a rotary mower, which cuts by brute force whacking instead of the neat scissoring action of a reel mower.

It isn't just the direct ability of disease organisms to enter the wound, although that plays a part. Compounding that are the other effects of the dull blade. Even with a sharp blade, the loss of leaf surface means reduced photosynthesis and reduced ability to take up water. These stresses make the plant weaker and less able to fight off diseases and slow root growth. When the cut is ragged and torn, the increased surface area open to the air means 10 to 15 percent additional water loss through evaporation and a longer time to heal. Diseases have an easier time entering a host with weakened defenses.

To make it even harder on your grass, mow when the grass is still wet. Not only are fungal populations higher when it is damp or humid, but the water on the grass impedes the lawn mower blade, leading to a poorer-quality cut. Rotary mowers are bigger offenders than reel mowers under these circumstances.

Cutting it right also means cutting it the right height. While grass may prefer never to be cut and we may prefer that golf-course-greens look, the best compromise for a healthy, good-looking lawn is to cut it 2½ to 3 inches high, year round.

Nasturtiums

'Creamsicle' nasturtium (Tropaeolum majus) *seeds planted in May in a large, east-facing windowsill pot get plenty of sun and will come up quickly. But eventually they quit flowering and become nothing but a great tangle of leaves and stems. You cut them back, and the foliage returns. You fertilize with Miracle-Gro every two weeks, but still you get only a few flowers. The temptation must be to do everything over again.*

Your nasturtiums would like to be left alone for a while, hopefully on the outside of that windowsill, to recover from all your kindnesses. Nasturtiums like a lean life: not much fertilizer; a porous, well-drained potting mixture such as Pro-Mix BX; and plenty of sun. Overfeed them, and they'll just grow lots of foliage. Shear the foliage back, and they'll do their best to replace it.

Soilless mixtures like Pro-Mix contain very few nutrients on their own, so some fertilizing is necessary. Miracle-Gro at one-quarter to half strength every three weeks is plenty.

Give them what they want, and they will flower, but not until they reach a certain size. Many nasturtium cultivars can reach 12 inches. If that is too large for your space, try a more compact-growing nasturtium, like the 'Tip Top' hybrids, which grow to only about 7 inches and hold their flowers above the foliage for a showier display.

Cultivar or Variety?

Two of the many botanical-naming terms that cause confusion are cultivar *and* variety. *They both come after the species name, but then it gets a little hazy for many people.*

Genus and species names are those two Latin words we glance at and promptly forget. They are actually the most common two in a series that places living things in a variety of pigeonholes, including kingdom, class, order, and phylum; they show what is related to what, and how close or distant the relationship is.

In the eighteenth century, when Linnaeus invented the naming system that is still used in biology and botany, he expected that every plant would have a unique and universally recognized two-word name by using just genus and species, one capitalized and one not. *Campanula cochlearifolia* refers to the same plant the world over.

But sometimes differences arise as a result of natural mutation and uncontrolled cross-pollination in the wild. These differences may be important, but not large enough to justify a new species name, and the plants need to be accommodated. They are called *varieties,* and their differences are likely (but not guaranteed) to reproduce well from seed. Variety names, in Latin, are not capitalized and simply follow the species name, sometimes set off by "var." *Campanula glomerata* var. *acaulis* is a dwarf form of its popular parent, *Campanula glomerata.*

Cultivars (a contraction of cultivated variety) are plants that have been bred or selected for desirable characteristics. They are propagated vegetatively, from cuttings rather than seeds, because their seedlings generally do not reproduce the parent. Cultivar names are capitalized, set in single quotes, not italicized, frequently not Latin, and more marketing oriented. *Campanula cochlearifolia* 'Miranda' is a stronger grower than *C. cochlearifolia.*

All this helps to avoid the confusion of common names, which change from place to place and generation to generation. All thanks to Carl von Linné, more commonly known by his Latin name—Linnaeus. You would think that he would know better.

Garden Maintenance

In early summer, cutting back some perennials can pay big dividends by encouraging reflowering or regrowth of foliage and helping them avoid that floppy, tired look.

Shearing lady's mantle right to the ground after it flowers will prod a new flush of leaves. To avoid legginess and splitting, shear Montauk daisy, and cut New England asters in half in early July.

Catmint and lavender will rebloom if cut by one-third after flowering. Shearing baby's breath after it flowers will promote another display in late summer.

African Violet Challenge

Once one of your older African violets develops an ugly neck, which pushes it up out of the pot, it's time to do something.

Take it out of the pot, and decide how brave you are.

One solution is to trim enough of the roots away so that the violet can be repotted with the neck below the soil line and the lowest tier of leaves just above the pot's rim. Scrape the neck before planting to encourage roots to grow.

If you are confident of your African violet propagation skills, just cut off the roots and most of the neck, leaving only enough so that repotting allows 1 inch of neck to be buried with the lowest tier of leaves back where they belong.

Horticultural Oil

Many people make the switch from using insecticides to using horticultural oil because they know it's safer. But they question if it can be used everywhere other products were.

Horticultural oil, highly refined, very pure, and made to evaporate quickly, is less toxic than other insecticides because it kills by smothering and leaves no residual poisons. Because horticultural oil is thought to be safe, however, it is treated cavalierly. Few gardeners read labels all the way to the bottom on poisonous products, let alone on "safe" ones. But reading may save a plant's life. Horticultural oil applied improperly, at the wrong time, or to the wrong plant, can cause severe problems.

Since oil can interfere with bud and twig growth, causing stunting and even twig death, it is used at different concentrations during dormant (winter) or growing seasons (summer). Oils should not be used in spring, when buds are open and shoots are starting to grow, or in fall, just after leaf drop, when plants are hardening off for winter.

Apply oil only when leaves can dry quickly (one to two hours). Conditions that prevent rapid drying—high humidity and temperature, overcast days—can cause leaf damage (yellowing, marginal burning, defoliation) or twig dieback.

Some plants should never be sprayed; these include aucuba, smoke tree, raspberries, cryptomeria, walnuts, and hickories. And if you spray a Colorado blue spruce, it will lose its blue color until new needles grow in. Avoid spraying hairy-leaved plants, which hold oil too long. Conifers sprayed in November or December will lose their protective waxy coating. No plant should be sprayed when it is under stress from lack of moisture.

Horticultural oil is valuable but not foolproof. As with all products, read the label and follow directions. Actually, reading the label may make you feel better. Compare the long list of pests that *could* be in your garden with the few that *are* there.

Watering Cacti

How often to water a cactus probably has more answers than nearly any other kind of houseplant. Mostly, the answers range from once a month to more often.

If you think the desert is a tough place for a plant to live, it's nothing compared with the conditions cacti find themselves in in most homes. Some people say to water cacti when it rains in Arizona. Since every other environmental factor is different, can this really make sense?

Dr. Ernest De Marie, former curator of the desert collection at

the New York Botanical Garden, says that the most common mistakes that people make are watering too little and too infrequently during the active growing season and thinking that cacti prefer infertile growing media.

From spring or early summer until October, when actively growing, cacti need plenty of water—enough to saturate the root ball completely. Let them dry out completely between waterings— only two or three days for a small pot— but they should not remain dry for more

Prickly Pear Cactus   than a week.

During the winter rest period, they need less water, as do most other plants. If kept cool—55 degrees during the day and 40 to 45 degrees at night (ideal temperatures for setting flower buds)—a thorough watering once a month or less is enough for most cacti, unless they begin to wrinkle noticeably.

The growing medium for cacti needs to drain well and to be well aerated so that the roots don't suffocate or rot. Commercial cacti mixes often look like the desert, but you can make a better mix at home. Mix two parts perlite with three parts of a soilless peat-bark mixture; then add 2 teaspoons each of limestone and superphosphate per gallon.

For larger, heavier specimens, add one part coarse builder's sand as a counterbalance; a tippy cactus can be downright dangerous. Use a balanced fertilizer (20:20:20) once a month, April through August.

Cacti may look rugged, but they like the good life, just like the rest of us.

Propagating Calycanthus

The large, fruity-scented shrub with reddish-brown flowers frequently found in the perennial borders of century-old houses is Calycanthus floridus, *known as sweet shrub or Carolina allspice. A great plant, it can be a little tricky to propagate for your friends' gardens.*

This is also known as strawberry shrub and by any name is a wonderful 6- to 9-foot-high, broadly rounded shrub that is hard to find at your local garden center. Individual plants vary widely in fragrance, so propagation is the best way to be sure of getting that same, distinctive fruity scent.

The easiest method is to collect the kidney-bean-size seeds after the leaves fall. They need a cold period (called stratification), so plant them in 4-inch pot and sink it in the ground for winter.

Carolina Allspice

The pot isn't necessary, but makes the plants easier to give away next spring.

Cuttings are more difficult, but some tips may help you. In July, early in the day while the plant is full of moisture, take cuttings 4 to 6 inches long from the current season's growth, and remove the bottom leaves. Just before planting in a 4-inch pot, with half perlite and half peat (premoistened), make a fresh cut and cover ¹/₂ inch of the stem with rooting hormone. The fresh cut is important because barriers that make the hormone less effective form quickly.

A 0.8 percent indolebutyric acid (IBA) rooting hormone powder gives better results than those that contain naphthaleneacetic acid (NAA), but indolebutyric acid is hard to find. Cuttings treated with indolebutyric acid take root in four to six weeks, but cuttings treated with naphthaleneacetic acid may take three months, with a lower success rate. Follow the label instructions; high concentrations of rooting hormone can burn the cutting's tissues.

Using the cutting to make the planting hole removes most of the powder, so use a finger or pencil instead. Place a plastic bag over the pot, and put it in a lightly shaded location. Leave the bag on until the cutting is well rooted, and remember to keep the mixture moist. Well-rooted cuttings can be transplanted in the fall. Gift pots can be sunk in the ground until spring.

The failure rate for cuttings is high, so start more than you need. Any that blacken should be thrown out. Young calycanthus is a slug's idea of heaven, so keep a close eye out for them.

If starting a small nursery isn't your idea of fun, here are some sources for calycanthus. Since every plant is different, see if you can get the nurseryman to smell the flowers and pick a good one to send out. Fairweather Gardens, P.O. Box 330, Greenwich, NJ 08323, (856) 451-6261, catalog; and Roslyn Nursery, 211 Burrs Lane, Dix Hills, NY 11746, (516) 643-9347, catalog. Fairweather Gardens has a yellow-flowered form as well as the traditional dark red.

Repotting Orchids

A gift orchid, like a phalaenopsis, can make even an experienced houseplant gardener nervous. New roots keep coming up out of the pot and the whole thing looks entirely too crowded to be comfortable. How and when to repot is always an issue.

Instead of taking your cues from the orchid, look at the growing medium. If it is rotted or deteriorated, soggy and broken down, it needs changing, usually every two or three years. The best time to repot is while the orchid is actively growing. May and June are good months.

Charles Marden Fitch, a recipient of the American Orchid Society Gold Medal, suggests the following method:

Water the orchid two hours or more before unpotting, so the

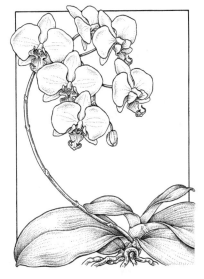

Phalaenopsis Orchid

roots will come out easily. After unpotting, remove the old bark mixture, except for any large chunks with roots adhering to them. Place a 1-inch layer of packing "peanuts" in the bottom to increase air circulation.

Position the plant in the pot at the same level that it was before. Fill the pot with new growing medium until the bark is level with the point where the plant's growth begins.

As you fill, keep rapping the pot on a hard surface to help the bark mixture settle, trying to get it firm and closely packed around the roots.

Misting or dribbling small amounts of water on the surface of the medium encourages rooting. Keep the plant in diffuse light for four to six weeks after repotting.

Chapters of the American Orchid Society (6000 South Olive Avenue, West Palm Beach, FL 33405) offer advice, demonstrations, and hand-holding for first timers. A source for orchid supplies is OFE International, 12100 SW 129 Court, Miami, FL 33186, (305) 253-7080, catalog.

Tree Wound Paint

When a storm brings tree branches crashing down, old-timers head for the hardware store to buy tree wound paint. Most likely you won't find it anymore since tree professionals no longer recommend it.

As far as the tree is concerned, wound dressings neither help nor hurt. Trees know how to seal off wounded areas without Band-Aids or iodine.

Whether the damage is the result of a woodpecker or a hurricane, once the protection provided by the bark has been interrupted, any wound deep enough to expose living tissue triggers a series of biochemical responses that protect nearby living cells from further injury by converting the cells surrounding the wound into an impermeable barrier. This process, called compartmentalization, shuts out possible damage by insects or disease.

Humans are the main beneficiaries of tree paints. If you can't stand the sight of blood or raw wood, a dark-colored dressing may improve the wound's appearance until it has time to darken naturally. Mostly, though, it's a way to feel useful without actually doing something useful.

Drying Hydrangeas

Drying blue hydrangea flowers, often an important part of a dried floral arrangement, often leads to faded or moldy flowers, sometimes both at once.

Hydrangea macrophylla cultivars, with their large, rounded blue or pink flowers, can be hard to dry well.

The weather is one factor. If it is humid, they take longer to dry, giving fungi an opportunity to damage them and spoil your efforts.

How well the color is preserved is related to the drying conditions and the cultivar of hydrangea. Some resist fading better than others, but drying them in the dark is necessary no matter which kind you are working with. Even normal room lights can cause the blooms to fade.

Don Mitchell, the president of Flora Pacifica in Brookings, Oregon, a major cut-flower drier for the floral industry, says the key to success is knowing when to pick. The flowers have to be at least 80 to 90 percent open. But most important is to feel the flowers. If the petals are a little rigid instead of soft, the veins have become prominent, and if the center structure (the true flower) in each group of petals feels a little rubbery, it is ready. This is a minor art form, and experience is helpful.

Hang the flowers in bunches of no more than three in a warm, dry, dark, well-ventilated place. An attic with the vents open will work. Add a fan to circulate air. Warmth speeds drying, darkness prevents fading, and lots of air reduces humidity and cuts down on fungi. Drying can take up to three weeks.

If you can wait until late September or early October, the *Hydrangea paniculata* cultivars, which include the familiar 'Pee Gee,' will be ready. When the 8- to 10-inch creamy-white cone-shaped flowers fade to a burnished rose, it is time to pick them. The weather is generally less humid, and the more open flower structure allows better air circulation, so they are easier to dry.

Pest Control Safety

Read the label before using any product that controls insects. Just because it comes from natural sources doesn't always mean it is safe. Insecticidal soaps and horticultural oils fix many insect problems, and environmentally conscious gardeners like them because they are generally safe for humans and pets. But they are not always safe for plants, especially during a hot, humid summer.

Soaps and oils can burn foliage if they are applied when the plant is in full sun or the temperature is above 85 degrees. Use caution on humid days, even when the temperature is lower. Since high humidity means long drying times, plants that are in shade when you spray may be in sun before they can dry. If the weather is making *you* uncomfortable, it's probably not a good time to spray.

Insecticidal soaps and horticultural oils work only on contact. Once they dry, they have no effect on insects, so use them when the insects are present. Remember that some insects may be on the leaf's underside, so try to cover all surfaces.

Make sure the soil is well watered before applying any pest control. And remember that no product is good for every plant, so read the fine print.

Yes, We Have No Berries

The doublefile viburnum serves two purposes in the garden. First, its lovely shape gives an oriental appearance. Second, its wonderful red berries in fall and winter provide food for birds that choose not to migrate. But when a few years go by and no berries show up, you have to wonder what's going on.

Dr. Michael Dirr of the University of Georgia in Athens said that there are several possibilities, but no easy way to know which one is right. If you have *Viburnum plicatum* var. *tomentosum,* and it didn't flower, it may not be quite old enough (if it is less than 3 feet tall, it's probably too young). However, if you bought a named cultivar, such as 'Summer Snowflake' (which is known for its heavy fruiting), age is not the problem since named cultivars are cloned from mature tissue.

If your viburnum bloomed but did not set fruit well, it will do better with a companion. Another clone nearby shouldn't really be necessary, but most doublefile viburnums seem to set more fruit if cross-pollinated.

It may still be getting over being transplanted, in which case another growing season should solve the problem—unless, of course, you have been pampering it with lots of water and fertilizer. Excess nitrogen promotes foliage growth at the expense of flowers.

If it isn't age, loneliness, transplant shock, or too much fertilizer, it could be lack of light. Some viburnums usually set fruit even in light shade, but they do better with more light. Of course, moving it means two to three years of waiting for recovery, but gardeners are supposed to take a long view of things. It will bloom and set fruit, and the birds will thank you. Doublefile viburnums must be especially tasty because the birds strip them right away, even before they have completely ripened. Others, including *Viburnum dilatatum* (look for the cultivars 'Iroquois,' 'Erie,' or 'Asian Beauty') and *Viburnum* x *rhytidophylloides* cultivars 'Alleghany' or 'Willowwood,' hold on to their fruit well into winter.

Pruning a Cactus

Columnar cactus, like other plants, grows. That cute 2-footer you bought is now 5 feet and growing. There are a couple of options.

You can prune, but if you are looking for an old desert saguaro with upraised arms, you won't get it. The cactus may throw out a branch or two immediately below the cut, but one may become a new leader, not a branch. The scar will remain obvious.

Lower the pot or raise the ceiling.

The Striking Gerbera

Gerbera daisies have a tendency to quit making those beautiful flowers and just grow leaves. The reason has to do with its history.

A striking flower, the gerbera has daisy-like rays surrounding a pincushion center and can be as much as 4 inches across. Gerberas practically light up a garden with their neon shades of pink and red or provide a gentle glow with the softest pastel yellow, salmon, or cream flowers, all held on sturdy stems above lower-growing foliage.

The history of *Gerbera jamesonii* is in its common names: veldt, Transvaal, or Barberton daisy. It was introduced to the horticultural world when Robert Jameson, a prominent Scotsman living in South Africa, followed the news of gold strikes to the area near Barberton in the Transvaal region in the 1880s.

I don't know how the gold hunt panned out, but he brought back specimens of the gerberas he found there and gave them to the Durban Botanic Garden. By 1912, commercial hybrids were being shown in England at the Royal Horticultural Society's Chelsea exhibition. Today it is hard to find a florist who doesn't carry a range of cut gerbera flowers—no leaves, just flower power.

The gerbera is a perennial in its native lands, and in the United States in Zones 8 or warmer, but it is most often grown as a tender annual or as a florist greenhouse crop. Like many other flowering plants, it needs cool nights to encourage blooming. Summers in the Northeast are usually too warm, both day and night, so the plants seem to tire out, hunker down, and wait for the end of the heat before continuing to flower. About the best thing you can do to help them is to pack them up and take them north, where the cool nights keep them blooming all summer long.

When to Water the Lawn

Lawn watering philosophies seem to generate nearly as many arguments as barroom political discussions. Lawns and family arguments go together. One side claims that you shouldn't water the lawn on a sunny day. The other wide believes you shouldn't water at night. There is a best way, but I doubt anyone is listening. In this case both sides are right, so no one gets to say "I told you so."

Dr. Noel Jackson, professor of turf management at the University of Rhode Island at Kingston, says morning is best, mostly because it isn't afternoon or evening. Watering during hot, sunny afternoons wastes water; some of it evaporates so quickly that it never gets into the ground.

There is no evidence of a magnifying lens effect (water droplets intensify the sun's rays and burn the leaves), but belief in that stubborn myth persists. Evening watering should be avoided because the water that lingers on the leaves encourages fungal diseases.

In case the family is tempted to fall back to arguing about how much water to give the lawn, let's settle that too. Water deeply two or three times a week for a total of 1 to 1½ inches a week. The idea that it is better to substitute frequent, very light waterings during high summer because it cools the plant is slightly misunderstood. Golf course greens, our most pampered turf, do benefit from a cooling surface misting, but they also have to get regular, deep drinks.

Keep your lawn at the right summer height (2 to 2½ inches for Kentucky blue and perennial rye grasses, 3 to 3½ for tall fescues) and the leaves will provide their own cooling shade for the base of the plant.

Mysterious Bark Splitting

Sometimes storms damage trees; other times insects or animals. But if a Japanese maple loses a 10-inch-by-3-inch chunk of bark on the lower trunk, nature doesn't seem to be responsible.

This sounds suspiciously like a case of power mower hit and run. Trim the rough edges back with a sharp knife to help promote wound closure, make sure the tree gets water when it is dry, and then leave it alone.

Pruning Fruit Trees

If you missed pruning your apple tree in the spring, you might be tempted to do it in the summer. Sounds reasonable, but you better think twice.

Summer and winter pruning accomplish different things, and if the goal is to shape and control the tree or to increase its fruit yield, procrastination has served you well.

A tree's response is different depending on when it is pruned. If it is pruned in the winter while dormant, the tree grows rapidly when it wakes up, using all its stored energy. By the end of summer the shaping you thought you had accomplished is gone. Winter pruning is used mostly on very young trees, where rapid growth is desired.

The response to pruning in late July through mid-August is one of frustration. After investing energy in producing leaves, the tree is finally ready to begin storing the food that mature leaves make. With production reduced, all the energy has to be saved for the coming fall and winter; it has little extra to push much replacement growth this season.

When pruning to increase yield next year, there are two things to remember. First, fruit grows on particular branches. Peaches and nectarines grow on year-old branches, while apples, pears, plums, and sweet cherries grow on two- to six-year-old branches. Make a mistake, and you end up buying fruit at the supermarket.

Second, buds need to be exposed to at least half of the available daily sunlight to develop into flowers, so the object of pruning is to let light into the tree, especially to the bearing branches. Since a dense canopy may shade three-quarters of the tree, that means pruning out some of those large, older branches inside and way up high. Encourage horizontal branches by pruning those that are weak and bend downward or are strong but vertical. Be careful on the ladder.

Saving Sunflower Seeds

Assuming you have guarded your sunflower from the deer all season, you might expect that it's time to look forward to harvesting and storing the seeds for the winter.

Forget the deer. It's time to start guarding it from the birds.

To keep seeds for growing or eating, you have to wait until they are mature. Birds will start lining up just before the petals fall, but the seeds don't mature until the bracts (the petal-like leaves surrounding the flower) turn brown and the back of the head turns lime yellow. Depending on the size and thickness of the head, this may follow flower petal fall by three or four weeks. During this time, you can protect the seeds by covering the head with a paper bag. (It is a choice between having a peculiar-looking garden and having sunflower seeds.)

Cut the heads off and hang them in a dry spot with good air circulation. Upside down or right side up doesn't matter, but it takes at least two weeks for the seeds to dry. They are ready when they come out of the head with a gentle rub. Store at room temperature in a sealed glass jar with a commercial desiccant because sunflower seeds are susceptible to mold in humid climates.

Seeds from hybrids may not grow up true to their parent, but they will still be sunflowers and are still worth having next year (or eating this year). Sunflowers such as 'Mammoth Black Russian,' which is not a hybrid, will reproduce the same sunflowers year after year.

Ripe Watermelon

Watermelon, long the most essential summer fruit, is reasonably easy to grow. But knowing when they are ripe and ready to pick is another matter.

The hardest part of painting is knowing when to stop, but the hardest part of harvesting is knowing when to start. Picking watermelon has a lot of folklore attached to it.

Some say that thumping is best. Use a sharp rap of the knuckle, and listen for a secondary vibration, or echo, underneath the main vibrato. This method is preferred by trained musicians and old farmers who have been doing it for many years. Others swear by a subtle change in the background color, from a light green to a yellow-green. Of course, individual melons may differ, as does individual color sense. How much green and how much yellow go into the right yellow-green is as much art as science.

The simplest way for the nonfarmer is to watch the tendrils growing from the vine. When the one that grows nearest to the melon turns brown and dies, the melon is ready. Watching something turn brown and die comes naturally to most gardeners.

String Bean Blues

Shriveled string beans are giving you a clear message.

They are thirsty. There are two reasons that they might not be getting enough water. First, you and nature might not be doing your part. Most vegetables are mostly water; if it hasn't rained regularly enough—at least 1 inch a week—you should have been watering. Second, if your beans are shriveling even with your good efforts, it may be that enough water isn't getting up into the plant.

One possibility is that the plants are not taking up enough phosphorus, which is essential for good root growth. It might be a lack of phosphorus in the soil, or it might be that the pH is too high or too low, which ties up phosphorus and other essential minerals in insoluble compounds. Test the soil: pH should be 6 to 7, and the phosphorus reading should be at least medium.

If the soil is okay, pull up a plant with shriveled beans and look for fine root hairs. If there aren't any, or are just a few, you could have nematodes or wireworms. Crop rotation—three or four years between replanting a crop in the same place—should reduce or eliminate the problem.

Who Needs Flowers?

Scented-leaved geraniums, which are wonderful to have inside all winter where you can brush against them, get repotted in the spring and placed outside. Then, of course, they grow magnificently but refuse to bloom.

You're not doing anything wrong, and neither is your scented-leaved geranium. It's just a misunderstanding. You think summer means flowers, but the scented-leaved geranium (actually it's a pelargonium) knows that spring is for flowering, while summer is set aside for growing lots of wonderful foliage.

Didn't flower in the spring? You probably didn't provide the right winter environment to ensure bud set. Pelargoniums are happiest on a south-facing, unheated porch where night temperatures hover around 50 degrees and days are short but very sunny. Flowering is triggered in late winter and spring when the number of

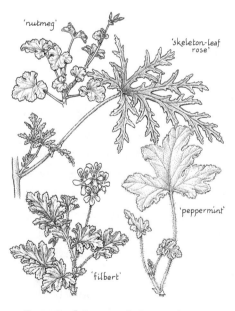

Scented-Leaved Geraniums

daylight hours increases. Where summers are cool, sporadic flowering may continue, but the foliage is the real interest.

Look past the flowers (pretty easy in this case) to see why people become obsessive collectors. Whether you crush the leaves for their unique aromas (lemon, peppermint, dusky rose) or admire them for their intricate shapes and colors, foliage is what these plants are all about.

The variety could keep you intrigued for years. Deeply cut, some almost skeleton-like, the leaves may be tiny and tightly crinkled, looking very sure of themselves and desert-like, or broad and fuzzy with gentle lobes that invite your touch. They may be blotched with purple-brown or edged in white, splashed with cream or just a perfect green, from light to dark. And while you're admiring, close your eyes and crush a few leaves. Suddenly it's an herb garden.

Two by Two

Small yards and big eyes sometimes lead to trouble. Planting, for example, one each of 'Golden Delicious' apple, Bartlett pear, and Napoleon cherry trees would seem enough to provide the average family with a summer full of fruit. But it's not enough to have one of everything, as Noah was smart enough to know.

Some fruit trees can live solitary lives; others cannot. If the bees are out, sour cherry, peach, European-type plum, and apricot are self-fruitful, so pollen from one flower can pollinate other flowers on the same tree or others of the same variety. But most apples, sweet cherries, plums, and pears are self-unfruitful, a phrase that causes frowns among both gardeners and grammarians, and means it's time to go shopping.

The 'Golden Delicious' is self-fruitful, but more and larger fruit will result if another apple variety is nearby that blooms at the same time, such as 'Paula Red' or 'Jonathan.' Your others require pollen from a different variety of the same fruit, and two would be even better, chosen for overlapping bloom periods, with one variety in flower and ready to donate pollen during your tree's early and middle bloom period, and the other ready during the middle and end of the period.

Don't buy the first cherry, pear, and apple that attract your eye. Plan carefully. If all the trees are to be productive, make sure the two apple, cherry, and pear varieties are capable of pollinating each other. It doesn't always work that way. Plant a 'Red Winesap' and your 'Golden Delicious' will be happy to pollinate it, but the favor will not be returned. 'Seckel' and 'Bartlett' pears won't pollinate each other, and your 'Napoleon' cherry will barely talk to a 'Bing.' Companion trees should be within 60 feet of one another. Since any crabapple with the right bloom period will pollinate any apple, you might be lucky enough to have one sitting in a neighbor's yard.

Flowering period and pollen compatibility are not found on tree labels, so check with a specialty nursery or local county cooperative extension office. Specialty sources for fruit trees include Southmeadow Fruit Gardens, P.O. Box 211, Baroda, MI 49101, (616) 422-2411, catalog; and Raintree Nursery, 391 Butts Road, Morton, WA 98356, (360) 496-6400, catalog.

Growing Garlic

Sometimes that spring-planted clove of garlic just never comes up, and people are tempted to repeat the planting in the fall.

If you grow tomatoes and basil, garlic has to be the logical next step. Many people attempt to grow garlic by putting a clove out in the garden, but sometimes grocery store garlic is treated to keep it from sprouting, so it won't grow. The clove rots, and one more person gives up, believing there's a secret to growing garlic. A better choice would be to use seed garlic from a local source. Any plant that has been cultivated, worshipped, and generally held in awe for 5,000 years is entitled to its secrets.

Part of the mystique of growing garlic lies in the abundance of contradictory information and the fact that the plant often changes, depending on the soil and microclimate. Different experts hold opposing views on many facets of growing garlic: genetics and environment will either have an effect on your crop, or they won't. Take credit for your successes, blame genetics for the failures, but at least try it.

Why bother at all? Because sulfur compounds common in the soil in the Northeast make the garlic more pungent and increase the production of compounds that many believe have health benefits. Local tastes better and may be better for you. On this, everyone agrees.

Unless you are a collector, botanist, or bore, garlic can be divided into two basic categories: the top-setting or hard-necked, grown in climates that have a winter cold period, and the soft-necked, typically grown in climates that do not. The experts' nod goes to the top-setters as being easier for most gardeners to grow reliably.

Plant cloves in mid-October, pointed end up, about 2 inches below ground, 3 to 4 inches apart in rows 15 inches apart. Garlic likes well-drained, fertile, neutral soil high in organic matter, and does better in dry weather than in wet.

Keep weeding until the end of June, because garlic is a poor competitor for nutrients and water. On top-set garlic, remove the scape (the round-stemmed seed stalk) that forms in early June. If you don't, your yield will drop since the scape takes energy to form bulbils, miniature bulbs on the top of the stalk. (There's a difference of opinion about this too, but I vote with the descapers). Foliage growth stops the third week of June, and so can your weeding and watering, as the plant concentrates on enlarging the bulb.

In mid-July, dig a bulb to check its condition. Look for bulbs with firm, tight outer skins. Harvest before the skin splits. Dry several weeks in a warm, airy place out of direct sun.

For a list of sources, send a stamped, self-addressed envelope to David Stern, director of the Garlic Seed Foundation, Rose Valley Farm, Rose, NY 14542-0149.

Caring for Ficus

Let's assume you have tried and failed with that Victorian favorite, the Ficus benjamina *tree. You try places in the house where there is sun but no drafts and you mist it regularly. And eight or nine months later it just seems to give up and die, with all the leaves dropping off at once. You would think that without some secret of long life, you were doomed to have the ghosts of ficus past haunt you forever.*

Could be you loved the Dickens out of them. Anyone who would stand there with great expectations hand-misting an entire tree may also have a tendency to overfeed and overwater, especially when a few leaves begin to fall.

After putting on new growth and new leaves during the summer, some leaves are going to turn yellow and fall off in autumn as hard times arrive, light levels drop, growth slows, and the tree can't support as many leaves. But that does not always mean trouble, and it certainly should not prompt extra feeding and watering. Cold drafts aren't great, but sitting near a radiator, especially in a bleak house, can be worse.

What may be wrong in this tale of two trees is that the balance of light, water, and fertilizer is out of whack. Our mutual friend the ficus is naturally a high-light plant, but will adapt to a well-lit house. Try to picture the amount of light found in a well-lit office, certainly more than is found in an old curiosity shop. To help them adapt, buy your next one in the spring when longer days bring more light inside.

If you can provide the right amount of light during active growth, water thoroughly after the soil has had a chance to dry out somewhat. (Dig your finger into the soil to check for moisture; it should be dry a couple of inches down.)

A feel for watering is the basic art of growing houseplants. If the growing medium is filled close to the pot's lip, watering once may not provide enough. But constantly soggy soil can rot roots and make leaves fall, and can even kill the tree. Reduce watering and feeding when the light drops in the fall, letting growth slow down.

Shallots

If you like onions, why not grow shallots?

Shallots, a cross between onions and heaven, belong to the category of multiplier onions. Over the growing season, they split and form a cluster of bulbs, typically four to twelve, providing both food and more bulbs for planting. They grow best in cool weather, and fall planting gives them time to develop roots and 2 to 3 inches of top growth that overwinters and regrows in the spring. In areas north and west of Boston, spring planting is more reliable.

'French Red,' 'Odetta's White,' and 'French Grey' are good varieties in the Northeast. Most mail order sources that grow their own will ship them only in the fall. Those that sell shallots imported from Holland ship only in the spring. Panic, however, is not necessary. Grocery stores and roadside stands often sell

'French Red,' which has reddish-pink bulb scales and purple-pink flesh. Buy some for cooking and some for planting.

In the Northeast, it's generally best to plant in early fall, in a sunny location where the soil is well drained and rich in organic matter. Plant with 1 inch of soil covering the bulb, spacing them 6 inches apart.

In the summer, shallots are kind enough to signal when they are ready. Stop watering when the tops begin to bend and fall down, and harvest when 75 percent of the tops have fallen, giving the laggards another week. Don't split them apart until they have cured for four to six weeks, or they may rot. Spread them out in a thin layer in an airy location out of direct sun.

Sources for fall shipping include Southern Exposure Seed Exchange, P.O. Box 170, Earlysville, VA 22936, (804) 973-4703, catalog. For spring shipping of Dutch shallots, sources include Cook's Garden, P.O. Box 535, Londonderry, VT 05148, (800) 457-9703, catalog.

Fall Asters

Fall-blooming asters can end up floppy, bending over nearly to the ground. It's tempting to cut them back to try to make them bloom again, with a little more starch in their stems. While they really are perennials, they have the habit of disappearing after just a few years in the garden.

In late August through fall, New England asters (*Aster novae-angliae*) and New York asters (*A. novi-belgii*) and their myriad hybrids provide abundant flowers in rich to soft shades of white, pink, blue, and purple in a wide variation in height (from 1 to 5 feet) and bloom time (late August to late September). Like prodigal sons, these native wildflowers had to travel to Europe for hybridizing before being accepted as desirable garden plants here.

Preventing the taller hybrids from drooping requires pinching them back in late May and again in late June or early July to encourage shorter, bushier plants. If necessary, taller ones can be staked, but use twiggy branches to look more natural. New York and New England asters should be divided every year or two in the spring to keep them vigorous and in full flower.

Fall is much too late to cut them, but actually a little fall flopping is good for the soul. All summer we demand chin-up, no-nonsense plants. Fall should be a more relaxed time, with a degree of untidiness as plants tumble into one another, enjoying the relaxation that comes with having made it through another summer. Asters, nearly smothered in bright flowers, sparkle in the fall light, accenting the reds and golds of leaves starting to turn. From the roadside to the garden, asters are autumn made tangible. And if there are secrets to ensuring their return, the asters aren't talking. Sometimes they make it through the winter; sometimes they don't. If they do, don't forget to divide them.

There are many other native aster species, and enough cultivars to provide endless variety in the garden. Sources include Heronswood Nursery, 7530 288th Street Northeast, Kingston, WA 98346, (360) 297-4172, catalog; and We-Du Nurseries, Route 5, Box 724, Marion, NC 28752, (828) 738-8300, catalog.

Repotting Hibiscus

Hibiscus, having spent the summer outside enjoying the sun and mild weather, sometimes responds to coming back inside by turning yellow. Everyone suspects that water is the problem, either too much or too little, depending on who you ask.

Most probably it is a case of too little water, but increasing your watering schedule is not going to help. Hibiscus grows quickly during the summer, and the increased root mass displaces the soil

Hibiscus

in the container. The water, as well as the fertilizer you probably applied religiously every two weeks, is traveling straight through rather than soaking in. You pour water in, see it come out through the drain holes, and naturally assume that the hibiscus has been watered and fed. Unfortunately, the soil around the roots remains dry, and the plant remains thirsty.

Knock the hibiscus out of its pot, and take a look. Overcrowded roots signal that moving to a larger container will be necessary. When repotting, score the root ball with a knife or pull through them with a hand cultivator and tease some away so that they will grow into the fresh medium. If you don't, the roots will remain wound tightly, occupying the center of the container, and you'll have the same starved, thirsty plant, just in a larger pot.

Of course, no matter what you do, hibiscus will probably sulk in the winter. It is a full-sun tropical plant, and the low light, short days, and low humidity that come with spending a northern winter indoors are even more depressing for it than for us.

One further note that may fall under the horticultural truth-in-packaging principle: small potted hibiscus frequently sold in the spring appear to be dwarf plants covered with large flowers. Most, however, are treated with a growth retardant to keep them small. When the retardant wears off after a month or two, the 2-foot plant is on its way to becoming a 6-footer. This can be disconcerting to anyone who has not seen the same phenomenon occur in a teenage boy.

Dividing Bearded Irises

Bearded irises should be divided right after they finish blooming. But if you've let them go too long, you might be tempted to just forget them entirely.

There is still time left, but you should get moving. At the Presby Memorial Iris Garden in Upper Montclair, New Jersey, Elizabeth Buckno, the curator, and her volunteers don't finish up until early August, but they have 4,000 varieties to look after. She was kind enough to take a breather and share her technique. (Remember that other irises are treated differently from bearded irises.)

After you dig up the clumps with a spading fork, hose off the soil and inspect the rhizomes for damage, watching for bacterial rot and for holes made by iris borer. Cut out and discard any damaged portions along with any roots that aren't a healthy white.

Bearded Irises

Cut the foliage down to 4 to 6 inches and the rhizomes into 3-inch pieces, each with some roots.

Dip the rhizomes in a 10 percent bleach solution, and let them dry in the sun for a day. Use a soil testing kit to check the pH to make sure the soil is neutral, adding lime if it is acidic.

To prepare for replanting, work compost into the soil along with an inorganic mix of 5-10-10 fertilizer, superphosphate, and bone meal, or an organic mix of rock phosphate, green sand, and blood meal. Plant the rhizomes so that they have an inch of soil cover, and water in well. After the first frost, cut the leaves down to 2 inches and mulch after the ground freezes for protection against their heaving up out of the soil.

Bearded iris like to be divided every four years, so you can use the presidential elections as a reminder.

Saving Seeds

Every year there's that one terrific tomato in the garden. If everything is labeled, you can just order more the following year. But since labels disappear, you might decide to save some seeds.

You can save them with a little effort, but I can't promise you'll like the results.

The hundreds, maybe thousands, of different tomatoes on the market fall into two broad categories: open pollinated or hybrid. Open pollinated are the results of free interbreeding courtesy of bees, wind, luck, or good intentions. Hybrids are the products of blind dates, arranged by breeders, that went exceptionally well. Unfortunately, their seeds contain a random set of the parents' genes, and the odds of getting exactly the same back are astronomical. You will get a tomato, but that's as much as I can promise.

Open-pollinated plants produce seed that comes true. To save them, take a ripe tomato (vine or window sill ripened; doesn't matter). Cut out the seeds, which are covered with a gel-like goo. Separate the goo from the seeds by fermenting the mess for three to four days.

Put the seed-goo mix in a small bowl, and sprinkle on just a little soil, cover with water, and let the microorganisms eat the gel. The soil is a source of microorganisms, but you can sprinkle on a little yeast instead to get the process started. Make sure it never dries out. The fermenting will smell exactly the way you think fermenting will smell: bad.

After three to four days, check to see if the seeds come away from the goo easily. Once they are ready, rinse and drain the seeds.

Now you have to treat the seeds to kill any tobacco mosaic virus present. This is a common virus, so don't go blaming the neighborhood smokers.

Soak the seeds in 1 part household bleach to 100 parts water for three minutes and rinse, taking care not to get the bleach on your clothes.

Fold the seeds loosely in paper toweling to dry overnight. They stick to the towel, so you have to scrape them off and into a plain paper envelope. Then label and store with a little packet of desiccant in a glass jar in the refrigerator.

They will last several years if kept away from heat and humidity.

Not Quite Figs

Given a little shelter, figs can even be grown in the northeast. Planted between buildings or near walls for winter protection, when September comes, the tree will be loaded with fruit. Unfortunately, hardly any of the figs will ripen before frost takes them.

Part of the problem is that northerners trim their figs back in the late fall because their plants aren't hardy enough to survive the winter. And that solution gets you every time.

When you are out there in the fall, whacking it back, do you ever notice tho se little swellings at the branch nodes? Not the pointed ones—those are just leaf buds—but the rounded ones, about the size of a pencil eraser? Some varieties of figs would bear two crops if the season were long enough, and those buds will become next year's first crop. If you prune selectively each fall, leaving the branches that have the most of those small buds, they will overwinter and will have time to ripen by the following fall, assuming you protect the tree during winter by wrapping it, burying it, or, if it's in a container, bringing it into an unheated room (25 to 45 degrees). The year's second crop, which grows on each summer's new growth, may not have time to ripen because northern summers are not hot long enough.

If careful pruning doesn't increase your yield and your tree is in full sun, you have one of the many varieties that won't ripen fruit in a northern summer. If so, buy one that will, such as 'Brown Turkey' (not 'California Brown Turkey'), 'Petite Negri,' 'Celeste,' or 'Magnolia.' When choosing from a catalog, look for words like *cool season, early ripening,* or *northern variety.*

Mail order sources for figs include J. E. Miller Nurseries, 560 West Lake Road, Canandaigua, NY 14424, (800) 836-9630, catalog; and Raintree Nursery, 391 Butts Road, Morton, WA 98356, (360) 496-6400, catalog.

Birdhouse Gourds

Usually seed packages give all the information you need—how to plant whatever's inside. The seed company figures you can take it from there. But with birdhouse gourds, there is a lot more to be desired. When to harvest, how to age or dry the gourds, and even how to transform it into a birdhouse are all missing.

Think small birds. Like most other hard-shell gourds, bottle gourds (*Lagenaria siceraria*), which are used for birdhouses or musical instruments, prefer a long, hot season to grow and ripen. Start seeds indoors, about three to four weeks before the last frost, and then plant outside in full sun once the night temperatures remain above 60 degrees.

I even know a northern gardener who helps his heat-loving vines along by letting them climb and sprawl on an arbor built over an asphalt driveway. The black asphalt captures heat during the day and releases it at night, helping them explode with lush, leafy foliage and fragrant, night-blooming flowers. It also helps the fruit mature.

Let the vines grow as long as they can, until light frost withers the plants. Harvest the gourds, including a couple of inches of stem. Hang them up to dry at room temperature, leaving room for good air circulation. Let the gourds dry until you can hear the seeds rattle around when you shake them—anywhere from six months to a year, depending on the size of the gourd.

For homemade maracas, you are done, except for the fancy painting. For a birdhouse, cut a hole far enough up from the base for a bird to feather its nest, but not up into the neck area. You want the birds to be able to get in without banging their heads against the back wall. The size of the hole depends on the birds. Chickadees, for example, need a $1^1/_2$-inch hole. Eagles will need a larger hole, and a larger gourd. Add one or two small drainage holes in the bottom, clean out the seeds and dried pulp with a spoon, and it's ready. Or don't clean it out and let the birds have the seeds as a moving-in gift.

Geraniums from Seed

People who grow geraniums generally take cuttings when they want to propagate them. But occasionally someone wants the secret to starting with home-grown seeds.

There is no secret. Unlike single-flowered seed geraniums, bedding geraniums (those upright, double-flowered hybrids—pelargoniums, actually—that we love to set outside each spring) cannot be convinced to make seed easily. They are bred for looks, not fertility. In many hybrids, some stamens—the organs that produce pollen—may be absent or may produce only small amounts of pollen.

If your flowers are complete, you can help nature by hand pollinating. Examine a flower to see if it contains both stamens (five small filaments topped by a half-moon-shaped structure called the anther) and a pistil. The pistil has a five-pointed structure, the stigma, attached to a swollen base (the ovary) by a thin filament, called the style.

The anthers open in the morning, revealing fresh, yellow pollen. Gently pull an anther off with a tweezer and touch it to the stigma, making sure that all five points receive some pollen. Dr. Ernest De Marie, who grows and breeds pelargoniums at the New York Botanical Garden, says that if the conditions are right (lots of sun, low humidity, and cool night temperatures), up to five seeds will be produced. Over three to four weeks, the petals fall and the ovary, now appropriately called a stork's bill, elongates to about 1¹/₂ inches, and then dries and turns brown. You may then pass out cigars and take some credit.

The seeds in the stork's bill are each wrapped in a protective cover. Remove the seeds, covering and all, and let them ripen at room temperature for two to three weeks. Then pinch off the covering with your fingernails, and there they are at last: teardrop-shaped pelargonium seeds, about the size of a rice grain.

Store in a cool, dry place. Before planting indoors in February, gently rub the sharp end with fine sandpaper and soak overnight in water.

Since these are hybrids, they rarely grow up looking exactly like the parent. There's no telling in advance what you'll get; it might be better, but most likely not. If this is all too much for you, or if you find it right up your alley, seeds and information are available from the International Geranium Society, P.O. Box 92734, Pasadena, CA 91109.

Well-Drained Soil

Beginning to garden means beginning to understand the shorthand that gardeners use, the inside language. "Well-drained soil" is a term that shows up everywhere, without a definitioin in sight or an explanation of what to do when you haven't got it.

Soil is a complex mixture made up of air, water, organic materials, and different-sized particles of sand, clay, and silt. The proportions of the particles and the organic materials determine the tendency of the soil to hold or move the water, air, and nutrients that your plants depend on. Gardeners refer to soils that let air, water, and nutrients move at a speed that lets plants make the best use of them as "well drained" or "loamy."

Clay soils, which have a high concentration of small clay particles and organic materials, are nearly impermeable to water and air. Sandy soils are the reverse—mostly large sand particles with very little organic material. Water moves quickly through them, but they cannot hold onto the organic materials the plants need. Loamy soils contain a proportion of the three particles that lets water and air flow through to the roots, but at a speed that keeps the nutrients available.

To test your soil, dig a hole the size of a 1-gallon milk container. Fill the hole with water, let it drain, refill, and see how long it takes to drain the second filling. If it takes less than 2 hours, the soil is too sandy and will need organic matter added when you plant. If it takes more than 4 hours to drain, the soil has too much clay, and will need both sand and organic material added.

Dehumidifiers

I have often been asked about using the water collected by household dehumidifiers for watering houseplants and outdoor plants. My answer is always the same.

Water away. The coils of a dehumidifier are cooled by expanding and contracting gas inside, and they condense water from the air just like the water that forms on the outside of a glass filled with a cold beverage on a warm day.

Growing Hosta from Seed

Hosta flowers, like others, become seed pods. Seed pods mean seeds, and seeds can always find someone who wants to plant them. As a project for a sunny winter window, you might be tempted into planting a dozen or more hostas to spread among your beds.

You can grow hosta from seed as long as you accept the idea of not knowing exactly what you'll get. The wonderful variegated and blue-leaved hostas available as transplants are all carefully selected hybrids. Self-pollinated or bee-pollinated hostas yield seeds that rarely produce plants that are identical to the parent.

Gather the pods in a paper bag when they turn brown and brittle and start to split open. The seeds can be teased out with a pencil point and planted. Place the seeds in compartmentalized growing trays with a commercial seed-starting mix that is well moistened but not soggy, and just barely cover them. Keep them at 60 to 75 degrees for ten to twenty days while they germinate. The plants begin to need fourteen to sixteen hours of light per day once the first leaves appear. Two or more cool-white fluorescent lights placed 3 inches above the plants provide the right light. Maintain good air circulation (a small fan will help), keep the soil evenly moist, and start watching for insects. Use a much-diluted fertilizer solution once the seedlings have two sets of leaves. Continue to let them grow, moving them into 3½-inch pots when the roots begin to fill the compartments.

Don't rush putting the plants outdoors; wait about a month after the last frost date. In the fall, they will be large enough to plant directly in the ground.

You never know where a bee has been; the odds are high that a hosta's seeds will produce plants with plainer leaves. But don't be too quick to judge. Leaf shape and color pattern may change somewhat as the seedling matures. And remember, plant breeders get to name their new creations. As long as you have no plans to sell them, no one can tell you that your seedlings aren't Hosta 'YourNameHere.'

When a Pot's Too Big

When you bring your ficus inside for the winter, you notice that it's time for a larger pot. Since it's so heavy and awkward, your natural inclination is to jump a few pot sizes, giving it plenty of extra room and avoiding the chore for several more years.

Your intentions are good, but the road to good gardening isn't paved with good intentions; it is paved with lots of dirty, hard work—like repotting only one size larger at a time.

Most plants coming indoors at the end of the growing season are looking forward to resting. The loss of light due both to being indoors and to shorter days slows growth to a crawl. Plants are on idle, just waiting, and not taking in much water or nutrients. Most of them prefer to be drier than during the active growing season.

Moving them to a much larger pot means there will be much more soil than before, which you might think would encourage root growth. But the extra soil will take longer to dry out between waterings, and the water pushes out the air between the soil particles. The roots should be able to take up air, which is vital to plant growth. If the soil stays too wet for too long, the plant will suffer and may die.

The next size pot (about 2 inches larger in diameter) is best. Remember at least some of your high school geometry: when the diameter changes a little, the volume inside changes a lot.

Transplanting Peonies

It's fall, and your herbaceous peony has grown too much and is beginning to overwhelm the rhododendron it shares a spot with in the garden. It needs to be divided and transplanted to other places, but you don't want to damage either it or the rhododendron.

This is the ideal transplanting time for herbaceous peonies because the ground is still workable.

After cutting down the foliage, lift the clump carefully and wash the soil from the crown and roots. If it is an old peony, the inside portion of the crown may be dead, so cut your new divisions from the younger, outer portions. Make sure each division has five to seven of the pinkish growth buds, or eyes. The new plants will probably not flower the first year, and those planted from divisions with fewer eyes could take even longer.

Since a happy peony can give pleasure in the same spot for fifty years, location is important: it has to be sunny with well-drained soil. Clay soils should be improved by digging a large enough hole (15 to 18 inches across and deep) to mix in plenty of well-aged organic matter. Dust the cut ends with powdered sulfur and plant so that the eyes are only 2 inches below the soil. Deeper is not better. Deeper will not bloom.

Shades of Astilbe

Catalog descriptions are generally accurate, but they sometimes take liberties when describing color. Your astilbes may not exactly match theirs. 'Peach Blossom' can be light lavender, and 'Federsee,' which is listed as carmine rose suffused with light purple, might be a simple rose-purple to you. Not an important difference, unless you had planned a bed whose theme is red. Bloom times can also differ from the printed word. 'Superba' was supposed to usher in late summer but bloomed for you in early July. And 'Finale,' which certainly sounds like the end note of the season, might have bloomed before August.

In gardening as in real estate, the three most important criteria for success are location, location, location. Catalog writers apparently live in a climate that is ideal for plants they write about, from desert dweller to swamp native. But real climates are usually less than perfect, and plants' reactions to them may be subtle.

Astilbes certainly grow in the Northeast, but a hot, humid summer has two effects. First, the bloom period is compressed. Catalogs may speak of early, middle, and late astilbes, but heat tends to blur the distinctions, and many will bloom over roughly the same period. Second, astilbe flowers seem to lose some color intensity in the heat, fading and not lasting as long as they do where temperatures are cooler. The common garden hybrids were developed from species that are native to cool regions in China and Japan, and most hybridizing was done in England and Germany, where summers are also cooler than they are in New York and the mid-Atlantic regions.

To keep your astilbes at their best, remember that they need water, and lots of it—enough to stay moist—combined with rich, well-drained soil. In warm areas, most do better in light or partial shade than in full sun. And unlike some other perennials, astilbes should be divided every couple of years to keep them looking good.

As far as color descriptions, it is my understanding that plant catalog writers are recruited from the ranks of former Madison Avenue lipstick and nail polish copy writers.

Forcing Hyacinths

You can have fresh flowers in the winter without owning a greenhouse. Bulbs, the fertile eggs of the plant kingdom, can be coerced (*forced* is such an ugly word) into flowering in the winter, when you need them the most. All you need to do is to make the bulb think the winter is over.

Fooling Mother Nature, however, takes more than just leaving a baseball glove lying around. You have to give a bulb what it needs to start its growth cycle: a cooling period to promote optimal elongation of the flower stalks. Roots also begin growing during this period.

Roman hyacinths can be forced faster and more easily than the traditional Dutch hyacinths and are nicer to live with. Instead of the dense mass of flowers hunkered down and looking like a purple gang fight, the simpler Romans offer three or four spikes that take their turn blooming, each with loosely spaced flowers that can be appreciated as individuals. They are grown in Israel and not easy to find except by mail order.

Roman hyacinths can be grown indoors, even in an apartment, if the superintendent is a little stingy with the heat. Put each one in a bulb vase or sitting atop a narrow-necked, 6- to 8-

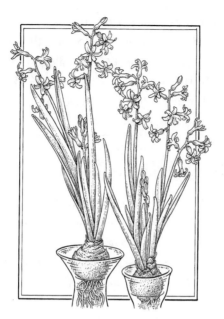

Roman Hyacinths

inch-tall glass jar whose neck is narrow enough to support the bulb. When the bulb is grown in this way, with water barely touching its bottom, you get a double show: beautiful blue or white scented flowers above and a mass of strong, bright-white roots below.

Keep Roman hyacinths on their containers in the dark at 48 to 50 degrees for ten weeks. An unheated closet on an outside wall works well; a refrigerator is too cold.

After the cooling period, bring them into sunny, direct light in normal room temperatures until the flower buds begin to show color. Then they can be moved into any bright area in the room. It usually takes about twenty-one days from the end of the cooling period until flowering.

Three mail order sources for Roman hyacinths, which you

may also see listed as French Roman hyacinths, are: McClure & Zimmerman, 108 West Winnebago Street, P.O. Box 368, Friesland, WI 53935, (920) 326-4220, catalog; Daffodil Mart, 30 Broad Street, Torrington, CT 06790, (800) 255-2852, catalog; and Bundles of Bulbs, 7091 N. River Rd., New Hope, PA 18938, (410) 581-2188, catalog.

Renovating Privet Hedges

Older properties often come with older privet hedges. Frequently they are quite woody toward the bottom and have meager foliage. If a hedge renewal is in order, you need to think about timing—whether to cut back in spring or fall—and how much you can cut back to maximize new thicker growth without worrying about killing the plants.

For major renovation of unshapely privet, wait until late March or early April, before new growth begins. The shrub can repair its wounds faster as the growing season begins than it can in the fall. Take a deep breath and whack the shrubs back to 12 inches from the ground. One thing you don't need to think about is how old the privet is. Even the oldest hedges respond well to this kind of renovation. Of course, it will require aftercare on your part. The privet will need fertilizer, mulch, and adequate water during dry spells as it regrows during the season.

Even though the rejuvenated hedge is small, don't let it get away from you. Maintenance pruning should be done every year in early spring before the new growth begins. Shear off half of the previous season's growth on the sides as well as the top to promote a dense wall all the way down without bare areas. Remember to maintain the correct shape—wider at the bottom and narrower at the top—so light can reach the lower foliage. Shape again in mid-July, and give it a once-over-lightly trim at the season's end. After two or three years, the hedge should be better than ever.

Propagating a Bromeliad

Moving in deserves a housewarming gift, and yours was a beautiful, vase-shaped houseplant with gray-green leaves that have powdery-white bands and a large pink flower on a stalk coming out of the center. The flower lasted for months but is now fading. Don't wait for another.

Your gift is an *Aechmea fasciata,* one of the bromeliads that is typically sold in flower because it blooms only once and then dies. To get more flowers, you'll have to do a little propagation.

The plant will continue to live on for many months, even a year or two. That will be long enough for the daughter plants, those small offsets at the base of the plant, to become large enough to survive on their own. Cut off the flower spike, and continue to water and feed the mother plant while the offsets grow. They can be severed and put in their own pots when half the size of the parent plant. Cut at an angle to include some of the mother's roots with each. Like most children, they do better if they take a few roots along. Or you can cut the mother plant out when it starts to look shabby and let the offsets continue to grow on in the pot. The young plants should bloom in two or three years, and the cycle continues.

Divide and Multiply

Plants don't talk, so you need to watch their body language. Perennials that are extending over their proper bounds, those whose flowers have decreased in size or number, and those that have stretched, flopped, or become lanky around sad-looking centers are telling you they need to be divided.

Spring- and summer-blooming perennials should be dug, divided, and reset in the fall, because time is running out before they (and you) settle in for the winter. Remember that the divisions won't have a full growth of roots, so they will need some protection against heaving during winter freeze and thaw cycles. After the ground freezes, mulch them with a layer of evergreen boughs from discarded Christmas trees.

Among the many perennials that are trying to catch your attention are astilbe, Siberian iris, heuchera, helenium, rudbeckia, and garden phlox.

Water Lilies in Winter

You wouldn't expect that tropical water lilies, or even hardy ones, would mix well with winter ice. That first winter for your new water garden needs a little planning.

Patrick Nutt, former assistant department head of horticulture at Longwood Gardens in Kennett Square, Pennsylvania, has grown water lilies for forty years and knows that hardy varieties are generally hardier than most people think. They do not need to be brought inside, but they must be protected against ice. He suggests cleaning them up in late October or early November, removing all of the old flowers and leaves, and sinking the entire plant, pot and all, deep enough so that it is entirely below any ice that forms. In the New York area, 2 to 3 feet is deep enough. In shallower water, a sheet of Styrofoam cut to the outline of the surface and painted black will absorb the sun's warmth as well as provide insulation. Be sure to secure it with weights and string on the surface of the water, black side up.

New shoots will begin to grow in mid-March, but the pots should not be brought up until after the last frost date for your area. Divide or repot in May.

Tropical water lilies are another story. They can be replaced each year or wintered over. The tuber, a walnut-sized body situated where the leaves emerge from the base, can be stored in clean, damp sand at 60 degrees at the same time that you prepare your hardy water lilies. Repot the tubers in mid-March, and move them outdoors after danger of frost is past. Or simply replant the tubers right away in 3-inch pots and grow them in an aquarium under cool-white fluorescent lights and a fluorescent light designed for plants, suspended right over the aquarium.

Water Lilies

With sixteen hours of light each day, blooms should form right around Christmas, and sporadically thereafter. In the spring, they can be moved outside to join their hardier companions.

If you are looking for an excuse to enlarge your water feature, make a summer visit to the Brooklyn Botanic Garden's Robert Wilson Aquatics House. It has the largest display of aquatic plants in North America and is bound to provide you with plant ideas.

Helping Agapanthus Bloom

Gardeners get into routines for plant care, and change can sometimes lead to disappointment. For example, if you grow agapanthus (lily of the Nile) in pots on your terrace, you probably bring them into a cool basement before the first frost, stop watering them completely, and bring them out again in mid-May. A change in your routine, like dividing some of them one fall, provokes a strange re-

Agapanthus

sponse—the next year both those that had been divided and those that had not will have fewer blooms.

Agapanthus are like fussy nomads who like to travel around but prefer to stay in their trailers. They enjoy going out for the summer and coming in for the winter, but resent being divided or repotted because their thick, fleshy roots are easily broken. They don't mind being potbound, but after several years, they are probably beyond their preferred comfort level and are signaling their need by reduced flowering.

It takes them a while to settle in after being divided, so the display should be back to normal next year. Divide carefully—only in the spring, as new growth is about to begin—but don't expect flowers that year. When they do flower, remove those great-looking seed heads to keep the plant's energy from going into seed production.

Agapanthus has deciduous and evergreen species, and while the evergreen hybrids are more common in the horticultural trade, check the label or ask which kind you are buying because their winter care is different. Deciduous species, whose leaves die down, go into dormancy and can remain dry and in the dark. The evergreen species slow down but don't really go dormant. They continue to need bright light and just enough water to keep the soil nearly, but not completely, dry. Both need temperatures of 40 to 50 degrees well into the spring. Once they are back outside, they need to be fertilized.

Well-grown agapanthus are a sign of an attentive gardener. They don't like to be in water-logged soil, but they don't like to dry out for very long either. With their need for well-drained soil, a pot full of roots, and much water during the growing season, agapanthus owners spend a lot of time with their finger in the soil. Luckily, the tall blue agapanthus flowers with their strappy leaves are worth the fuss.

Storing Dahlias

You planted dahlias last spring, ignoring the issue of what to do with them in the fall. Now it's fall, and you have to face the fact that you still don't know what to do with them. You know that dahlias are not hardy in cold climates and that they have to be dug up and brought inside for the winter, but you have heard that dahlias are difficult to store.

Nonsense. Anyone can do it with a little time and care. Tag each plant with the variety name or flower color before you do anything because tubers all look alike in the spring when you go to lay out the new planting plan.

When frost has blackened the tops, cut them back to 2 inches above the soil. The tubers are easily damaged, so dig about 10 inches from the stalk and lift carefully. Shake off the soil, place them on a tarp, and let them dry for a day or two.

Pack the tubers in dry vermiculite in a sealed container or in peat moss that is just barely damp in mesh or plastic bags with lots of holes. Dahlia tubers rot if stored too

Dahlias

moist but shrivel if stored too dry. Store in a cool place that will remain around 40 degrees. Check them in February, partly to look for signs of rot or shriveling, but mostly because seeing and touching them will remind you that winter can't last forever.

Grapevines to Go

When the house you grew up in is being sold, you might want to preserve some of those memories. Long Islanders often had grapevines, which can be a real touchstone between you and the parent who tended them. So take some cuttings for your own house, and keep the memories alive.

The procedure is easy; the hard part is remembering which end is up. After Thanksgiving, when the vines are fully dormant, cut several pieces 12 to 18 inches long, each as thick as a pencil, with two to three buds from the canes that grew this past season.

Grapes

Alice Wise, the viticulturist for Cornell Cooperative Extension of Suffolk County, New York, first cuts straight across 1 inch below the lowest bud (the end toward the trunk of the vine) and then at an angle 1 inch above the upper bud. The difference in cuts is a guide when planting; once you cut the vine, it is difficult to tell which end is which, and upside-down grape cuttings don't grow. The extra inch at each end protects the nodes from drying out.

Bundle the canes and store at around 40 degrees. You can keep them in the refrigerator—wrapped in damp paper towel and placed in a plastic bag with holes—but if you do, you have to give up fruit for the duration. The ethylene gas emitted as fruit ripens is toxic to the buds. Better yet, bury them outside in a shallow trench, covered with 8 to 10 inches of soil—no bag, no paper towel, no fruitless winter.

When you can work the soil next spring, prepare a well-drained spot in full sun. The pH should be 6 to 7.5. Plant 5 feet apart, keeping them upright, with one bud just above the soil line and the others below. County offices of Cornell Cooperative Extension have fact sheets with information on growing and on pest management for grapes.

If a Cherry Weeps Too Much

Weeping cherries are a favorite ornamental tree, but most people are afraid to do the basic maintenance—the pruning that keeps the branches from growing right into the ground. Not only does it make lawn mowing difficult; it also ruins the graceful lines of the tree. The key issues are when to prune and how to go about it.

Reluctance and patience are your best tools when thinning weeping trees.

Ideally, the effect should be more of a see-through Victorian beaded curtain than a solid wall of branches. Go inside, near the trunk, and look outward to make your decisions and your cuts. Don't remove more than a third of the tree's total wood; if necessary, leave some pruning for next year.

Some branches can be removed entirely to lighten the tree's appearance; others should be cut to different lengths, beginning as high as you can reach, 6 or 7 feet, to encourage the new growth to come downward with a natural grace rather than a uniform, artificial look. Branches that you want to keep long but that touch the ground should be pruned back to 6 to 8 inches off the ground.

The best time to prune is right after the tree is finished flowering; otherwise you will lose some of next year's flower buds.

Pruning trees takes some courage because each cut seems so final, but don't let the fear of making a mistake lead you to the biggest mistake of all: doing nothing.

Fall Planting Hazards

Alas, there never seems to be a simple answer or a rule without exceptions. Most, but not all, trees are good fall planting candidates. The exceptions are called fall digging hazards, and they are touchy about being moved or planted in the fall because they have fleshy, nonfibrous roots that are slow to regenerate.

It is best to wait for spring for varieties of birch, hawthorn, beech, tulip tree, dogwood, flowering cherry and plum, ornamental pear, and magnolia, among others. Besides, waiting is like a long engagement—hard on the passions, but better for cool judgment. It gives you a chance to be sure the tree and the spot are right for each other over the long haul.

Planting a Tree

How large to dig the hole and how much to prune after planting are two of the most confusing things about planting trees. The confusion comes from the wide range of answers that have been put forth over the years.

Simply put, make the hole wide, not deep, and don't over-prune. The current recommendation is to dig a hole three to five times wider than the root ball, but just deep enough to bring the top of the ball to the level of the surrounding soil. This has replaced the older practice of making a hole deep as well as wide, digging a $5 hole for a 50-cent plant.

The advice used to be to prune the tree back hard after planting, to the same diameter as the root ball, supposedly to compensate for the roots that were cut off when the tree was dug up. Both practices sound reasonable, but studies show that they make adapting harder, not easier.

Tree roots generally grow out and away, not down. If they hit hard-packed soil or clay just past the ball, they take the path of least resistance (don't we all?) and begin to circle around. Container-grown trees are a special concern, because any roots that have hit the side will have already started turning. Before planting, open up and spread out the roots, especially any that are encircling.

Planting a tree too deep can cause problems. Roots that grow over and around the trunk, called girdling roots, can strangle the tree as the trunk and roots grow larger. Squeezing a tree into a hole that is too small rather than expending the effort to enlarge it is just asking for trouble.

The only pruning you need to do is to remove broken branches or those that cross and rub against each other. Transplanted trees need as many leaves as possible to produce food to regenerate their roots.

Colorful Latin Visitor

Iresine herbstii, *commonly known as blood leaf, beefsteak plant, or chicken gizzard, is a subtropical South American (it hates frost) plant that should stay moist and loves humidity. To have dried out one and frozen the other is just adding insult to injury.*

Iresine is a plant well loved by people without enough light in their apartments or homes for flowering plants. Its magenta leaves make a lovely accent. Occasionally one even sees them in window boxes. When they get leggy, it is easy to cut them back and start new plants from the cuttings. But they can be difficult to find. When you lose one, either from forgetting to water it enough or by leaving it outside when a frost is due, finding a replacement can become a small emergency. Or an opportunity. If I tell you where to get it, will you promise to keep an extra cutting at a safe location?

Small and shrubby, iresine has waxy, variegated leaves that are frequently puckered. What makes it a standout is that the leaves are magenta with pinkish midribs and veins, providing color even without flowers. If your color sense tends away from the Crayola, try the variety *I. herbstii* 'Aureoreticulata,' with green leaves, yellow veins, and bright red stalks and stems. Both need the same care: plenty of light with some direct sun to keep the colors bright and keep them moist without being soggy. Pinch the tips occasionally to keep the plants bushy.

Sources for iresine include Avant Gardens, 710 High Hill Road, North Dartmouth, MA 02747, (508) 998-8819, catalog; and Davidson-Wilson Greenhouses, R.R. 2, Box 168, Crawfordsville, IN 47933, (765) 364-0556, catalog.

Sprawling Lavender

Fall cleanup is the time you are likely to discover all sorts of things to do. Your lavender, for instance, may be getting sparse and leggy and look ready for pruning.

Sharpen your pruning shears. Then put them away. You are way behind on your pruning, but hardy lavender should be pruned in spring, when the small nodes along the branches begin to swell, but before actual growth starts, or in summer right after it flowers, not in the fall.

Pruning back about one-third to one-half the length of the branches every year encourages branching lower down and keeps lavender growing upright, avoiding the sprawl that goes with its tendency, after about three years without pruning, to become woody and open up in the middle. This isn't just a question of aesthetics; sprawl can be risky. It leads to leaves that touch wet soil, a great point of entry for any enterprising fungus looking for work to do. Disease, of course, weakens a plant, making it more susceptible to winter damage.

A dressing of sand around the base is beneficial when growing lavender because it warms the soil and keeps water away from the leaves.

Spring is also the time to embrace your lavender: just before pruning, run your hands up through the dead leaves, letting them fall away. You get that stick-garden look, but in a few weeks the flush of new growth will show off the spring in your garden.

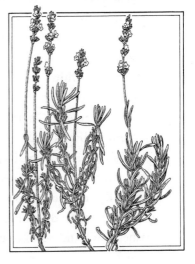

English Lavender

Perlite and Vermiculite

Many of the recommendations you see for soilless mixes call for both perlite and vermiculite. Since they appear to do the same things—hold water and create spaces—you might be tempted to substitute the one you have for the one you don't.

Perlite and vermiculite are not interchangeable. Considering how simple they are and how long they have been around (since the 1940s), it's surprising how confusing they are. The most common misconception is that perlite is a form of plastic or polystyrene. Both, however, are minerals that are processed at high temperature to make them explode into small, lightweight, puffy pieces.

They do share many traits that make them valuable components in a growing medium. Their size and shape make channels for the flow of air and water, helping aerate and providing drainage. Both prevent the growing medium from drying out too quickly because they hold onto water, though they do it differently, and the difference is important. Perlite holds water only on its surface, by capillary action, but vermiculite absorbs water, as much as sixteen times its weight, thereby making a much wetter growing medium.

Perlite is white, small, and nearly round and comes in several sizes, or grades, from a grain of sand to about 1/4 inch. No matter where it is mined, all perlite is the same chemically.

Vermiculite is also small, but it is boxlike, and has a shiny brownish metallic color. Depending on where it is mined, vermiculite may range from neutral to strongly alkaline. Perlite is chemically inert and neutral, and remains intact, while vermiculite is active, binding or releasing various minerals. It eventually crushes down and needs to be replaced.

Fooling Hyacinth

Forcing Dutch hyacinth bulbs for winter bloom, even buying those special glass vases, often leads to more disappointment than flowers. The result is always the same—tiny flowers hidden among the foliage. You have to wonder why even with plenty of light they won't come up where you can really see them.

They hide because they haven't gone through a full cycle of seasons. Give them a short winter, and they'll be ready to act more as if it's spring. Dutch hyacinths, like many other bulbs, need a cold period to prepare them for spring bloom. Often catalogs and nurseries offer "prepared" bulbs, which have been given a controlled temperature treatment. Unfortunately, that sounds as if the bulbs are ready to bloom. They're not. The preparation reduces the needed cold, dark period from at least fourteen weeks at 40 degrees to only ten weeks.

Without that period, the flower stalks will fail to elongate, and the flowers, hidden in the foliage and much less spectacular than they could be, will open from the top of the short stalk downward. With a proper cool period, the stalk will grow longer, and the flowers will open in the right sequence, from bottom to top.

Put the bulbs in their forcing jars, and put the jars in the back of your refrigerator for the right amount of time. Give them winter, and they'll give you spring.

Prepared Dutch hyacinth bulbs are available from McClure & Zimmerman, 108 West Winnebago Street, P.O. Box 368, Friesland, WI 53935, (920) 326-4220, catalog.

Winterizing Tree Roses

Hybrid tea rose standards, kept in pots on an outdoor terrace or patio, are fabulous the first summer you buy them. Then you realize that winter is coming, and they have to be prepared for it. The temptation, of course, is just to bring them inside.

Rose standards, or tree roses, are modern roses grafted onto a single trunk-like understock. The understock might be winter hardy, but the head and especially the graft union are not, and must be protected from the vagaries of winter.

Nelson Sterner, director of horticulture at Old Westbury Gardens on Long Island, suggests lightly pruning the rose, watering it well, and applying an antidesiccant spray to the canes before wrapping it. Put two 2-by-2-inch wooden stakes a foot taller than the standard in the pot, and staple burlap to one. Circle the plant, stuff the enclosure with salt hay, and staple it closed. Use lots of hay: it is going to be a cold winter out there. Now lay the whole thing down next to a wall, sheltered from the sun and wind, and say goodnight.

Do not think you can get away with bringing it inside. This is not a houseplant, and it will probably respond to your kindness by dying.

Hold Your Seeds

It's itchy time for gardeners. The Christmas blizzard of J Crew and Lands' End catalogs has been replaced by Burpee and Johnny's, seed orders have gone out, and packages are in hand, on the way or on display in the garden centers. Garden centers, supermarkets, and even hardware stores have put out their seed displays, and gardeners everywhere are looking at their calendars. To put their seedlings outside at the earliest moment, they count backward from whatever the last frost date is for their neighborhoods to find the seed-planting day.

Pots and seed trays are ready and everyone is at the starting line, waiting for the call, "Gentlemen, start your tomatoes." And heaven help the gardener who misses and has to set them out a week past the last frost date.

At the risk of incurring the wrath of winter-weary gardeners, will everyone please put your seeds away and go back to the couch? The last frost date is a statistic, not a license to move cold-tender transplants outdoors with impunity. Remember that the dates are based on averages, and in any given year there may be a frost weeks after that date. Even though nights are not expected to drop below 32 degrees, temperatures in the 40s aren't any better for seedlings.

Tomato

But most important, it's the temperature of the soil, not the air, that counts. Many seedlings (tomatoes, eggplants, peppers, and other frost-tender annuals) just won't take off in cold soil.

Starting seeds early but waiting to plant them when it's warm will result in stretched, pot-bound seedlings. To have seedlings ready to go out when the world is ready to welcome them, do your counting back from at least two weeks after the last frost date.

Tomatoes should be planted outside when the soil warms, and they will catch up to and surpass those that survive being first outdoors. Remember that bragging rights come from the flowers and vegetables, not from shivering seedlings.

Last frost dates vary. Check with your local county cooperative extension service for the date in your area.

Moving Rosemary Indoors

Rosemary is a wonderful plant, but it is one that most people have difficulty wintering over indoors.

Rosemary can survive indoors if you remember that it is not a typical houseplant. Taking it inside, where light levels are lower and the air is warmer and drier, is a shock. Ease the transition by taking it in before night temperatures are low enough to make the heat go on. And try to remember that water is not the answer to everything. Rosemary responds to excess water by gradually turning brown and dying. Of course, it responds to underwatering the same way.

Tom De Baggio, owner of T. De Baggio Herbs in Arlington, Virginia, points out that rosemary also hates being poorly drained. He prefers a coarse, free-draining mixture: one part sphagnum peat to one part perlite, plus 1 teaspoon of lime for a 6-inch pot. Rosemary needs a nearly neutral growing medium, and lime reduces the peat's acidity. Using this mixture, along with clay pots, allows rosemary to dry out more quickly between waterings.

Brown or black leaf tips or leaf shedding, starting at the base of the plant, are signs of overwatering; droopy stem tips or leaves that are a little grayer and angle up more sharply than normal are signs of underwatering. Keep spindly winter growth pruned, leaving one branch of soft, new growth as a water meter. The soft growth will wilt when the rosemary is too dry.

De Baggio never prunes the roots or moves rosemary into larger containers in the fall. A larger pot holds more growing medium and therefore more water. The additional time to dry out is more dangerous than the stress of being a little pot-bound. In the spring, he whacks off a third of the roots on the bottom and sides, and repots in the same or a slightly larger container.

Finding the right formula for overwintering takes trial and error. Balance water and temperature. Cooler rooms, around 55 degrees, keep the growth compact but lengthen the time to dry; warmer rooms let the rosemary dry out more quickly but encourage spindly growth. Rosemary prefers lots of sun. Artificial light can be used to extend day length.

Powdery mildew, a common problem for rosemary, can be fought with good air circulation, by keeping a small fan running. It's a small price to pay for the pleasures rosemary provides to eye, nose, and mouth.

Paperwhites for Winter

With refrigerator space at a premium, it's nice to know that here is a bulb that can be started without a cold period.

Nothing comes free. For paperwhites, a generic name for those narcissus that can be forced without a cold period, the price is their pervasive sweet, musky fragrance. The most commonly sold cultivar, 'Ziva' (usually just labeled "paperwhites"), can be overpowering. Israeli breeders, who supply the world, are trying to breed narcissus with shorter, sturdier stems and a lighter fragrance, but until the perfect paperwhites come along, experiment.

Fragrance is in the nose of the beholder, and while all are strong, some may have more appeal than others. Look in stores and nurseries that typically sell holiday plants and gift items for others, including 'Galil' (also called 'Galilee,' all-white petals), 'Israel' ('Omri,' creamy white petals with a yellow cup), 'Jerusalem' ('Sheleg,' white), and 'Nazareth' ('Yael,' creamy yellow petals, yellow cup). 'Grand Soleil d'Or' (lemon-yellow petals with a yellow-orange cup) and Chinese sacred lily (white petals with a yellow cup) are narcissus that have a reputation of being unpredictable because their bulbs may not bloom at the same time.

Grow in pebbles or soil in full sun to help keep them from flopping over. Some may need staking. Those potted in late fall will take four to five weeks to bloom, but in February they will take three weeks because of their genetics. They normally bloom in December or January when grown in the field, and this timing urge is powerful even indoors.

Putting them in a cool, airy room will help keep the fragrance from building up to agonizing levels. And don't plan on transplanting them, because they are not winter hardy. Throw them out.

Paperwhite Splendor

Let's say you've done your best with paperwhites. Twenty-five bulbs of the cultivar 'Ziva' were watered thoroughly, kept in the dark in a 55-degree room for five or six weeks, then planted in three bulb pans in a sunny spot. You don't quite end up with the display you wanted. You have about eight flower clusters in each tray, but the catalog you ordered the bulbs from had an awful lot more in their picture. It doesn't sound like you forgot to do anything.

When you think about how many bulbs, rhizomes, and what-nots are stuffed in the average gardener's refrigerator or out on the porch this time of year, paperwhite narcissus are just about the friendliest; they are very agreeable to work with. Dr. August De Hertogh, a professor of horticulture at North Carolina State University in Raleigh and author of *Holland Bulb Forcer's Guide*, the floricultural industry's bulb bible, says that paperwhites, unlike most other bulbs, don't need any dark or cooling period when you buy them. Just pot them up in pebbles or a well-drained potting medium, water, and put them on the windowsill.

My suspicion is that your bulbs were on the small end of the size range. With smaller bulbs, one stalk per bulb is about it. This year look for what the industry calls top-size bulbs, about 6½ to 7 inches around. At that size, the norm is two stalks per bulb, with the occasional third. Or look for 'Galil,' which produces more florets but is shorter than 'Ziva.'

For a real eye-popping display, do what some catalog photographers have been known to do: cut a few extra stalks and prop them up in the pot alongside the other bulbs. Looks spectacular, at least for the time it takes to snap the picture.

Suppliers for 'Galilee' paperwhites include the Charles H. Mueller Company, 7091 North River Road, New Hope, PA 18938, (888) 594-2852; and French's Bulb Importer, P.O. Box 565, Pittsfield, VT 05762, (800) 286-8198.

Turning Leaves to Mulch

Before raking those leaves out to the curb, think about other possibilities. They may not look like much, but they have more to offer than just taking up space at the local landfill. They can be put through a shredder or mulching mower. That way they won't blow around, and they take up a lot less space while you wait for the ground to freeze before putting the mulch around your plants. Three inches of mulch lessens plant heaving and provides an attractive appearance on otherwise bare soil. (Unless the mulch is battery powered, it does not keep the soil warm; it just slows cycles of freezing and thawing.) In the summer, shredded-leaf mulch looks great, helps the soil retain moisture, and makes weeding a breeze. As it breaks down, it provides organic material and improves the tilth, or structure, of the soil.

Anybody who has a compost pile should see that no leaf ever

leaves the yard. Stockpile them to add in next summer, along with fruit and vegetable scraps, grass clippings, and other green trimmings. The leaves provide a source of carbon, and the scraps and clippings provide nitrogen. Both are necessary to produce good compost quickly.

In the forest, fallen leaves are an important part of soil enrichment. Our gardens should not be denied the same benefits.

Jasmine in Winter

Jasminum polyanthum is not a plant for the casual gardener. Getting it to bloom regularly is difficult, even when you try your best to control day length, feeding, and other variables. It might tease you by blooming once, accidentally, and then never set flower buds again.

Winter-blooming jasmine is a houseplant that refuses to adapt its life to ours. The highly fragrant display of pink buds and starry-white flowers in February requires a specific temperature range that is hard to match in most houses. From November until the buds are fully set in January, *Jasminum polyanthum* must have very bright light with some sun and night temperatures between 40 and 50 degrees, with days not much warmer. It benefits from staying outdoors late into the fall, but must acclimate slowly to the drop in temperature.

The need for a particular amount of darkness each night is less certain, and growers' opinions vary. To be safe, strike a compromise. Keep the plant in a cool room, wear an extra sweater, and read with a flashlight until the buds are set.

The buds form on the growth made after July. Don't prune until after flowering is over, even though it looks as if it needs it. Whether it is cold and dark or cold and light, this is not the kind of a houseplant that one gazes lovingly at on the mantel while turning pages curled up before a roaring fire. The warmth of a typical room will shorten the flowering period even after the buds have set. But in February, it will be worth the effort to bundle up with hat and gloves and slip out into that unheated room to gaze at the display.

Pruning Hydrangeas

Your hydrangeas are magnificent, with lush foliage. Unfortunately, over the last few years they have given you none of the big blue blossoms you cherish. They have full sun, regular fertilizing, and seem quite happy. At the end of fall you even cut off all the stalks fairly close to the ground because the branches are unsightly. Well, well.

Imagine how frustrated the hydrangea must feel. It spends the season storing energy, getting ready, and finally producing buds for next year's flowers, and the next thing it knows, all of its work is in the compost pile.

Hydrangeas (*Hydrangea macrophylla*) should be pruned just before growth starts in the spring. They are barely hardy in Zone 6, so some branches or buds may die back from very cold winters or late spring frosts. Leaving the dead flowers on may provide some winter protection for the new buds.

Next year's flowers will be carried on twigs that grow from buds produced on this year's woody growth. Pruning back beyond the uppermost set of buds eliminates not only the spent flower but also the ones to come. The only clear-to-the-ground cutting necessary is for stalks that are more than three years old. All other branches should be pruned one at a time as you locate the buds. Take a cup of tea out to the garden with you. If you can prune a hydrangea before the tea cools, you are working too fast.

Helping Clivias Bloom

Your cliva, now six or seven years old, bloomed about four years ago for the first time and then again the next year. That was the end of that. You treat it well but you don't get any flowers in return. It doesn't seem fair.

When winter is at its worst, *Clivia miniata,* with a cluster of striking trumpet-shaped orange flowers held on a spike, can take the place of a Florida weekend, although the rarer clivias can cost nearly as much.

Although it is possible to kill a clivia (pronounced CLY-vee-uh), it isn't easy. Clivias live in a variety of temperatures, tolerate shady windowsills, like to be pot-bound, and are immune to most insect pests. What they do not do is bloom on command. Like many other plants, clivias don't recognize winter by looking out the window or watching the Weather Channel; they need to experience it for themselves.

Clivia

A rest period of eight to ten weeks in a cool room where temperatures are 40 to 50 degrees at night and only 10 degrees warmer in the daytime, with a reduced water supply and no fertilizer, is necessary to trigger flowering. Experts disagree on whether to allow them to stay completely dry or just nearly dry during the rest period. But they all agree that the cold period is necessary.

For the rarer yellow-flowered and peach-colored cultivars, a blooming-sized plant can cost more than $500, but plants that provide many years of wonderful orange flowers can also be purchased for about $35.

Louisiana Nursery, 5853 Highway 182, Opelousas, LA 70570, (318) 948-3696, has an extensive range of selections listed in their catalog.

Softened Water

You may prefer softened water for drinking and washing, but everyone tells you not to give it to your plants. What they don't tell you is why not.

The things that make water hard are minerals like calcium and magnesium. Water softeners remove these minerals (which plants like) by exchanging them for the sodium part of the salt (sodium chloride) that you load into the softener. Not enough sodium goes into the water to affect its taste, but much more than would be there naturally.

Sodium is a very active chemical. It not only exchanges places with the calcium and magnesium, it does the same with potassium in plant cells. Potassium is necessary for dozens of cell enzyme functions. When it is replaced by sodium, these functions can't happen, and the plant could die. Different plant species have different tolerances to sodium, but eventually the sodium buildup will get to all but those that grow naturally at the seashore.

Is November Too Late for Sod?

After finishing home renovation work in November, the contractor has left your lawn a disaster. The timing of the next step is up to you.

September and October would have been better, but you can do it now, provided you can find sod this late in the year. There are drawbacks, of course. Below 45 degrees, the roots won't grow much and the pieces will not knit together or grow into the soil layer below, making them vulnerable to drying out. However, since sod, like other grass, goes dormant during the winter, it will just sit there waiting for spring.

Sowing seed at this time probably would be unsuccessful. Even if it germinates, the small amount of root growth would not anchor the plants against the heaving that comes with cycles of freezing and thawing.

The least you can do is give the sod a fighting chance. Prepare the site properly before laying the sod by removing any remaining grass and testing the soil pH. Rototill in organic matter, superphosphate, and lime if the pH needs to be raised. Rake the site level, and, most important, butt the sod pieces as close together as possible. They have to fit tightly to prevent the edges from drying out and shrinking, and the sod must have good contact with the soil. Make sure you water it in well.

Winter's drying winds pose the greatest danger, so pray for good, thick snow cover.

Red-Twigged Dogwoods

Their beautiful twigs make red-stemmed dogwoods a valuable plant in the winter landscape. To keep them at their best, however, a little maintenance is in order.

Few other things look as good as the bright red stems of *Cornus alba* cultivars and the red or yellow-green stems of *C. sericea* cultivars against a snowy background.

The trick to maintaining the display at peak color is to understand that the stems turn corky-gray as they get older, so annual pruning anytime in late winter (up to late March) is critical. Since the shrubs send up their new growth from the base, prune as close to the ground as your cutting tool allows.

The most recent growth has the most vibrant color; two-year-old stems are not as bright, and after three years the stems have lost nearly all the color that you planted the shrub for in the first place.

Removing the three- to four-year-old gray stems each winter provides a shrub that displays a mass of colored twigs, not just a few bright stems among a dull majority.

Cultivars of these two common red-stemmed dogwoods are hardy in zones 3 to 7, but *C. alba,* which has the brightest forms, prefers the cooler climates and does better at higher altitudes in the New York area. *C. sericea* is a tougher shrub, less prone to forming stem cankers, and handles the warmer end of the planting range better.

By the way, while you are out there trampling around and pruning in the March snow, try to avoid stepping on those spring bulbs.

Helping Amaryllis Rebloom

Amaryllis is one of those plants that people have to buy year after year because they just can't seem to get them to rebloom.

Amaryllis, which are actually hybrids of *Hippeastrum,* are willing to give their all (some people find their all to be a little too much), but they do ask for special treatment in return. Allen Merrow, who breeds amaryllis at the University of Florida in Fort Lauderdale, says the bulbs require a lot of raw ingredients—sunlight and nutrients—to produce those long leaves and large flowers. During the growing season, fertilize once a month, water regularly, and make sure they get as much sun as you can provide.

Without adequate sun, the bulb will produce leaves, but not flowers.

Put the bulbs to rest between September and November. Withhold water, and let the leaves turn yellow before cutting them off. Then they need eight to ten weeks of storage in their pot with bone-dry soil. Keep the amaryllis in the dark, at 45 to 50 degrees, ideally in a humid location so that the bulb itself does not dry out too much.

Growing media can break down after as little as two years. The best times to repot amaryllis are just after the dry rest period begins or at the beginning of the growing season, just as the flower stalk and leaves peek out of the bulb scales.

Wood Ashes in the Garden

Recycling fireplace ashes in the garden seems a natural—what could be more organic than ashes? But actually, it's not a great idea.

Sometimes it's hard to remember that "organic" does not mean "harmless" and that moderation is not a bad idea, even with natural things.

Wood ashes may be natural, but they are not chemically neutral. Although they have no ability to improve soil condition, they do contain some potassium and a high amount of calcium. Exposed to weather, the calcium changes to hydroxide and carbonate forms.

Gardeners know calcium carbonate as limestone, used to raise the pH of acidic soils. Wood ash can be worked into the soil as a substitute for ground limestone, using twice the weight as the amount of limestone required as determined by a soil test. Too much wood ash in one place can raise the pH to the point at which plants will have trouble growing.

If the ashes are always spread over the same areas, check the pH every two years to make sure the soil does not become too alkaline.

Avoid putting ashes around plants that prefer acid soils, like azaleas, rhododendrons, heaths and heathers, blueberries, mountain laurels, pierises, leucothoes, and andromedas.

Winter Mulch

Perennials planted late in the fall can be a worry. What will the winter bring? The most common solution is to mulch them.

Mulch is the chicken soup of gardening—soothing to the roots in summer, protection against the damages of winter. Applied after the ground freezes, mulching prevents the rapid cycles of thawing and freezing that can happen if warm, sunny days are followed by cold nights. Cut-up Christmas tree boughs allow air to circulate but moderate the speed of change in soil temperature by keeping the ground in shadow.

The freezing and thawing can heave young perennials or those with shallow roots out of the ground, exposing roots to the bitter, drying winter environment. Don't be in a rush to remove them all at once on the first sunny day in March. Boughs should be removed in stages to prevent late damage from one of those miserable surprise late freezes.

Moving Houseplants

Moving during the cold months is not only hard on you; it is also hard on your houseplants. Protecting them depends on understanding them.

Remember that most houseplants are tropical natives and can get cold-induced injuries starting around 45 degrees. The amount of protection they will need depends on how long, and how cold, the trip will be and on how quickly the plants cool off. From house to heated car, a closed paper or plastic bag will trap warm air long enough.

For overnight trips, Dr. Charles Conover, a professor of environmental horticulture at the University of Florida's horticultural research center in Apopka, suggests wrapping each plant with ten to twelve sheets of newspaper (or with plastic foam or bubble wrap) and placing them in cardboard boxes that can be closed. Wrapping with thin plastic bags does not insulate well enough. Keep the plants in the car (not in the trunk) where they can get some heat, and never leave them in the car overnight if the temperatures threaten to fall below freezing.

Remember that most moving vans heat the movers, not the moved, and that a few hours in a below-freezing van will probably result in severely damaged plants. It might be better to give your plants to friends and start over at the new house.

Plants damaged by cold will wilt and look lackluster, but other signs may not appear immediately. Leaf drop, yellow mottling, and curled or browned edges after one to three days are common responses.

Blooming African Violets

African violets have the reputation of being constant bloomers. But they frequently slow down or stop for the winter, and people wonder what is wrong.

Probably nothing that a little more light won't cure.

In their native habitat, African violets (*Saintpaulia* species, although only cultivars and hybrids, not the true species, are found in the horticultural trade) root where they can find high humidity, warmth, and indirect sunlight. In this part of the world, from

October through February, there is much less strength to the daylight and the days are shorter. During this period they should be placed where they can get full sun, or fluorescent bulbs should be used to supplement their day length to fourteen to sixteen hours.

In the spring, move the plants back to indirect light. Light is the single most important factor in flowering (assuming you don't forget their need for warmth, humidity, water, and fertilizer). So adjusting the light year-round should be rewarded with nearly constant flowering.

Christmas Cactus's Nap Time

Getting a Christmas cactus to bloom takes a bit of work and a bit of planning. One 6-year-old that I know has bloomed only once, even though it constantly puts out new growth. It sits near a north window where the temperature is sweater-weather cold in winter. The year it bloomed, its owner lived in a drafty loft that got lots of heat in the morning and evening but not much in between. The result? Tons of pink-red flowers.

Once the rent was doubled and the owner and cactus had to move, nothing. Something about that loft experience was just right for the Christmas cactus.

Christmas cacti (*Schlumbergera* x *buckleyi* hybrids) need it cool during fall in order to initiate flower buds: night temperatures of no more than 55 degrees. But what makes them particularly persnickety is their love of the dark. Starting around the end of September, they have to snooze undisturbed for 12 to 14 hours every night until the buds are set. Any exposure to light will prevent bud set and convert that energy into vegetative growth. Sometimes moving to a new neighborhood has its drawbacks: any bright streetlights or all-night diners nearby?

A Bonsai Epiphany

Bonsai trees for Christmas. There's nothing like giving something that usually needs a lot of specialized knowledge but comes without any instructions.

A gift bonsai is a little like a gift drum set for a five-year-old: it's a gift that never stops giving, but it's not always what you want to hear. Bonsai, miniaturized woody plants grown in shallow containers, are more demanding than a typical pot of pothos. Since bonsai plant material can range from subtropical plants through temperate deciduous and evergreen trees, it is important to find out what you have, because the care requirements differ markedly.

Subtropical plants may be able to remain indoors all year, but conifers and deciduous trees need that winter cold period that their larger relatives get in nature. Because the small amount of soil in the pots will freeze and damage the roots, bonsai trees cannot simply be put outdoors for the winter. Enthusiasts often have cold frames or cool greenhouses, and some people even board their bonsai trees for the winter at specialty nurseries.

To keep your bonsai healthy and well shaped, you will need to become familiar with the mysteries of shoot and root pruning, training branches with copper wire, and water and fertilizer regimens. It is worth the effort. With proper care and time, bonsai trees grow old gracefully, becoming more beautiful and more valuable, unlike that spider plant taking over your window.

Bonsai enthusiasts love to share their knowledge. You can take your bonsai to a meeting of a local chapter of the American Bonsai Society, P.O. Box 1136, Puyallup, WA 98371. The American Bonsai Society Web page (http://www.absbonsai.org) has a wealth of information.

There are many excellent books on bonsai care, including *The*

Japanese Art of Miniature Trees and Landscapes: Their Creation, Care, and Enjoyment, by Yuji Yoshimura and Giovanna M. Halford (Tuttle, 1958). Yoshimura taught classical bonsai techniques for many years at the Brooklyn Botanic Garden. He died in 1997, but his memory lives on in the Brooklyn Botanic Garden bonsai collection and in his many New York area students.

Ivy's Own Timetable

Not everything is a pass-along plant. A friend has a wonderful English ivy, with unusual leaves and lush blue-black berries. Nothing about it looks like a typical ivy, and you try to take cuttings, but they fail. There must be something you can do to make it root.

Nothing. Your friend's English ivy (*Hedera helix*) has decided to stop fooling around and grow up. It has changed phases, from juvenile to adult, and is more interested in its responsibilities to the future than to rooting. Peter Del Tredici, director of living collections at the Arnold Arboretum of Harvard University, says that English ivy has phases in its life that are controlled by changes in the balance between various growth-regulating chemicals.

Juvenile ivy creeps, growing adventitious rootlets (those that grow in unusual places, such as from stems, for example) to help it climb and spread. As an adult, its form changes, becoming more erect, with thicker stems, but without rootlets. Most important, the adult form is sexually mature, and the plant concentrates energy on flowering and producing berries for reproduction. The leaf shape also changes, becoming more regular, without the indentations or the white veins seen on juvenile leaves.

Important to you, although probably less so to the plant, Del Tredici says he believes it is impossible to get a cutting from an adult to take root.

One English ivy that may interest you is called '238th Street,' after the location in the Bronx where it was first found. Like a teenager with a moustache, this ivy is an immature form with adult characteristics. It is available from Carroll Gardens, 444 East Main Street, Westminster, MD 21157, (800) 638-6334, catalog.

6

Doing It Differently

New things are the sparkle in life. New plants and new ideas bring more enjoyment out of a garden. Trying new things is the logical next step for someone who is reasonably comfortable in the garden. Partly it's experimentation for its own sake; partly it's a desire to change from the run of the mill to the extraordinary. Not just exotic-looking plants, although that is certainly of interest to many gardeners. More often people are looking for subtle improvements—plants that take less maintenance or, especially, fewer chemicals, because they are adapted better to the region. Native plants, disease-resistant cultivars, drought-tolerant plants—you name it, people have an interest in it.

One of the benefits of a newspaper column is the opportunity to write about plants that I like and to give people different ideas about plants to solve problems. But just because I like them doesn't mean you will, or that they will be the right plant for your needs. If you can, go see full-grown plants in landscaped situations—botanical gardens, display gardens, garden tours. Like a

Christmas puppy, plants sometimes have a way of taking over their living space.

It's your garden. Fool around before you settle down.

Do-It-Themselves Garden

Take advantage of those hardy annuals—especially Shirley, red corn, and bread seed poppies; love-in-a-mist (nigella); and larkspur—that reliably return because the seeds they release each year overwinter until spring. But it's best to let them do it their way since they are not only rugged, they are cantankerous. They resent the inevitable root disturbance during transplanting, especially the poppies, with their taproots, and often don't make it. They prefer to start outside, without much help from the gardener.

It may be shaky sociology, but tough love really is best for these tough annuals. Their seeds can be sown in the fall or early spring right where you want them, and they will grow stronger and more vigorous than transplanted seedlings. Fall sowing is problematic because seeds and clear garden patches are hard to find. Early spring sowing, even right into the snow cover, lets you do some useful gardening without too much actual work.

These plants' tiny seeds are difficult to sow uniformly and thinly by hand. To avoid crowding, which produces weak plants, or having to thin ruthlessly, mix the seed with sand or use a pepper shaker and a controlled flick of the wrist. Scatter seed once, carefully, and they will take it from there. Poppies and larkspur look best in patches, while fragile, ferny love-in-a-mist works better as a weaver, coming up among other foliage.

Part of the music of a living garden is the way your point is answered by its counterpoint. Year after year self-seeded volunteers will move about, finding unexpected places. Over time the pastels of the Shirley poppies slowly revert to the vivid red of the parent corn poppy, while the range of colors in the bread seed poppies reverts to a natural mauve. Composing a garden should be a joint effort between you and the plants.

Ivy-Covered Wall

I have met people who have long, tall, very blank walls that they would like to cover quickly with an evergreen ivy. They ask for a particular recommendation and a time frame, but I can only tell them to think before they order anything.

Whether you are starting a new university or just softening a surface, consider carefully the conditions your English ivy (*Hedera helix,* the only climbing ivies reliably hardy in the Northeast) will face as it grows and then choose among the many cultivars that will thrive in those conditions. In the end, is a long, high wall covered with something you do not like any better than the original blank face?

The first thing Sabrina Mueller Sulgrave, director of research at the American Ivy Society, wanted to know was in what direction the wall faced. Most hardy ivies do well on walls that face east or north, which get less direct sun in winter, causing fewer leaf-scorch or dieback problems. Choices could include 'Buttercup,' a variegated ivy with yellow-green leaves; 'Harrison,' with its very narrow lobes and white veins, or 'Wingertsberg,' which has a wonderful maroon-purple winter color.

A wall that faces west or south and does not have some protection, such as nearby buildings or trees, demands the hardiest ivies you can find. Here Sulgrave suggests choosing 'Woerner,' a vigorous grower with dull-surface leaves and light-color points at the end of each lobe, or 'Tom Boy,' which has unlobed, egg-shaped leaves that are waxy and bright green.

Cultivars differ in growth rate and their ability to climb, and individual conditions also make a difference, but any ivy will take at least several years to cover a wall.

Regardless of your choice, increase the success rate by choosing large plants, stripping off the leaves halfway up the stem, and planting deep in soil mixed with organic matter. Deeper planting increases root formation. Since it takes a year to settle in, plant as soon as the ground warms up, and for the first year water whenever the soil dries out. Once established, most ivies are drought tolerant, but everybody needs a good start.

Two sources for ivy: Hedera, Etc., P.O. Box 461, Lionville, PA 19353, (610) 970-9175, catalog; and Sunnybrook Farms, 9448 Mayfield Road, P.O. Box 6, Chesterland, OH 44026, (440) 729-7232, catalog.

Home-Grown Ginger

With the rise of health food stores, it becomes tempting to try growing a piece of fresh ginger root to make your own. After all, it's just the chemical treatment to stop it from sprouting that kept you from trying it years ago, right?

Health food store or otherwise, all fresh ginger root should grow, because the U.S. Department of Agriculture does not require any treatment for ginger (*Zingiber officinale*) imported for culinary use. But, of course, the ginger has its own requirements. As a native of the tropics, it grows well only with plenty of warmth and humidity.

If you have a warm, humid, sunny place indoors, you can give it a try, but don't expect to become ginger self-sufficient. Buy a plump, fresh rhizome in early spring, when it would normally be getting ready to sprout, and plant it horizontally about 1 to

2 inches deep, in a well-drained potting medium rich in organic matter.

Start it in a sunny window, and move it outside to a spot in the garden with dappled shade when the weather warms up. If you plan on keeping it inside all summer, use a 5-gallon pot because by fall that cute little rhizome is going to turn into a 4-footer with roots to match, assuming it likes the conditions (at least 75 degrees, bright light, and very humid) and doesn't suffer too much from spider mites and the various other ills that affect plants held indoors against their will.

By October, you will realize that this lanky, rangy plant is not particularly attractive, won't survive outdoors, and should probably just be harvested. Reduce watering, stop fertilizing, and wait for the foliage to turn yellow. In November, dig the rhizome up. It will have grown, although you will think it should be much larger based on the size of the plant. It's hard to store without drying out, getting moldy, or both, so just use it in a curry and buy another piece to plant next year.

Choosing Grass Seed

When the choice is to renovate a lawn or live with a dirt yard, the season doesn't matter—fall or spring—you just have to do it. Most people simply head for the garden center looking for a grass seed that promises to do well in shade and give a beautiful lawn without fertilizing or mowing too often.

Considering the time, expense, and work that go into starting or renovating a lawn, it is surprising how little thought most of us give to grass seed selection. After following the whole rigmarole of preparation—testing soil pH, killing the old lawn, rototilling, incorporating organic matter, liming, fertilizing, grading, not to mention sweating, cursing, and panting, all to prepare the perfect seedbed for that "low-maintenance" lawn—a quick trip to the garden center shelves results in a basic choice: grass seed for sun or shade. And for many people, that's all the information they can handle because they did the physical preparation but not the mental.

Some gardening work is best done on the couch now, before the garden chore season begins. Choosing grass seed can be as complicated as a moon shot, but a little reading can help.

Grass, or turf to the professionals, is one of the most heavily studied subjects in horticulture. With the huge market provided by golf courses, parks, athletic fields, home owners, and commercial landscaping, demands for better turf have led to the development of scores of named cultivars of Kentucky bluegrass, perennial ryegrass, tall fescue, and fine leaf fescue, each with its own characteristics. Among the considerations are looks (color, texture, density, and growth rate), tolerance to disease (leaf spot, dollar spot, red thread, stripe smut, and various patch diseases), and adaptive traits (winter color; spring greenup; how easily it establishes itself; tolerance to heat, cold, drought, and shade; fertilizer needs and mowing height).

With some basic knowledge about the site conditions, the publications, fact sheets, and advice available from the local office of the extension service can provide the background necessary to judge how appropriate each commercial grass seed mixture is. To find county cooperative extension offices, check the telephone directory under the sponsoring university—for example, Rutgers in New Jersey, Cornell in New York, and the University of Connecticut.

Adonis Forsaken

I have always been surprised that no one ever asked about one of my favorites, *Adonis amurensis*. No one mistaking this early blooming perennial for a spring bulb. No one wondering about the identity of that mass of bright yellow 2-inch buttercup-like flowers erupting from the ground atop bronzy olive-green foliage which is tightly furled, then expanding into a feathery crown.

Named for the beautiful Greek god Adonis, who spent his winters in the underworld only to be resurrected each spring by Aphrodite, this Adonis also dies back and goes dormant at the end of June, leaving only its memory, and an anticipation of next spring's show.

Adonis (the plant, not the god) prefers sun at least part of the day and well-drained soil. They can be hard to find at nurseries, possibly because they take several years before developing a sizable clump with lots of blooms and therefore do not fit into today's idea of "instant gardens." But if spring is worth waiting for, so is Adonis.

One source for Adonis is Kurt Bluemel, Inc., 2740 Greene Lane, Baldwin, MD 21013, (410) 557-7229, catalog.

Home-Grown Chicory

Chicory as an additive for coffee has a long history. While you can buy blends, you need the right variety to grow your own.

Cichorium intybus 'Magdeburg' and other chicories described as large rooted are the coffee chicories. It gets confusing because *C. intybus* varieties, and their relatives the *C. endiva* varieties, have almost as many common names as uses, and the common names seem to wander across species. For example, among the *C. intybus* varieties are several used in salads: red heading chicories, including the one known as radicchio; cutting chicories, whose young, tender leaves are picked for salads; and 'Witloof,' which is also grown for its roots. Dug up after frost and trimmed of leaves, the roots are stored at 32 to 40 degrees and a month later are forced

Chicory

to regrow in the dark around 50 degrees. The new growth forms the tight, white head (or chicon) known as Belgian endive.

But Belgian endive isn't the true endive. That's *C. endiva,* whose varieties are also known by the culinary names escarole (a broad-leaved form) and frisée (a fine cut, curly-leaved form). Ask for chicory in a salad, and anything might show up, except probably coffee.

To flavor, extend, or substitute for coffee, grow the 'Magdeburg' variety until late fall. A long growing season allows the plant to develop large roots. Dig up the plant, discard the leaves, and wash the soil off the roots. Cut into pieces ½ to 1 inch long, and place on a cookie sheet. Bake at 250 degrees until they are brown and brittle, but not burned. Grind the pieces well in a mortar or blender. Experiment to find the proportion you prefer; for most people it is usually about one-third chicory to two-thirds coffee. While waiting for the roasting to finish, make a salad and relax.

Mail order sources for 'Magdeburg' chicory seeds include Richters Herb Catalogue, Goodwood, Ontario, Canada, LOC 1AO, (905) 640-6677; and Seeds Blum, HC33 Box 2057, Boise, ID 83706, (800) 528-3658, catalog.

Preserving Easter Lilies

Keeping an Easter lily is possible, but requires some work.

Easter lilies, varieties of *Lilium longiflorum,* are forced into flowering at Easter time, which takes a lot of food energy out of the bulb. Forcing the same bulb again next year requires special techniques, but this year's bulb can be saved for the garden. Do not cut the stems and leaves, which will make food for the bulb. Keep the plants in a sunny, cool place indoors, and water regularly. They can be planted outdoors in a sheltered site after danger of frost is past. Plant them so that there is 6 inches of soil above the bulb. The plants should recover and grow as "permanent" perennials, although hardiness is questionable in the Northeast, depending on the severity of the winter. They may bloom as early as the next year, in late summer.

Starting Seeds

Go out to buy your seeds for annuals this spring and a salesman might insist that along with seed-starting mix and covered trays you should buy special grow lights. If your window sills have only minimal light, buying them will give good results. But after looking at the price, you may wonder about using regular lights instead, and what exactly is it that makes a grow light different.

It's good that you recognized that your window light wasn't going to be adequate. Even the sunniest window is sunny for only a short period each day, and not much good at all on cloudy days. That is hardly the 16 hours of consistent bright light needed to grow sturdy seedlings that are ready for transplanting into the garden on time.

Sunlight contains the full range of light from ultraviolet and blue through red and infrared, and plants have adapted to use nearly all of it.

The question is, How close to sunlight is close enough? Specialized grow lights come much closer to reproducing sunlight than do regular incandescent bulbs, which produce mostly red light, but very little blue. Fluorescent bulbs have varying amounts of all colors, with cool-white bulbs producing a bit more blue and a bit less red than warm-white bulbs. Special fluorescent grow lights do better at the red-blue balance than either cool white or warm white alone, but one cool white plus one warm white, 40 watts each, will do a perfectly reasonable job of raising seedlings.

What's just as important is the amount of light. Two bulbs in a standard 4-foot shop fixture suspended 2 to 4 inches over the plants and left on sixteen hours a day will do the trick.

New Plants from Old

Rubber plants don't stay the way we like them. They lose their bottom leaves, leaving all the foliage at the top.

Schefflera, dracaena, croton, dieffenbachia, ficus, philodendron, and many other plants that have stems that have gotten too tall or straggly lend themselves to air layering, a technique that allows the top of the plant to grow new roots while still getting nourishment through the stem.

Pick a point on the stem where you want new roots to grow, and make an upward-slanting cut one-third to halfway through the stem. Keep the wound open with a toothpick or wooden match to prevent it from closing. Rooting hormone may be dusted on the cut to help speed up rooting.

Wrap thoroughly dampened long-fiber sphagnum moss (available at garden centers) around the area, forming a softball-sized mass. Wrap clear plastic around the mass, and tie or tape it shut top and bottom to keep the moisture in and give the new roots a medium in which to grow.

Check the moss periodically to make sure it stays moist. Root formation can take several months on plants with nonwoody stems. Plants with woody stems can take as long as a year. When the new roots fill the moss, cut the stem just below the roots and pot up the new plant immediately. The part left behind, while looking horrible at the moment, will eventually develop new shoots.

Double Digging

High achievers and type A's are out there every spring double digging their gardens. They seem to like the pain, but I no longer sympathize.

I used to like to dig, but then, I used to like to run, too. Now I like to sit and stare and let the worms and roots do my digging for me. I like to think that it's not just laziness, but that spring preparation doesn't really require the pain and energy of turning every piece of soil over yet again. So I'm always glad to find other, smarter gardeners that agree with me. One of my favorites is Lee Reich, whose book *A Northeast Gardener's Year* (Addison-Wesley, 1992) divides gardeners into two camps—diggers and nondiggers—based on their soil preparation beliefs, and comes down squarely on the side of the nondiggers.

Diggers are those gardeners that turn the soil over using rototillers, spades, or garden forks. The benefits of digging are physical and emotional. Turning soil, especially if organic materials are mixed in during the process, promotes aeration. The emotional benefits come from the hard work, which satisfies the soul and makes the land look fresh and ready for a new year.

The dangers in digging come from working the soil too much or too early. Overtilling reduces the soil aggregates into a fine powder that prevents air and water from reaching plant roots. Working soil too early in the year, when it is too wet, also ruins the crystalline structure of the soil.

Digging has its drawbacks, though the tradition dies hard. Working soil brings a rush of oxygen into contact with the organic material, speeding up the decay process and removing those materials. Turning also destroys worm tunnels and old root channels, which serve to conduct air and water through capillary activity. Dormant weed seeds are brought to the surface, where the light helps them germinate. And, of course, digging may put the gardener's back out of commission, delaying planting.

Nondiggers add 2 or more inches of compost, and sometimes a bit of lime, to the beds each spring. The compost retards small weeds while using the activity of worms and microbes in the soil to incorporate the additional organic materials. The lush growth seen along roadsides, in pastures, and on the prairies where no hand has ever turned a shovel should give us pause to remember that Mother Nature knows how to do these things and that she will help our gardens along if we just let her.

Honoring the Radish

Considered an ideal crop for children to grow because they are quick and easy, radishes can nonetheless be disappointing if not planted with care. Their growing needs are simple but must be met to get the best crop. Loose, well-drained soil allows the radishes to grow in the shape they want to, unlike clay or heavy soil, which can cause them to become misshapen.

Plant early, when the forsythia is in bloom. Radishes that mature during hot weather and longer days are sharp-tasting and pithy, and may be small and hollow because the plant is concentrating on growing its above-ground stalk. Plant in the garden or in a container, and thin until the seedlings are 1 inch apart. Make sure they get 1 inch of water every week after they germinate, or they will end up tough. Cover early plantings with polypropylene row-cover material to retain warmth and protect against cabbage-root maggots.

Varieties that do well in the Northeast include the following: 'Cherry Belle,' 'Champion,' 'Scarlet Knight,' 'Improved Red Prince,' and 'Sparkler.' Sowing seeds every week for three or four weeks will provide fresh radishes all spring.

Radish

One More Time?

Terrace gardening, even just a few containers of annuals and herbs, is a pleasure, but third-floor walk-ups and heavy bags of potting soil or planting medium just don't mix. There is another possibility.

Reusing soil or, rather, reusing the soilless growing medium that should be in your containers instead of soil, is a matter of weighing your options. (Actually, soil belongs in the earth, not in containers, especially shallow ones like window boxes. The fine particle size means tiny spaces in between, which retard water and air movement.)

One hard and fast rule is that the mixture should be replaced if your previous year's plants had any fungus disease that wasn't completely eradicated. Many disease pathogens overwinter in the soil and will come back as soon as you provide another suitable host.

Compaction is another issue, but one that can be managed if you are diligent. Plant roots, especially in crowded, successful containers, will fill all the available space, packing the mixture into a tight, intertwined mass. If you were patient last fall, pulling all the roots out and saving as much planting medium as possible, you may have nearly enough for this year. Break up any clumps, fluff it out so it has nice spaces that can pass water, nutrients, and air to the roots, and just mix in enough new medium to make up for any losses.

The other basic rule is that the higher up you have to carry the bag, the more you should try to reuse the mixture.

Tulips versus Daffodils

Assuming that you can't resist bringing in bouquets of freshly cut spring flowers from your garden, keep in mind that daffodils and

tulips make terrible vase mates. Some of the chemicals that daffodils release when their stems are cut block the ability of tulips to take up water. Since cut tulips absolutely crave water for the first day, the result is a tulip in shock, sitting in water but dying of thirst. Meanwhile the daffodils are smirking and looking forward to having the vase all to themselves.

To avoid the problem, condition the daffodils and tulips separately before introducing them. Put each in its own vase of water overnight. Then rinse the flower stems well before putting them together. A quicker way to condition daffodils is to

Narcissus

> soak them for one to six hours in a solution of twenty to twenty-five drops of bleach to a gallon of water, then rinse well before putting into another vase with the tulips.

Looking for Epimediums

Once you have one or two species of epimedium doing well in the shady edges of your northern perennial garden, you'll start looking for more. Books list a couple of dozen species, with varied flowers. The problem will be finding a grower who supplies them or a garden center that stocks these underused plants.

So I'm always glad to push epimedium, a terrific ground cover that by all rights should put pachysandra on the compost pile.

Epimediums thrive in all types of shade, including the dry conditions under a Norway maple, and compete well with tree roots. They will grow where little else has a chance, but prefer moist, well-drained soil.

Some are clump forming and slow to spread, and look good in small, intimate groups or planted in wide swaths or as a border edge. Others, such as *Epimedium pinnatum,* E. x *perralchicum* 'Frohnleiten,' and E. x *rubrum,* spread faster and make better ground covers.

Species and hybrids range from 6 to 12 inches high, with delicate, heart-shaped foliage that is tinged red in the spring on some species and often turns bronze in the fall. Early spring, shy, columbine-like

Epimedium

flowers, which may be rosy pink, yellow, white, violet, or bicolor depending on the species, are held aloft on wiry stems.

Cut down old foliage in the spring before new growth begins, so that the flowers may be seen more easily. Epimediums should be planted or divided after flowering when the foliage is mature, or in the fall.

Sources for epimedium include Busse Gardens, 5873 Oliver Avenue S.W., Cokato, MN 55321, (320) 286-2654, catalog; André Viette, P.O. Box 1109, Fishersville, VA 22939, (540) 943-2315, catalog; and We-Du Nurseries, Route 5, Box 724, Marion, NC 28752, (828) 738-8300, catalog (be sure to ask for the separate specialty list of epimediums).

Crabapple Choices

I am often asked to recommend the best flowering crabapple for someone's yard. I usually respond by saying that there is no one best crab.

One of the most popular ornamental trees, there is a bewildering number of crabapple hybrids, offering a huge range of possibilities. Selecting the right tree is just as important as proper planting and should never be an impulse decision.

Choosing a crab requires juggling so many characteristics that one might even feel the need for a computer spreadsheet program, preferably one that works in several dimensions. Many people decide based on the flowers, which run the gamut from white through pink to red, in single, semidouble, and double forms. But the flowers last only two weeks, while the tree is there all year.

The tree itself can be upright, rounded, shrubby, columnar, or weeping, and range in height and spread from under 10 feet to 30 feet when mature. Fruit may be small ($^1/_4$ inch in diameter) or large (as much as 2 inches). Fruit colors can extend from lime green to yellow to dark red, and the fruit persists late into the winter or is quickly eaten by birds. The tree bears fruit annually or alternately (every other year).

But not all characteristics are so pleasant to think about. Crabapples appeal to more than just humans and birds. Keep in mind apple scab, fireblight, cedar-apple rust, powdery mildew, and Japanese beetle, all of which are common and provide their own distinctive damage, ranging from disfiguration to defoliation.

Disease resistance and size should be the major concerns when choosing a crabapple. While remembering that resistance is a relative thing, not a guarantee, some of the better cultivars include 'Adirondack,' 'Coral Cascade,' 'Donald Wyman,' 'Harvest Gold,' 'Narragansett,' 'Professor Sprenger,' and 'Profusion.' But resistance is just about the only characteristic they share.

One source of helpful information is *Flowering Crabapples: The Genus Malus,* by John L. Fiala (Timber Press, 1994).

How to Grow Vines

Over the last few years many gardeners have become interested in adding vines to their gardens.

Vines are back in the garden fashion cycle, between water gardening (the last rage) and ferns (my prediction for the next rage). Remember that vines require suitable companions—something to climb onto.

Vines climb in three basic ways. Most twine around a support, either twining their stems (wisteria, hyacinth beans, morning glories, moonflowers, and honeysuckle) or with tendrils that reach out and curve around anything they touch (sweet peas, passion flowers, grapes, and clematis). A flat wall is as much a barrier

Hyacinth Bean

Sweet Pea

to these vines as it is to us. They need a support thin enough to coil around.

Other vines, like English ivy, Boston ivy, trumpet creeper, climbing hydrangea, and Virginia creeper, grow rootlets modified into sucker-like disks that adhere onto flat surfaces. Wire fences and string supports are as challenging to them as a high wire is to an acrophobic.

Still others, like the wild vine catbrier, grow thorns that act like grappling hooks, helping them pull themselves up and over nearby shrubs. Polling these neighbors does not provide high marks for popularity, and they are seldom planted on purpose.

How a vine climbs is as much a consideration as any of the visual characteristics. If a particular vine is desired, an appropriate support will have to be supplied. If the support is there already, pick a vine that knows how to use it.

When to Spray

Using insecticides effectively requires two pieces of information: which insects are they effective against and when to apply them. By law, products have to list which insects they work on, but hardly anyone tells you when to use their product.

With insects, as with comedy, timing is everything. Insects and plants know just what time of year it is without calendars.

Plants begin growing after a particular amount of heat has warmed the air and soil, telling them that spring has arrived. Since species are consistent every year, relationships between them remain consistent. Insects are synchronized to their favorite plants because survival depends on being ready to dine just when their hosts are ready to be dinner. Showing up too soon or too late may be fatal.

Phenology, the study of recurring, weather-related biological phenomena, provides two ways to know when pests are vulnerable. The first is to watch for plant phenology indicators—plants that bloom at the same time that pests are present on another species. For example, birch leaf miner is vulnerable when the common lilac is not quite finished blooming, and peach tree borers are best treated when the mock orange blooms. Eastern tent caterpillar larvae are active and vulnerable in early May, when the redbud and saucer magnolias are in bloom.

The second way is to track growing-degree days. Beginning March 1, a cumulative total is kept of the season's warmth. Each day's minimum and maximum temperatures are added and divided by 2; 50 is then subtracted, because there is little insect activity below 50 degrees. The degree-day total shows how much heat has accumulated in the season. Particular insects are active during particular ranges. Euonymus scale is vulnerable as an overwintering adult between 35 and 70, or as a crawler between 70 and 120, while spruce spider mite eggs can be treated between 7 and 121.

Local county cooperative extension offices can provide information on figures for growing-degree days and plant phenology indicators, including the season's daily degree-day totals in your area.

Growing Herbs Inside

These days any cook worth her salt grows at least a few of her own herbs. Even grown indoors many herbs will taste just as good as outside.

Small culinary herbs, such as chives, oregano, and thyme, can be grown on a bright windowsill or under fluorescent lights. Be sure to use a good soil mix containing either perlite or vermiculite to increase drainage. Herbs can be grown in separate pots or all in one window box, but keep each type together so that taller ones don't shade shorter ones. For growing under lights, use two 40-watt cool-white fluorescent bulbs kept 4 to 6 inches above the plants.

Aphids are the most likely pests, and they can be rinsed off with a water spray. Keep an eye out, and they won't have a chance to build up a significant population. Herbs grown indoors will taste just fine—certainly a lot better than dried ones.

Scents in the Night

During the day, evening scented stock is disguised as just another weed, but in the evening the very small, pinkish-lavender flowers open up and one of the most beautiful scents you will ever smell begins to fill the garden. It used to be more common than it is now, and you might have trouble finding seeds.

As much as we appreciate the colors and fragrances of flowers, we are not the intended beneficiaries. The purpose of a flower is to aid pollination, usually by attracting the attention of bees or other insects, and plants have devised different strategies for success. Plants that bloom in daylight can use color and pattern, but those that bloom at night must depend mostly on fragrance to attract moths and other night visitors.

Evening stock (*Matthiola longipetala,* sometimes sold as *M. bicornis*) is generally not planted right up front in the garden because it isn't much to look at. But at night, when the flowers open and the scent begins to waft across the garden, building as the evening passes, the fragrance more than makes up for its daytime looks. Lemon, rose, musk, and spices are part of the scent, but only part. It is best described as indescribable.

If work occupies most of your day and only evenings are available to enjoy the garden, you might consider other night-fragrant plants like dame's rocket (*Hesperis matronalis*), *Nicotiana* 'Fragrant Cloud,' *Petunia integrifolia,* tuberose, moonflower, four o'clocks, brugmansia, and night phlox (*Zaluzianskya capensis*). There's no reason why a garden can't be enjoyed twenty-four hours a day.

Sources include Thompson & Morgan, P.O. Box 1308, Jackson, NJ 08527-0308, (800) 274-7333, catalog; and Select Seeds, 180 Stickney Hill Road, Union, CT 06076-4617, (860) 684-9310, catalog.

Pest Management

Preventative spraying of insecticides, done regardless of the actual situation, is becoming much less popular. Replacing it is a process called integrated pest management, and landscapers are becoming "scouts."

In the largest park or the smallest patio, every garden guardian faces choices about how and how much to intervene in nature's process. Wanting to protect plants from the ravages of insects and diseases and, at the same time, wanting to act "green"—the shorthand phrase that represents sound ecological practice and respect for all life, not just the portion that we paid for and enjoy—are desires that are not easily balanced.

Between the extreme positions (nuke everything at the first chewed leaf, or share a weed-filled plot with an entomological wonderland) is the practice of integrated pest management, a set of principles to control pests and diseases while limiting the use of chemicals. It means using chemicals when needed but trying to prevent their need through other means.

The first principle is to maintain good cultural practices. Proper planting and care encourage healthy plants that can fight for themselves. A diverse plant population supports beneficial insects (there should be more to a landscape than the overused taxus, arborvitae, and juniper). Most important, choose disease- and pest-resistant cultivars. After deciding what plants you want, ask a local county cooperative extension office if cultivars that are resistant to the most common problems are available.

Second, monitor for problems. This is what your landscaper means by "scouting." Using growing-degree days (a method of tracking cumulative temperatures), indicator plants (plants that bloom at the same time that pest is active), and frequent inspection, home owners and landscapers can be aware of potential pests and watch for signs of damage.

Third, when you find a problem, treat it with the least toxic method that will work. That may mean pruning out infected areas, spraying with horticultural soaps or oils, or, as a last resort, using traditional chemicals.

Choosing the right plants, finding problems early, and treating when the pest is most vulnerable can reduce both chemical use and damage.

Making Stone Troughs

*With the price of stone troughs where it is, you might think they
were lined with gold. They look so good on a terrace, though, that
you should be tempted to make some yourself. Put away the carving
chisels—you don't need them.*

Real stone troughs are hardly used anymore because they are
too heavy to lug around and have a tendency to crack if they are
left full of soil all winter. Making troughs that are lighter and
more resistant to winter damage is easy but time-consuming.

Robert Bartolomei, the director of outdoor gardens at the
New York Botanical Garden, begins with a cardboard box to set
the trough's shape. Support the outsides of the box with cin-
derblocks, and coat the inside with motor oil so you can peel it off
more easily later.

He mixes equal parts of dry Portland cement and perlite and
a handful of polypropylene fibers for strength, and some polymer
concrete hardener, according to the label. The hardener and the
polypropylene fibers are available at a builders' supply outlet.
Add just enough water to make stiff mud, stir, and trowel it 2
inches deep in the bottom of the box. Place half-inch dowel rods
into the mixture to make drainage holes. Now, place an oiled box
that is 2 inches smaller inside, and fill the space between the two
boxes, firming as you go.

Let it sit for twenty-four hours. Then remove the cardboard
and the dowels, and add texture with a wire brush. Burn off any
protruding fibers with a propane torch. Cement has to cure
slowly, so wet it and keep it in the shade wrapped in plastic for
about two weeks. Then leave it out in the open for a month or
two so the rain and sun can leach out the lime that forms during
the curing and may harm your plants.

The Handbook on Troughs, available from the American Rock

Garden Society (P.O. Box 67, Millwood, NY 10546), is filled with information on making and enjoying troughs and trough gardens.

If you make only a single trough, it becomes easier to see why they cost so much. But with nearly the same time and effort, you can make several to keep for yourself or give to friends.

Hardy Evergreen Ferns

Every garden with a shady area, and that's a lot of gardens, is probably a good place for ferns. There are even evergreen ferns that look good most, if not quite all, year.

Not *too* shady, however. A good site is mixed, with some direct sunlight in the morning and dappled protection in the afternoon. Rich, loose, humusy soil with good drainage, to which organic matter is added when planting, is ideal. Add compost or mulch each year to help retain moisture.

Fronds are replaced every year, so even those ferns that remain green in the winter brown out just as the new fronds, called croziers or fiddleheads, are emerging in the spring. Four of the hardy evergreen species commonly available are Christmas fern (*Polystichum acrostichoides*), evergreen wood fern (*Dryopteris intermedia*), marginal wood fern (*D. marginalis*), and autumn fern (*D. erythrosora*). All of these have fronds 1 to 3 feet long.

Autumn fern is the best of these because it stays upright during the winter (unless the snow is too heavy). Its fronds begin bronze, changing to dark green as they mature, and have brilliant red sori, or fruiting dots, on the backs. The others remain green but get mushy at the base of the stalk and collapse, looking pretty much like the rest of us during a long winter.

To see two outstanding collections of hardy ferns, visit either the F. Gordon Foster Hardy Fern Collection at the New York Botanical Garden in the Bronx or the Fern Garden at Lyndhurst

Museum Property of the National Trust for Historic Preservation in Tarrytown, New York. To read about ferns, look for *Ferns for American Gardens,* by John Mickel (Macmillan, 1994), a definitive guide to more than 500 kinds of hardy ferns.

Fern sources include Fancy Fronds, P.O. Box 1090, Gold Bar, WA 98251, (360) 793-1472, catalog; Foliage Gardens, 2003 128th Avenue S.E., Bellevue, WA 98005, (425) 747-2998, catalog; and Wild Earth Native Plant Nursery, P.O. Box 7258, Freehold, NJ 07728, (732) 308-9777, catalog.

Switching Azaleas

When your life begins to relax a bit, you may want to do the same for your garden—make it a bit less formal. But that doesn't mean giving up on azaleas, a dependable flowering shrub.

Use this as a chance to eat your cake and have it too. Switch those stiff, overpowering hybrids that explode into color and then fizzle out early for our native, deciduous azaleas.

All azaleas should not be judged by their loud-mouthed relatives. Native species offer benefits that the hybrids can't match. Flowering does not have to be restricted to spring; by choosing a selection of natives, you can have blooms the entire season. Long, graceful, tubular flowers range from subtle to bright with noticeable feathery stamens and spicy-sweet fragrances. The foliage of many deciduous natives turns orange-red in the fall.

Their range of growth habit, color, and period of bloom make natives more useful in the natural garden than those bright but ultimately boring hybrids planted next to every house since the 1920s.

Of course many natives also flower in April and May. But in summer, when the hybrids are just a memory, there are natives that will flower in every month. June and early July bring *Rhodo-*

dendron arborescens (sweet azalea, 6 to 8 feet), with very fragrant, bright-white flowers with long red stamens and glossy green foliage. *R. viscosum* (swamp azalea, 5 to 6 feet) blooms later in June and July, with fragrant, white flowers. In late July or August, you can be enjoying *R. prunifolium* (plumleaf azalea, 10 to 12 feet) with showy orange-red flowers. The flowers are bright, but against the foliage they become more subtle. As late as September or October, *R. serrulatum* (Florida hammocksweet azalea, 5 to 6 feet) will be providing lovely white flowers for the breakfast table.

Remember that azaleas are classified botanically as rhododendrons; they are usually found together in catalogs. Mail order sources include Eastern Plant Specialties, Box 226, Georgetown, ME 04548, (732) 382-2508, catalog; and Woodlanders, 1128 Colleton, Aiken, SC 29801, (803) 648-7522.

Biennial Foxgloves

Biennial foxgloves are peculiar plants. Sometimes they seem to grow well past their two-year life span. There are rumors that you can make them perennials by pruning.

If it finds a site it really likes, the biennial foxglove *Digitalis purpurea* sometimes settles in as a short-lived perennial, but it's not something you can talk (or prune) them into. Foxgloves are willful. The biennials will "walk" around the garden finding locations they like (well-drained, moderately moist soil high in organic matter in a lightly shaded site), usually popping up where you would never have thought of. Because they are biennial, they produce a low rosette of leaves the first year, sending up a 2- to 4-foot flowering stalk the second year. They broadcast seed and then die, unless they decide to live another year.

Although you can't make them behave like a perennial, you

can extend the bloom by cutting the spike below the nearly spent flowers. This will force several side shoots to form and flower, although the new stalks will be shorter and the new flowers will be smaller than the originals.

For perennial foxglove, try *D. lantana,* the 2- to 3-foot Grecian foxglove. Its small, gray-purple flowers with faint brown markings have a protruding lower lip. *D. grandiflora* has a 3-foot stalk of yellow flowers whose throats are speckled cinnamon.

A source for foxgloves is Milaeger's Gardens, 4838 Douglas Avenue, Racine, WI 53402, (800) 669-1229, catalog. Seeds are available from Ron's Rare Plants and Seeds, 415 Chappel Street, Calumet City, IL 60409-2122, (708) 862-1993, list.

Small and Wide Shade Tree

Small yards dictate small trees. There are lots of small trees, but you can't always have what you want. For example, gardeners often want a tree only 15 feet tall, but with a wide canopy full of spring flowers and the ability to cast cooling shade.

Since a 15-foot tree's branches will start somewhat close to the ground, I assume you don't mind bending low when you go to sit in its shade. One problem with meeting your requirements is that to be a tree, you have to look like one, and 20 feet tall is about the minimum. But there are a few crabapples that Kris Bachtell, curator of the collection at the Morton Arboretum in Lisle, Illinois (with over 200 species and cultivars of crabapples), has some suggestions.

Malus floribunda (Japanese flowering crabapple) is 20 to 25 feet high and wide with pale pink, nearly white flowers. Its yellow fruit, blushed with red, attracts many birds, so watch where you sit. *Malus* x *zumi* var. *calocarpa* (redbud crabapple) grows 20 feet high and 25 feet wide. It has pinkish-white flowers and red-orange fruit. *M.* 'Weeping Candied Apple' grows 15 feet high with picturesque horizontal branches 15 to 20 feet wide. Its white flowers, edged in pink, are followed by bright red fruit.

Unlike the other two, redbud crabapple is an alternate bearer, with heavy flowering years alternating with lighter displays. Alternate bloomers cause much consternation and discussion among their owners as to what's wrong with the tree every other year.

Giant Pumpkins

'American Giant' is the pumpkin cultivar that usually holds the world's record for size. If you think you're up to the challenge, that's the one to try. But obviously there is more to it than just starting the right seed.

Serious pumpkin growers—those who figure anything under 250 pounds is fit only for pie filling—have their own methods. The World Pumpkin Confederation publishes growers' hints in its newsletter, but I would not be surprised to find out that some secrets never reach print. (For membership, write to Ray Waterman, 14050 Route 62, Collins, NY 14034.)

Start with fertile, well-drained soil with a pH of 6.8 to 7.0. Mix compost and 1 pound of 5-10-5 fertilizer into an 8- to 10-foot-square plot. Big pumpkins are always feeding and need room to grow.

Bright yellow male flowers appear on the vines first as they start to run. Female flowers, with a small swelling underneath, follow. Remove the first two female flowers on each vine, keep the third and fourth. Once these flowers set fruit, remove the rest of the female flowers as they appear over the season.

When fruit begins to grow, remove all but the strongest one. World-class pumpkins are not for the fainthearted. One pumpkin, one chance for fame. Put that pumpkin on a large, sturdy support to keep it off the ground. A bed of straw on a wooden pallet is good if you are going to use a forklift to move it. Don't try to turn it to make it grow round; big pumpkins flatten out, and you might snap it off the vine.

Growing huge pumpkins means paying serious attention to watering, especially as the pumpkin gets larger. Give it a lot of water and fertilize (follow label instructions for a liquid fertilizer) every two or three weeks as it grows. A soaker hose two hours a day will provide enough water and keep the foliage dry and free of powdery mildew. But don't overdo it: too much water will drown the roots, and too much fertilizer can burn the plant.

The grail of pumpkins is to be the first to grow a 1,000-pounder. Don't forget to water. And you better pick up a few hundred pie shells.

Oriental Poppies

The brilliant red-orange and pink blossoms of oriental poppies are wonderful in bloom, but once they're done, they're done. And then all the leaves turn black.

There's nothing quite as spent as a spent oriental poppy, and there's nothing quite as obvious as the hole they leave behind once you clean up the mess. Since they disappear in midsummer, plan on using neighboring plants that will move in to cover the space and begin their bloom around this time. For this summer's bare ground, consider a birdbath.

Daylily Day Trips

With almost 15,000 named cultivars of *Hemerocallis*, or daylily, available on the market, it's easy to understand the trepidation

Daylilies

that accompanies filling out an order form. Imagine how pleased you'll be next summer when the daylily you picked out because of a catalog picture of the bloom provides only a few flowers, each held on a low stalk, or scape, half hidden in the foliage.

What the catalog pictures don't tell you may be the things that are the most important. How well will any particular daylily do in your part of the world, and what does the whole plant or, better yet, a grouping of daylilies really look like? How soft is that soft yellow? Can you depend on a catalog photograph to render subtle colors accurately?

Since daylily flowers last only a day, the number of buds on a stem is a good indicator of how long the plant will bloom. And where are the scapes held: above the foliage or half-buried inside? And what does the foliage look like anyway? After all, you are going to live with the foliage a lot longer than you live with the flowers.

How a daylily affects you, how it tugs at you or leaves you cold, is something that needs to be determined in person. The members of the American Hemerocallis Society understand all this and try to make it easier to fall in love with daylilies by assessing private, public, and nursery display gardens. Gardens that they consider qualified, all open to the public, contain a wide variety of well-grown daylilies, each labeled with the cultivar name. Be sure to bring a pencil and paper along; you'll probably want to try more cultivars than you can commit to memory.

Missing Butterflies

Along with global warming, some gardeners are worried about their missing butterflies. They planted the favorites (butterfly bush, heliotrope, verbena, Sedum spectabile, *joe-pye weed, and phlox) to attract them but still don't get the numbers they think they should.*

It's not all nectar and glimmer being a butterfly. It's easy to forget that a good part of their lives is spent in a larval stage as humble, sometimes downright ugly, caterpillars, not as shimmering adult butterflies. For every butterfly sipping nectar, there was a caterpillar chewing leaves and keeping one eye open for indignant gardeners. After all, hardly anyone plants gardens specifically to attract caterpillars, and most caterpillars are treated as unwanted guests. The host plants for larvae (like milkweed and black cherry) either are not typical garden plants or are plants that we prefer unchewed (like carrot foliage, parsley, and dill).

To make your garden more attractive to butterflies, be sure to include water for drinking and a wide variety of flowers for nectar. It is especially important to choose plants that don't bloom at the same time, so that the butterflies can feed all summer. Remember that monarchs and others that face long migrations need nourishment right up until they leave in the fall.

Whether to include some plants for the caterpillars depends on the balance you choose between garden and butterfly, since most caterpillars prefer those plants that we consider weeds. Milkweed, for example, provides nectar for forty butterfly species adults. More important, it is the sole host for monarch larvae.

On a sadder note, the introduction of a parasite to help control gypsy moth is proving once again that messing with Mother Nature has unforeseen consequences. *Compsilura concinnata,* the parasite, was first brought from Europe in 1906. Unfortunately, it attacks not only gypsy moth but also more than 200 different species of butterflies and moths.

For a Bouncier Lawn

Are "Keep Off the Grass" signs doomed? Not exactly—but there is a cure for overused turf, whether in a stadium, on the tee boxes at the golf course, or even in that area by the fence where the dog runs back and forth. The grass dies in these areas because the soil becomes too compacted. Home owners may give up, but professional groundskeepers have to replace sod several times a season.

Dr. John N. Rogers III, an associate professor of turf science at Michigan State University, and J. Timothy Vanini, one of his graduate students, have found that this compaction can be prevented on high-use areas by sprinkling rubber "crumbs"—pieces no bigger than the period at the end of this sentence—that are made from used tires. The rubber clings to the base of the grass blade, so the treatment lasts indefinitely. No harmful side effects have been found, Rogers said, and, in fact, treated grass seems to green up faster in the spring.

As often happens in science, a desire to solve one problem leads to many unforeseen benefits. Rogers's goal was to reduce high school football injuries by reducing soil compaction, thereby softening the blow when body meets field. But other uses keep popping up. Rogers said the spectator areas at the 1996 U.S. Open were treated with the rubber, and the lawns were saved even though hard rain flooded the area only days before the Open began.

Crumb rubber costs 15 to 25 cents per square foot of lawn and could help use up some of the 253 million tires thrown away each year. If you own a football team, a golf course, or an energetic dog, you may want to contact the university's marketing licensee, Jaitire Industries in Denver, (800) 795-8473. The company can direct you to a distributor.

The Other Kiwis

The word is getting around about hardy kiwis. At least some of the word is. People still don't know much about their taste or their growing habits. Rumors spread, of course. I have heard their taste described as being as insipid as that of mulberries. It's not.

Hardy kiwifruit (*Actinidia arguta*, hardy in Zones 4–7) and superhardy kiwifruit (*A. kolomikta*, hardy in Zones 3–7) are smaller and smoother than their fuzzy grocery store cousins. They have a similar taste but are even sweeter. Hardy kiwifruit are about walnut size, while the superhardy tend to be marble sized. Perhaps as compensation for the lack of size, both have edible skins to go with their emerald green flesh and tiny black seeds. No muss, no fuss, put a handful in your pocket and go (just be careful how you sit).

Both species need well-drained, slightly acid soil, light shade, strong supports, and plenty of room. These are twining woody vines. In their native humid mountain forests in Asia, they can grow to be 100 feet long, although 20 to 30 feet is more likely in the Northeast. Perhaps in embarrassment for being so large, they tend to hide their fruit under the leaves, so you'll need to hunt a bit at harvest time. One benefit is that the small, green fruit are almost completely overlooked by birds. Cats, on the other hand, may eat the leaves and stems, which make them act a little dopey—the same effect as catnip.

Except with the *A. arguta* cultivar 'Issai,' both male and female plants are necessary for fruiting. Plant the male within 35 to 40 feet to make it easier on the bees. *A. kolomikta* typically starts producing fruit when it is two years old, but *A. arguta* may wait until it is three to five years old. Both species are beautiful foliage plants, especially *A. kolomikta,* whose variegated leaves are shades of pink, white, and green. The cultivars *A. kolomikta* 'Krupnopladnaya' and *A. arguta* 'Ananasnaja' are particularly heavy bearers.

Sources for hardy kiwifruit include Burnt Ridge Nursery and

Orchards, 432 Burnt Ridge Road, Onalaska, WA 98570, (360) 985-2873, catalog; and Edible Landscaping, P.O. Box 77, Afton, VA 22920, (804) 361-9134, catalog.

Van Fleet's Roses

With the number of people working on plant breeding over the years, it's not surprising that we run into their descendants once in a while. A Marylander named Van Fleet thought his grandmother was kidding when she called one of her roses a Van Fleet. An article in the paper made him think twice.

You should always pay attention to grandmothers. Walter Van Fleet (1857–1922) was one of the world's most important hybridizers of climbing roses, breeding such classics as 'American Pillar' and 'Silver Moon.' He worked for the U.S. Department of Agriculture and lived for many years near the USDA trial grounds at Glenn Dale, Maryland. Your grandmother's rose may have been 'Dr. W. Van Fleet,' named for him in 1910 by Peter Henderson, whose nursery introduced it. Van Fleet wanted to name it 'Daybreak,' but Henderson insisted that the delicate shell-pink rose honor the man who really invented the "dooryard rose," vigorous climbing roses that are tough and beautiful.

Or her rose might have been 'Sarah Van Fleet,' a medium pink hybrid rugosa rose named for his wife and introduced after his death. Both namesakes are still popular, but neither is as well known as 'New Dawn.' Introduced in 1930, 'New Dawn' is a sport of 'Dr. W. Van Fleet.' A sport is a mutation that causes a single branch of a plant to look or behave differently from the rest of the plant. Discovered on a plant years after his death, 'New Dawn' has all of the wonderful properties of 'Dr. W. Van Fleet,' but it also repeat blooms. 'New Dawn' was granted the first U.S. plant patent, so you may want to check the family tree in your old Bible and bask in a little horticultural glory.

Bold Colors in the Garden

Is there a hole in your late summer garden? Are the same old annuals beginning to bore you? Next year try something unfamiliar.

Tithonia rotundiflora, the Mexican sunflower or torch flower, isn't an annual for wimps. Instead of quietly sitting there, anonymous, at the edge of the border, tithonia is big, bold, and brassy, catching your eye, and the eyes of bees, butterflies, and hummingbirds all around the neighborhood.

Tithonia cultivars range from the 3- to 4-foot orange-flowered 'Goldfinger' and fiery orange 'Sundance' to the 6- to 7-foot cultivar 'Torch' (deep red-orange). Each has a bright yellow half-pincushion center made for pollen gathering. With a riot of 3-inch-wide velvety blossoms, it is a plant that loves the hot weather of high summer and blooms from midsummer to autumn frost if deadheaded regularly.

Use it as you would its similar cousin, the sunflower, at the back of a perennial border, or bring it right up front and go eye-to-eye with color before the quiet of winter sets in.

Seeds are available from Pinetree Garden Seeds, Box 300, New Gloucester, ME 04260, (207) 926-3400, catalog; Stokes, P.O. Box 548, Buffalo, NY 14240-0548, (716) 695-6980, catalog; and Burpee, 300 Park Avenue, Warminster, PA 18991-0001, (800) 888-1447.

Prime Looking Season

Too many gardeners think only of spring and early summer show and neglect to include late summer and fall in their garden plans. Late summer is the time to take a good look at as many gardens as you can. Seeing new combinations can inspire you to make changes that were hard to imagine back in the spring when you were looking at tiny starts at the nursery or pictures in a catalog.

If you saw "*Hemerocallis* 'Lusty Lealand,' bright red tetraploid to 36 inches" in a catalog, would you know how to use this plant in your garden? What would look great next to it? Do you have an instinctive feeling for tetraploids? If so, you're better at this than most others. Even when accompanied by a photograph, catalog descriptions are best for people who already know what the plants look like.

Visit public gardens with a pad and pencil to note what various plants look like in full summer growth and among their friends.

The Versatile Allium

As you order bulbs for fall, there ought to be room in your garden for some of the 500 or so species of allium, the genus that includes the culinary standbys onions, chives, garlic, leeks, and shallots.

Alliums can vary in size from the 4-inch *Allium oreophilum* to the 4-foot *A. giganteum*. *A. christophil* flowers in May, with a globe of purple-metallic-blue stars about 8 inches in diameter on a stalk 2 feet tall. When the flowers die, the seed head remains, looking like a see-through garden sculpture atop a stalk, punctuating space here and there as it rises above its neighbors. How many other flowers look as good dead as they do alive?

A. moly, which blooms in early June, is a 6-incher with yellow flowers. *A. sphaerocephalon,* the drumstick allium, flowers in late June or July, with egg-shaped red-violet heads waving atop 2-foot stalks. Its flowers last a long time on the plant and up to ten days in water as cut flowers.

Curly chives, *A. senescens* var. *glaucum,* have twisted leaves forming a gray-green swirly mound, with small lavender flower heads in August. It is a great plant for a border.

Alliums can tie a garden together, forming the musical notes on an invisible scale in four dimensions: height, color, size, and time of bloom.

Two sources for alliums are McClure & Zimmerman, 108 West Winnebago Street, P.O. Box 368, Friesland, WI 53935, (920) 326-4220; and the Daffodil Mart, 30 Broad Street, Torrington, CT 06790, (800) 255-2852.

Novelty Daffodils

In a competitive gardening world, sooner or later one of your neighbors will brag about spending $15 each for her new daffodil bulbs. Has the world gone nuts? Have daffodils?

I can't answer the first question, but the second is more interesting anyway. Your neighbor is about to enter the world of rare or novelty daffodils, and may have trouble getting back.

While the large Dutch growers concentrate on propagating huge numbers of traditional daffodils, such as the 'King Alfred' type, small American breeders are developing new cultivars with better growth and flower characteristics in new shapes and colors. Prices can rise to $100 for a single bulb for the most basic reason—supply and demand. The number of people who avidly collect or show daffodils is tiny compared to those who buy traditional bulbs. But the number of bulbs available of a new daffodil is even smaller, and remains small for years.

Dave Karnstedt, who has bred daffodils for forty-five years at Cascade Daffodils in Minnesota, explains that the process of developing a new cultivar is long and not very promising. New cultivars come from seed produced by careful cross-breeding experiments. In four to six years the first blooms appear, and the breeder begins to have an idea of the results. Promising cultivars are moved into a test bed where they grow for another three to five years, to see if the first year's bloom repeats or changes, as some do, and to see if it has good growing characteristics. After more than ten years, the grower has a half-dozen identical bulbs. Since bulbs multiply every one to two years, depending on conditions, it can be another ten years before the breeder has fifty bulbs—enough to sell some and reserve others for propagation. If the flowers have done well at shows during this period, there will be a waiting list of collectors willing to pay the high prices.

With a fifteen-year investment and a success rate of 1 percent of trial cross-breedings that are good enough to be selected and named, a new cultivar is costly until the supply of bulbs increases enough to meet the demand.

You can see the latest cultivars, as well as older, high-quality daffodils, at shows put on by the American Daffodil Society and its local chapters each spring, generally in April. For information about the American Daffodil Society and its local chapters, contact the executive director, Mary Lou Gripshover, 1686 Gray Fox Trails, Milford, OH 45150, (513) 248-9137.

Catalogs of specialty daffodils are available from Cascade Daffodils, P.O. Box 10626, White Bear Lake, MN 55110, (651) 426-9616, and from Grant E. Mitsch Novelty Daffodils, P.O. Box 218, Hubbard, OR 97032, (503) 651-2742. No matter what kinds of spring bulbs you want to see, order in time for fall planting.

Moss for the Terrace

Building the subgrade for a new bluestone terrace in a shady area where there was an abundance of moss means removing the moss.

But moss growing between the stones adds character to the terrace. Encouraging moss to grow takes a bit of work, but the old gardeners' tale of using buttermilk should be discounted.

If bluestone is set in concrete, you will not have much luck, because moss needs a site that will hold some moisture. *Ceratodon purpureus,* or the purple horn-tooth moss, is one of most common mosses in the United States and will grow well in relatively dry, compacted sites, such as terrace cracks. You won't find it in any catalog, but it is abundant on roadside embankments, in vacant city lots and open fields, and on roof shingles.

After collecting it, let it dry out and then pulverize it in your blender. Sprinkle the resulting powder along the cracks, water regularly, and it should be established and lush within two years. Forget the buttermilk, but don't forget to wash out the blender.

Winter Aconite

Tell friends you are thinking about planting winter aconite to have its lovely early flowers and your friends will tell you that it is impossible. That's only partly true. There are things you can do to improve the odds.

Winter aconite, *Eranthis hyemalis,* suffers a bad reputation, only partially deserved, but like a risky stock, when it pays off, it more than compensates.

Blooming in late winter around the same time as snowdrops, eranthis helps shorten February and March, which can seem to be very long months. The bright yellow flowers, similar to buttercups, sit atop a fringy collar of green leaves, seeming to melt the last snows and provide assurance that spring is coming. But you won't see them in the spring unless you plant them in September. Eranthis tubers resent being harvested, packaged, and left lying around on the shelf. The shorter the time between harvesting and

Winter Aconite

planting, the more likely they are to respond.

When you get the tubers, don't send them back because they look so awful. They just do. Small and shriveled, looking like dried-up raisins or ancient deer droppings, they don't even seem to have a proper top or bottom. Rehydrate them overnight by wrapping in dampened peat moss.

Plant within a day because the rehydration process may make them susceptible to fungus diseases. Don't worry; the tuber can figure out which way to send stem and roots. Find a site that gets sun and moisture during the winter. Plant tubers 2 to 3 inches deep and the same distance apart.

About that bad reputation: Eranthis rewards the patient and punishes the greedy. Don't be surprised if four out of five are never seen again after planting, although they multiply readily by self-seeding once they settle in. Plant lots—hundreds if you can. Not just because many won't make it, but because the late winter needs that kind of display.

Fall Cover Crops

At the end of the vegetable growing season, that nice, fertile plot of open soil is just ripe for a weed takeover. But it's not necessary to use herbicides to keep them down.

Why not do what farmers have done for many years? Fall cover crops, planted now and turned back into the soil in the spring, not only keep weeds down and prevent erosion, but also enrich and recondition the soil, benefiting next year's vegetables.

Annual ryegrass can be sowed from September through late

October, on bare ground or around existing plants. Cultivate lightly and sow at a rate of 4 to 6 ounces per 100 square feet. Since annual ryegrass dies when the temperature goes below zero, it will be a ready-made mulch in the spring, all set to be tilled in.

Winter rye (the grain, not the grass) and winter wheat can be planted until mid-October and still have time to grow enough to be effective cover crops. They survive the winter, and the more you let them grow in the spring, the more organic material will be available as "green manure." Of course, larger plants are harder to till in, especially if you are going to be turning them over with a spading fork.

All cover crops improve the tilth, or structure, of the soil, reduce erosion and mineral leaching, and improve the soil's water-holding ability. They also make looking at the winter vegetable garden bearable.

In addition to your local garden center, mail order sources for cover crop seeds include Johnny's Selected Seeds, 1 Foss Hill Rd., RR1 Box 2580, Albion, ME 04910, (207) 437-4301, catalog; and Mellinger's, 2310 West South Range Road, North Lima, OH 44452, (330) 549-9861, catalog.

The Versatile Clematis

You can bring interest back to areas of your garden in late summer and early fall. Climbing small-flowered clematis can be planted to grow up, over, and through your shrubs and small trees. Unlike the large-flowered hybrids commonly stocked by garden centers, many of the small-flowered clematis species and hybrids bloom later in the growing season and nicely complement rather than feud with the plants they grow on. Some can even be tied in and trained to cover a fence or arbor.

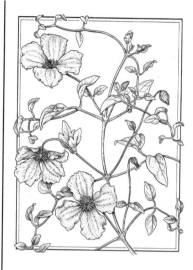

Clematis

Some clematis are considered subshrubs because they have woody bases, grow to about 4 feet tall, and have shoots that die back in the winter. They are not climbers and can be planted to tumble over old tree stumps, run across rocks, or imitate a sprawling ground cover. If planted behind perennials that finished flowering earlier in the growing season, they will spill over and around them, adding life to an otherwise empty area.

Plant clematis from mid-September through October, placing the crown (where the stem meets the roots) 3 to 4 inches deep. Make sure they go into winter well watered, and for protection, cover them with evergreen boughs after the ground freezes. To provide shade for the roots, plant the clematis on the north side of, but not directly under, the plant you want it to grow over or under. You can guide the clematis as it grows. One of the species' most attractive qualities is that they all bloom on new growth, so in the early spring they can simply be cut down to about a foot tall without one's having to remember complicated pruning rules or figuring out how old each stem is.

Here are just a few small-flowered clematis to whet your appetite:

Climbers

Clematis rehderiana—loose clusters of $^{1}/_{4}$- to $^{1}/_{2}$-inch pale yellow, tubular flowers; fragrant

C. serratifolia—nodding, small, lantern-like pale yellow flowers
tinged green with purple stamens, followed by silky seed heads

C. terniflora (formerly *C. maximowicziana*)—sweet autumn clematis;
many small, white flowers followed by silky seed heads

C. texensis hybrid, 'Gravetye Beauty'—ruby-red, bell-shaped, 2-
inch flowers

C. viticella hybrid, 'Royal Velours'—very deep purple, velvety 2-
inch flowers

Subshrubs

C. heracleifolia var. *davidiana*—clusters of fragrant, deep blue,
hyacinth-like flowers

C. stans—clusters of narrow, tubular ³/₄-inch fragrant light-blue
flowers whose tips flare backward

Small-flowered clematis are not usually found at garden cen-
ters. Mail order sources include Completely Clematis, 217
Argilla Road, Ipswich, MA 01938, (978) 356-3197, catalog; and
Heronswood Nursery Ltd., 7530 288th Street N.E., Kingston,
WA 98346, (206) 297-4172, catalog.

Before you order, make sure that the particular clematis is
rated for your hardiness zone. Don't be in a hurry; it takes a couple of growing seasons before you see the display that you
thought you were going to see the first year. Give the plants a
chance to settle in.

Different Snowdrops

Travel around England with your eyes glancing downward and
you'll find yourself seeing masses of snowdrops that are different
from any you have seen before. Pay attention and you'll want some
of the many different types available.

Snowdrops are much more popular in England, having first been brought there by the Romans. There are many species, and since some of them hybridize freely, countless garden variants are found there. In the United States, forms of *Galanthus nivalis* and *G. elwesii* are the most commonly seen, but there are a few others available also.

Galanthus are among the first bulbs to bloom, and they can brighten an otherwise gloomy February day.

Like parents at a twins convention, true galanthophiles recognize distinct differences where others see only the similarities. The subtle differences in flower markings (you'll have to bend over, lift the head, and look for markings on the inner segments), leaf color and form, and height make it fun to have several different ones in the garden. Since they are small (most are about 5 inches), they should be planted in the fall in groups of at least twenty for the best show.

Because *G. elwesii* has been overcollected in the wild, it is covered by Appendix B of the Conventions on International Trade of Endangered Species agreement. All bulbs covered by the agreement are required to have an export certificate from their country of origin. It is important that you choose a supplier that offers propagated, not collected, bulbs. *G. elwesii* bulb sources may be on the package label or on the display box. If you don't see the listing, ask. If in doubt, take a pass.

Roses from Canada

Gardeners in colder climates may find what are called "Canadian roses" at local garden centers or nurseries. You may not find them in your books and assume that the garden center is trying to pull a fast one. They aren't.

Since the early 1900s Canadian agriculture researchers have been breeding shrub and climbing roses that combine the winter hardiness and disease tolerance of rugosa roses with the desirability of modern roses—prolific flowering and a repeat or long bloom period. The resulting hybrids have become popular in extreme northern climates, where they can survive without protection. To find them, look for specialty catalogs that give breeder or hybrid series information. Listings showing "Canada" or "Ag Canada" (for Agriculture Canada), or roses from the popular Parkland or Explorer series may appear under sections for rugosa hybrids, climbers, or shrub roses.

To produce salable plants more quickly, a few nurseries are grafting Parkland or Explorer roses onto other root stocks. Neville Arnold, a scientist at the Agriculture Canada research farm in L'Assomption, Québec, says winter hardiness and disease resistance drop in grafted plants, so be sure your plants are grown on their own roots.

In the New York region, roses, bought either bare root or in containers, can also be planted in the fall, through late November, giving them a good head start. Bare-root Canadian roses are available from the Roseraie at Bayfields, P.O. Box R, Waldoboro, ME 04572-0919, fax (800) 933-4508, catalog; and Royall River Roses, P.O. Box 370, Yarmouth, ME 04096, (800) 820-5830, catalog.

Can't find a specific rose? Beverly Dobson and Peter Schneider's *Annual Combined Rose List* gives sources for every rose being sold. It can be ordered from Peter Schneider, P.O. Box 677, Mantua, OH 44255.

Narcissus

Rising Bulbs

After a number of years in the ground you may find that clumps of your narcissus bulbs are working their way to the surface in the late fall. Of course you want to immediately divide and replant them, spaced 8 inches apart like the books say, but you and your narcissus will be better off if you don't.

Don't dig, that is; mulch. Dr. August De Hertogh, a professor of horticulture at North Carolina State University in Raleigh, says tests show that bulbs are as well protected under 6 inches of shredded bark mulch as in the ground. Besides, digging them in late fall will probably damage their fragile roots, which begin to grow at this time of year.

Heretical as it may sound to any gardener who grew up on English gardening techniques, De Hertogh said that narcissus never need to be dug up and divided. They will go on happily multiplying and flowering for many decades if they get the water and nutrients they need. Since narcissus roots dig in and pull the bulb deeper, he said he believes they are working toward the surface because the soil under them is too compacted, not because they need to be divided.

Falling for Pansies

If your bright pink annuals are beginning to look a little out of place as the rest of the natural world heads into autumnal shades of yellow, red, and brown, your alternative is not just a patch of emptiness. Pansies—yes, pansies—the embodiment of spring, also come in great fall colors. Deep velvety purples, mustard yellows, oranges, and maroons in single, bicolor, or tricolor work very well with the changing colors of the fall garden.

Even better, they last. They'll survive the kind of frost that browns a chrysanthemum. The next day, curled leaves usually straighten and bowed heads lift their plain or blotched faces into the sunshine. And if you cover pansies with a single layer of discarded Christmas tree boughs after the ground is frozen to reduce the danger of heaving and winter foliage burn, they'll be there in the spring when you uncover them or when the blanket of snow melts. Of course, you'll have to decide if you want to look at fall colors next April.

Fall Color at Your Feet

Ground covers are a frequently neglected part of garden design. How else to explain the overwhelming use of *Vinca minor,* English ivy, and pachysandra when so many other interesting ones are available?

Instead of thinking only of very low-growing evergreen selections, broaden your definition to include other plants that can be massed to provide unifying structural or textural connections. The relationship between the ground cover and the location and usage should determine the appropriate height, not some limiting idea that anything more than 4 inches high cannot qualify.

Fall color is an important part of garden design, and it should be part of your ground cover selection process, just as it is with trees and shrubs. Here are a few plants to think about as ground covers:

Fragrant sumac (*Rhus aromatica* 'Gro-Low'). The glossy, deciduous leaves, which are aromatic when bruised, turn a fiery orange-red in the fall. The low, wide-spreading shrub grows 2 feet tall and works very well, even on a slope, in full sun or partial shade.

Bigroot cranesbill *(Geranium macrorrhizum)*. This semiever-green, mound-forming perennial has distinctively fragrant leaves that turn reddish in the fall. (The strong medicinal fragrance will let you know if the dog has been tramping through it.) It grows from 12 to 15 inches tall and spreads well through a thick, rhi-zomatous root structure. It is easy to grow, and is heat and drought tolerant. Different cultivars have different spring flower colors.

Leadwort *(Ceratostigma plumbaginoides)*. Fall color and flowers at the same time. The shiny green leaves turn strawberry tints, then bronze-red, in fall, while the cobalt blue flowers last from late summer until frost. Cut back the bare wiry stems in late win-ter. Leaves appear late, just after you're convinced it's dead. Growing 8 to 12 inches tall, it works well in full sun or shade, al-though it colors up better in the sun.

Siberian carpet cypress *(Microbiota decussata)*. This wide-spreading evergreen grows to 2 feet tall, with arching scaly, feath-ery foliage that turns bronze after a frost. It is unusual in that it is an evergreen that tolerates shade. It really is from Siberia, and very cold hardy.

Rockspray cotoneaster *(Cotoneaster horizontalis)*. The dark, shiny, deciduous leaves turn orange-red, complementing orna-mental red berries growing along the stems. This low-growing, densely branching woody shrub grows 2 to 3 feet high, spreading to 6 feet. Its arching habit makes it look like the perfect refuge for rabbits or chipmunks as it covers and cascades down a bank. Lower-growing cultivars are also available.

Evergreens in a Hurry

Speed is on everyone's mind, even gardeners. Which evergreens are the fastest growing is a common interest.

It really depends on your needs. Most requests for fast-growing evergreens come from people who discover that the new neighbor collects junk cars. If that's the case, then white pine might not be a good choice. Although it grows fast, as much as 50 feet in twenty-five years, it eventually loses some lower branches, letting the glint from those old hubcaps shine through. It is also sensitive to salt, making it a poor roadside choice if your community uses salt in winter.

Is your site wet? The tall, slender Atlantic white cedar (*Chamaecyparis thyoides*) will do just fine.

Are you making a hedge? Canadian hemlock *(Tsuga canadensis)* works well, but wooly adelgid attacks mean a high maintenance obligation.

I know you see it everywhere, but eastern arborvitae (*Thuja occidentalis*) does make an effective, quick-growing hedge. A more handsome version, the western or great arborvitae (*T. plicata*), does well from Boston to Cincinnati to Raleigh, North Carolina, despite the western connotation of its common name.

A grouping of three to five tall, pyramidal Japanese cryptomeria (*Cryptomeria japonica*) forms a screen, not really a hedge, although it works better as a single-specimen tree.

The feathery Leyland cypress (X *Cupressocyparis leylandii*) gives a more columnar screen and grows in coastal areas from Massachusetts to Florida.

For large, single specimens, Norway spruce (*Picea abies*) and Atlas cedar (*Cedrus atlantica*) grow quickly when young, then slow down.

Spend a little time looking before you buy. Large evergreens are a strong presence in the landscape, summer and winter. Go to public arboretums and botanical gardens and look at mature examples. Do you have the room? Is it as cute at 30 feet, or 80, as it is in a 1-gallon container?

Growing Cherimoyas

Cherimoya, an uncommon fruit with a flavor somewhere between strawberry and pineapple, is not yet a grocery store staple. Americans who know them either discovered them on a trip to warmer territory or found them in a street vendor's stall in Chinatown. As delicious as they are, some people try to grow them from seed, but without luck. They soak them or nick them with knives in an attempt at having a cherimoya in the backyard.

You can grow cherimoya if your backyard happens to be in a subtropical, frost-free region that doesn't get too humid in the summer. Israel would do, or Egypt, Chile, or parts of South Africa or California.

It's too humid in Florida, but Jonathan Crane, a specialist in tropical fruit crops at the University of Florida's Tropical Research and Education Center in Homestead, has experimented with growing cherimoyas from seed. He found that the seed seems to have an after-ripening requirement. Well-cleaned seeds (don't want any fungus) should be left to age in a plastic bag at room temperature for at least three months (six is even better). Soaked for a day and planted ½-inch deep in well-drained growing medium and kept moist, they will germinate in three to four weeks—if the pot has bottom heat so that the medium is kept at 80 degrees.

That's the easy part, and it will result in a large, full-sun foliage plant. Fruit is another matter. After three to eight years as a juvenile, your cherimoya may flower, but the species of beetle that pollinates it will not be around; Food and Drug Administration inspections keep it out of the country. And hand pollinating is tricky because the male and female flowers bloom at different times. Well, you've got a few years to figure out how to imitate a beetle.

Mulching Leaves

Sometimes gardening gets easier. Research shows that you don't have to rake leaves off your lawn. Frank Rossi, assistant professor of turf science at Cornell University, reported that no ill effect on lawn quality was found on a test plot at Michigan State University, where for four years ankle-deep oak and maple leaves were mowed with a mulching mower instead of being raked off. Some may be disappointed that the "instant compost" does not improve the grass; the rest of us are happy that it does not hurt.

Make sure the leaves are cut fine enough for the pieces to fall between the blades of grass. Nothing should remain on top of the lawn. A good mulching mower should do it in one pass, but even two or three cuttings in different directions with a regular mower can cut the leaves fine enough.

Who knows? Maybe someday scientists will breed hybrid trees and shrubs that can be left on top of the soil and will dig themselves in.

Bring 'Em Back Healthy

Traveling out of the country, it is always tempting to bring back a few living souvenirs. But there are rules about bringing plants home, and good reasons for them.

Traveling gardeners want to bring back plants or seeds to remember a vacation or their homeland. Customs officials, on the other hand, are responsible for preventing plant diseases or pests from entering the country and for enforcing international agreements on endangered species. Preparation can reduce the time and discomfort of passing through customs for both human and plant travelers.

All plant materials must be inspected; bring them in bare

root, washed clean of soil. Soil hampers inspection and shelters unwanted organisms. Seal the plant in a plastic bag so the roots won't dehydrate. Even seeds must be inspected, so they cannot be encapsulated with fungicides or anything else. Individuals can bring in twelve plants without a written permit from the Department of Agriculture.

Phytosanitary certificates from the country of origin can help you through U.S. customs by showing that the plant has already been inspected. To get them, ask the nursery where you buy the plant. Local agriculture departments can certify plants you collect yourself, if they are not endangered. The certificates are not yet required, but the Department of Agriculture may mandate them, so check before you leave.

Many plants are difficult or impossible for individuals to bring back. The Animal and Plant Health Inspection Service of the Department of Agriculture in Beltsville, Maryland, (301) 734-8645, provides information about importing plants on the endangered species list (orchids, cacti, and others), plants that require quarantine periods (fruit trees, hydrangea, chrysanthemum, and carnations, among others), and forbidden plants (citrus, potatoes, and others).

Try not to arrive at customs late in the day. Inspection stations at the major entry ports are closed after 5 P.M. and on weekends, which means leaving your plants and returning for them later.

Fragrant Houseplants

There are houseplants that bloom and are fragrant during the winter, to ease those blues.

Fragrance is one of the hardest things to describe, and one person's simmering-oranges-with-a-dash-of-rose-and-a-hint-

Mitriostigma

of-lavender is another's overheated-gymnasium-with-a-soupçon-of-bear-in-heat. But however described, fragrant flowers in the house gentle the winter and ease the symptoms of gardening withdrawal.

With the understanding that one has to smell them for one-self, I can suggest four: *Murraya paniculata* (orange jasmine), *Osmanthus fragrans* (fragrant olive), *Mitriostigma axillare* (wild coffee), and *Cestrum nocturnum* (night-blooming jessamine). All except cestrum have glossy dark green leaves, and all have many small, white flowers and like average house temperatures during the day.

Murraya, mitriostigma, and cestrum bloom well with night temperatures of 65 degrees, making them ideal for most homes. Osmanthus needs night temperatures of about 50 degrees, so it may be harder to find a place for.

Buying any fragrant plant for the first time is a small gamble because tastes and tolerances vary. On the bright side, they make wonderful gifts, so you need not be stuck with something you don't like.

Mail order sources include Plumeria People, 910 Leander Drive, Leander, TX 78641, (512) 259-0807, catalog; and Logee's Greenhouses, 141 North Street, Danielson, CT 06239, (888) 330-8038, catalog.

Winter Window Boxes

Once the window boxes are emptied in the fall, diehards always want to just keep going. Surely there must be something that can be planted in them for the winter, some sort of green or greenery that would last until spring.

Window boxes do not hold enough soil to insulate plant roots from cycles of freezing solid, then thawing, which can injure or kill plants as well as heave them right out of the soil. Instead of growing live plants, try making arrangements with cut material that will bring you the pleasures of the season every time you look out your window.

Take a walk in the woods (or down to a florist's) and look for evergreen boughs (cut-up Christmas tree branches are available on every street in January). The range of materials that can be poked into the soil, nestled among the evergreens, can accommodate any mood.

Winterberry (*Ilex verticillata*), with its gray stems lined with bright orange-red fruit; shrubby dogwood branches, both red- and chartreuse-stemmed varieties; the dormant catkins of black alder branches; dried seed heads of roadside weeds or garden perennials; or the contorted branches of Harry Lauder's walking stick (*Corylus avellana* 'Contorta') can provide color and bold textures, yet made delicate by a light coating of snow or a tracery of ice.

Even in New York City, winter has a quieter, softer look, with more muted colors and a more subtle beauty. Let your window boxes reflect the season.

Impressive Ivy Geraniums

If you visit Germany, you'll notice many terraces from which blankets of ivy geraniums (Pelargonium peltatum) *drape down, some of them several feet long and almost as wide. If you come home fired up and rim the terrace with 3-foot-by-6-inch wooden boxes planted with ivy pelargoniums, the usual results are some blossoms but not to the extent you saw in Europe. In fact, they'll hardly drape at all. There's more to it if you want to achieve that lush spread you remember.*

Fine food and displays of ivy geraniums are the strongest memories for many visitors to northern Europe. Many people fail in their attempts to reproduce either once home because they require attention, a bit of skill, and the right ingredients.

For the ingredients, 'Balcon Royale' (red), 'Princess Balcon' (light orchid), and 'King of Balcon' (light coral) are commonly used cultivars, said Gary Barnum, the director of horticulture for the Clark Foundation in Cooperstown, New York, whose midsummer displays could bring tears to a German eye. He advises using a soilless mixture to promote good drainage and packing the container with enough plants to be pot-tight right away.

Since these cultivars of ivy geraniums tend to be rangy, pinch them back at the second node (second set of leaves from the base) to encourage lateral growth. Then pinch at the second node of each lateral, continuing until the number of laterals has you completely confused and unable to keep track of which have or haven't been pinched. When to stop? Since it takes six to eight weeks for flowers to appear after you stop pinching, it's a trade-off between early flowers and big spreads.

Pelargoniums are sensitive to both drought and inconsistent moisture. With a container full of roots in a relatively small volume of growing medium, they will need watering and feeding daily, using an all-purpose fertilizer diluted much further than the label advises.

Start the food and water when you plant, and continue the daily regime until you are fed up and ready to rip the whole thing out. And if you really want to match the European displays, don't forget to come home at lunchtime to water.

Balcon ivy geranium plants are available in spring from Thompson & Morgan, P.O. Box 1308, Jackson, NJ 08527, (800) 274-7333, catalog.

Growing Popcorn

Popcorn roping on Christmas trees is a fine, old tradition. If you already raise a few vegetables, you may want to consider raising your own popcorn for next year's tree, especially if you have gardening-age children. But you better know what makes it pop.

To pop, a kernel of corn needs three things. It needs enough moisture inside to build up 135 pounds per square inch of pressure when heated to 400 degrees. It has to contain a hard starch that turns gelatinous and is carried along when the moisture becomes steam and bursts through the hull. And it needs a hull hard and strong enough to hold in enough pressure, but not so much pressure as to turn a bowl of kernels into a weapon of mass destruction. Only special varieties of corn provide the right combination.

Plant popcorn in the spring, after the danger of frost is past. Popcorn has to grow past the time when sweet corn is ready, so that the kernels can become hard and mature. Some varieties are ready in September; others may need to grow through October. To judge, pick a bright, hard kernel. Scrape the tip where it joined the cob, looking for a thin, black layer that forms when the corn is ready.

Husk the corn, and let it dry on the cob in a dry, airy place. It can take several weeks to reach the right moisture level. Removing some kernels occasionally for a test pop is the only way to tell. Shell and store the kernels in an airtight jar.

There are only a few varieties sold for home gardens; commercial growers have about forty choices. There must not be much taste difference; otherwise at the movie theater one would be hearing, "I'll have the Idaho-grown 'Robust 10-84' with double butter, no salt, and she'll have the Kansas varietal 'White Cloud,' half butter half margarine with the salt substitute."

Popcorn varieties are available from Johnny's Selected Seeds, 1 Foss Hill Road, RR1 Box 2580, Albion, ME 04910, (207) 437-4301, catalog; and Stokes Seeds, Box 548, Buffalo, NY 14240-0548, (716) 695-6980, catalog.

Growing Pineapples

Why is it everyone tries to grow a pineapple top at least once and fails? Whether in water or in soil, everyone has trouble turning this fruit into a houseplant.

As a traditional sign of welcome and hospitality (do you think all those pineapple doorknockers are just a coincidence?), pineapples add a nice tropical touch for visitors. Try the method used by commercial growers, who do not suspend the top on toothpicks over a glass of water—the amateur method of choice for avocado pits.

Using a fresh top, trim off any remaining fruit close to the stem (leaving a slice of fruit still attached is a common reason for failure because it rots and kills the top). Remove about a quarter of the lower leaves by pulling them downward. Roots grow from those small brown bumps in the exposed rings on the stem, called root initials. Removing the leaves eases their way.

Let the top dry overnight; then plant up to the base of the remaining leaves, using a well-drained growing medium in a 6-inch pot.

Enclose the plant, pot and all, in a plastic bag, and set in a bright, warm place out of direct sun, keeping it moist but not soggy.

Remove the bag when new leaves start to grow, move the pot to a sunny window, and begin to apply a half-strength fertilizer solution twice a month during active growth. As the roots fill the container, transfer to a larger pot.

After two to three years, it may be ready to flower and perhaps produce a tiny pineapple.

Feeding Goldfinches

Goldfinches, living up to their name, prefer one of the most expensive of all bird seed—Niger. You can raise it yourself, but you won't save much.

Niger seed, most commonly labeled thistle seed when sold as bird feed, actually comes from a tropical annual called Niger (*Guizotia abyssinica*), not from a thistle. Niger belongs to the Compositae family, along with sunflowers, thistles, and asters. Its yellow flowers are daisy-like—about 3/4 inch in diameter.

Niger is cultivated as an oil-seed crop in India and Africa, especially Ethiopia. The seeds sold as bird feed are sterilized before being imported, but it would take a 10-foot-by-10-foot Niger garden to raise just a single pound of seeds.

Fortunately, goldfinches enjoy many seeds that you can grow. Zinnias, cosmos, and asters—common garden flowers—will attract them once the flowers go to seed. If you are willing to give up part of your salad greens, let some lettuce or chicory bolt and produce seed. Some tree seeds, such as birch and alder, and the perennial coreopsis, also attract goldfinches. But the true test of a finch lover is the person who is willing to leave the dandelions alone and to bring in goldenrod and burdock, guaranteed to make the neighbors stare in disbelief.

When Tomatoes Are Not Red

Among other things husbands and wives argue about are tomatoes. Generally, women would like to liven things up with some odd-colored ones while men say nothing tastes like the red ones.

Tomato taste is second only to politics as a cause of heated discussions. Everyone agrees that home grown is better than store bought but that's where agreement ends, especially with regard to nonred tomatoes.

The funny thing about taste is that sight is also involved. Taste tests of red and nonred tomatoes show very different results when conducted under red light (where they all look red) as opposed to normal light (where the true color is apparent). So plant what you want and feed your husband in the dark.

Richard Robinson, a tomato breeder at Cornell University's Geneva Research Station, says that primary taste differences between tomatoes are caused by different balances of acidity to sugars, not color. Commercial tomatoes bred for high yields really don't taste as good. It takes leaves and photosynthesis to make sugars. With more tomatoes on the plant sharing the wealth, each gets a smaller amount.

Many of the nonred tomatoes are heirlooms, and there are nearly as many heirloom tomatoes as there are grandmothers who raised them. In addition to the legendary pink 'Brandywine,' you might want to try 'Persimmon' and 'Many Moons' (orange-yellow), 'White Wonder' and 'White Beauty' (creamy white), 'Purple Cherokee' (purple-pink), and 'Evergreen' and 'Green Zebra' (they stay green, even when ripe).

Sources for tomatoes of all colors include The Cook's Garden,

P.O. Box 535, Londonderry, VT 05148, (800) 457-9703, catalog; and Fox Hollow Seed Company, P.O. Box 148, McGrann, PA 16236, (724) 548-7333, catalog.

Storing Leftover Seeds

At the start of the gardening season or just before, we all go through the great seed package inventory. There are always leftover partial packages, but, not knowing how long a seed will last, we buy more anyway. You can't just throw them away, but you don't want to take a chance and lose a crop.

Those of us with limited space for flower and vegetable gardens, but unlimited desire to grow some of these and some of those, usually bind these leftovers in rubber bands and store them haphazardly.

Lists are available that show general viability terms for most common seeds, but the length of time a seed remains viable also depends on storage conditions. Packages kept in a hot, humid garden shed or tucked into a gardening book may not live up to expectations.

A good way to store seeds is to place the packages in a glass jar with a tight-fitting lid. A package of commercial desiccant or an inch of powdered milk in the jar keeps the humidity low and the seeds dry. Seal the jar, and keep it in the refrigerator—not the freezer.

Test for viability by placing ten to twelve seeds between sheets of damp paper towel. Put these test beds in a closed plastic bag in normal room temperature. Check every few days to see if the seeds have sprouted and that the paper is still damp. If more than half of the seeds sprout in the germination time shown on the package, the seeds can be used. When testing several packages, make sure to write which is which on the plastic bags.

Avoid the leftover problem by sharing seeds with friends or by purchasing smaller packages. Two companies that offer smaller packages (at smaller prices) by mail are Fox Hollow Seed Co., P.O. Box 148, McGrann, PA 16236, (724) 548-7333, catalog; and Pinetree Garden Seeds, Box 300, New Gloucester, ME 04260, (207) 926-3400, catalog.

A Different Valentine

Valentine's Day doesn't have to mean the same old things every year. Pull your catalogs out from under the bed and take a careful look.

Between the pounds of chocolate and the bouquets of flowers, the oversize cards and the overpriced jewels, lies the path to a unique gift. There are a surprising number of "chocolate" plants—offering the advantage of standing out from the crowd while simultaneously testing the recipient's sense of humor. If a relationship is solid, it ought to withstand any of these.

Coral bells (Heuchera) 'Chocolate Ruffles' and 'Chocolate Veil' offer dark chocolate leaves with purple undersides ('Ruffles') or silver patches ('Veil'). The chocolate flower, *Berlandiera lyrata,* has yellow daisy-like flowers with the scent of chocolate. *Cosmos atrosanguineus,* chocolate cosmos, is a rich burgundy with a strong chocolate fragrance.

'Chocolate Drop' and 'Chocolate Cake' are available for gladiolus lovers, while those who need to sink their teeth into something might prefer the bell pepper 'Sweet Chocolate' (referring to color, not taste, thankfully). Herb lovers can choose a chocolate mint (*Mentha* x *spicata* cultivar) that smells and tastes like a peppermint patty. For brand-conscious sweethearts there is *Pulmonaria* 'Milky Way.' Or scented geraniums in 'Chocolate Mint' or 'Cocoa-mint Rose' might win her heart.

Since none of these is in flower in February, gift-wrapping a package of seeds, a handful of corms, or a cutting may be necessary to set the heart on fire. If the explanation is drawing a blank stare, having a gooey card and a large diamond nearby will probably save the day. Sources include specialty mail order plant catalogs and Cartier.

Forgotten Bulbs

Midwinter basement cleaning sometimes turns up a few bulbs that didn't get planted in the fall. If you can dig them in, there's still a chance for spring flowers.

Generally spring flowering bulbs need a continuous cold period of twelve to thirteen weeks at 35 to 40 degrees to produce a flower. Without a long-enough cold period, the biological mechanisms inside the bulb recognize that something is not normal and that it is better to take the easiest road to survival. For bulbs, that means aborting flower production and concentrating on producing bulb offsets, which take less energy. Flowers may be better in the long scheme of evolution because of the opportunities for improving the species through cross-pollination provided by wind or insect visitors, but making more bulbs is the most important task.

If you want to place a bet that the ground will still be cold enough in April, go ahead and plant them. But put them in an out-of-the-way spot where a failure won't put an obvious hole in the rest of your spring display.

Wildflowers from Seed

The New England Wild Flower Society sells seeds or spores of more than 150 varieties of wildflowers and ferns. There are easy-to-grow perennials, like black-eyed Susans, blazing stars, and foamflowers. Experts may want to try ferns, gentians, Canada lilies, or swamp-pinks.

All requests for seeds must be received by March 15 each year. To obtain their catalog, contact the New England Wild Flower Society, Garden in the Woods, 180 Hemenway Road, Framingham, MA 01701, (508) 877-7630.

Black-Eyed Susan

7

The Endless Path

Gardening can be many things to many people, but for every-one it's a chance to touch the earth again. Sometimes our civilization makes us lose daily touch with something that goes way back in our history. There's no good reason that we should be surprised at how satisfying gardening is, but we always are when we first start and have our first successes. Even if you raise the same lettuce that is sold in the supermarket, yours will taste better—not just because it actually does taste better (long truck rides can hardly help any vegetable), but because you did it with your own hands. Of course, the woodchucks will agree.

Much of the best garden writing of the past century has been about the pleasures and deeper meaning of gardening, not about how to do it or about what plants to use. They are more musings than instructions. It is an essential part of the experience.

On the days when everything is going well or, even more im-portant, on those days when the slugs decimate your favorite hosta, pause a while in the garden, take a deep breath, calm down, and remember why you do this.

Touching Your Roots

Every spring it happens. After a winter of snowfall, windstorms, and too many days trapped indoors, garden centers and mail order companies brace themselves for a rush of cabin-fevered gardeners, eager to buy. And in the rush to load up with the latest and greatest—those 12-pound tomatoes, the rose with tricolored frizzy petals, the apple tree grafted to produce five different varieties—let me put in a plea to save a little space for comfort plants.

Comfort plants, like comfort foods, are different for each of us, but share certain characteristics. Whether the plants are garden balsam, annual candytuft, four-o'clock, or lily-of-the-valley, we typically learn to appreciate them at our mother's or grandmother's knee. They usually are slightly bland, out of favor, and a touch embarrassing to the tragically hip. And always they evoke a memory that more than compensates for all of that.

Gardening is about connections—to the earth, to the past, to

Old-Fashioned Flowers

the future. Try to remember those plants that first fostered a love of gardening in you, and save a little space between the new and improved for the old and unimproved.

Garden Tourists

Judging by the increasing size of each edition of The Garden Tourist *by Lois G. Rosenfeld (Garden Tourist Press), the whole country is gardening.*

Plant sales are happening practically day and night, whenever and wherever the weather allows. With stamina, a van, and deep pockets, one could shop the Northeast and not come home for weeks. Whether it's an Earth Day Celebration and Plant Sale in New Jersey or the annual Spring Plant Sale at the William Paca Garden in Annapolis, Maryland, in May—call for information, (410) 267-6656—something is happening somewhere all season long.

Private gardens are also on view. Secret Gardens of Newport, Rhode Island, for example, offers tours in June: for dates, call (401) 847-0514. And special gardening events are popping up like mushrooms. Take the tour of Johnny's Selected Seeds in Albion, Maine, in August, and you can see where those catalogs come from. For date, call (207) 437-9294.

The Garden Tourist lists international events for those who have shopped and toured out the United States. The book, which is arranged alphabetically, provides dates, hours, fees, and addresses.

As with all of life, moderation is suggested. One can easily overdose on gardens and overspend on plant sales. Remember how big, or small, your garden really is.

Back into the Garden

Spring is the time to remember exactly why anyone is willing to suffer through the gardener's Four Horsemen: insects, diseases, woodchucks, and drought. Gardening, in addition to its obvious pleasures, has always been a quiet source of knowledge, not just about nature but also about the place of humans in the scheme of things.

There's nothing quite like a slug for a solid lesson in humility. Of course, if you don't spend time in your garden, hearing about the damage from secondhand reports does not have quite the same impact. Humility is a hands-on sort of thing. I doubt that those medieval man-as-the-center-of-the-universe philosophers ever seeded a lawn and then watched a flock of sparrows stuff themselves silly.

Before jumping into the annual who-gets-the-first-tomato race, realize that the true contest is the attempt to beat the elements, not other gardeners. This year try keeping a simple notebook, recording the rainfall, the temperatures, the disasters, and the things that make you smile. Put the picture books full of impossible gardens back on the coffee table where they belong, and go outside. Pick up a handful of soil and smell it. Does it smell familiar? It should. It should frequently be found under your nails and rubbed into your pant knees. You need your garden as much as it needs you. Spend some time out there every day, even if it just means looking around. Your garden changes constantly and won't repeat itself.

Gazing Globes

Are gazing globes back? They go in and out of fashion quicker than the image shifts as you approach one. Over the past few years, the popularity of gazing globes—those mirrored balls in various colors that are commonly seen on concrete pedestals in the middle of a lawn—has been rising.

Glass globes should not be included in the same class as plaster gnomes and pink flamingoes. Globes date at least to thirteenth-century Venice, where they were seen as symbolic of fertility. The colors used in the glass also contained meaning: red was said to preserve love, green guaranteed a good harvest, and blue prevented war (if only it were that simple). They became basic equipment for witches, who would stare into them and enter a trance.

In a more mundane use, glass globes became garden ornaments sometime before 1625, when Francis Bacon suggested letting the sunlight play on them. By the 1870s they were being made in America and were especially popular in southern gardens. These days, the globes are thinner glass, coated inside with a reflective powder, mirroring and distorting over a huge angle.

One reason that they are popular may be the variety of ways we can use them. Sitting in isolation on a pedestal out on the lawn, they become an object in themselves, and a pretty weird one at that. But gardeners with more imagination place them on the ground among the plants or on the bank of a pond, where they can have an effect on the viewer of condensing and changing the garden itself. Moved on whim and contemplated with some leisure, mirrored globes can change the perspective of garden and gardener alike.

A Public Look at Private Gardens

Great private gardens are created in all sorts of places by all sorts of people. Those of obvious public interest, either local or national, are maintained in many ways—as national treasures (Jefferson's gardens in Virginia) or as local gems (Wave Hill in Riverdale, New York), by public or private financing.

But great modern gardens can fall through the cracks of inheritance and disappear without help to replace the financial and aesthetic support of their creators. Unlike buildings, which tend to decay slowly, or wild places, which maintain themselves if undisturbed, gardens are fragile and will deteriorate quickly unless cared for.

The Garden Conservancy, a national nonprofit group, was created in 1989 to identify great gardens still in private hands. Rather than purchase the properties, it provides advice to owners on how their gardens can be turned into nonprofit community resources with the proper mix of money and garden management. The conservancy then sees the process through until the private garden has become a locally managed public resource.

Starting in 1989 at the Ruth Bancroft Garden in Walnut Creek, California, where more than twenty years of collecting cacti, succulents, and native California species had produced 4 acres of spectacular gardens, the Garden Conservancy worked to develop a preservation plan, oral history of the garden, and a friends' group. In Mill Neck, New York, it helped preserve the Humes Japanese Stroll Garden when it was about to close because its endowment was nearly gone. Now this tranquil, 2-acre garden, honoring both the Japanese reverence for nature and their philosophy of design, will remain intact and open to visitors.

In 1995, the conservancy began persuading gardeners to open their private efforts for public viewing on selected weekend days as a way of promoting gardens and gardening. The guide, the *Open Days Directory,* quickly sold out, and more than 10,000 people were welcomed through the garden gates during the season.

Every year, the conservancy has expanded the open days to include first gardens in New York and Connecticut, and now gardens around the country. Gardens are open to visitors on specific weekend days from May through September. Each garden is selected for its strong design or interesting plant collections.

Proceeds from the tickets benefit the conservancy. The current *Open Days Directory,* which also includes information on membership, is available by calling or writing the Garden Conservancy, P.O. Box 219, Cold Spring, NY 10516, (914) 265-2029.

Children in the Garden

If you developed a love of gardening even though you were told to stand out of the way while the grownups did the work, Michael Levine, the Ruth Rea Howell Family Garden coordinator at the New York Botanical Garden, has some better ideas about introducing small children to the joys of gardening. He suggests keeping two things in mind: gardening should be fun, and you should be the guide, not the boss.

What's fun, of course, varies with age. A four-year-old may prefer pouring water or digging for worms to planting straight lines of vegetables (and who says straight lines are better, anyway?). At age five or six, children are better at using tools and sticking with something for a while, and actual gardening, the kind adults recognize, is a possibility.

Since a whole backyard can be overwhelming to a small child, use a raised bed, child-made sign, or stick fence to clearly mark off a child-sized area, about 2 feet square, that is just theirs. Then let them follow their instincts. Quick crops, like radishes and lettuce, and bright flowers, such as marigolds and zinnias, are good, but they are still typical plant-and-wait crops. If more space is available, consider what the world might look like from the inside of a 15-foot-tall allée of sunflowers. A bamboo or stick tepee of scarlet runner beans would provide a secret place to take a break from weeding. And don't ignore the rest of the senses. The smell of mint or lemon verbena and the touch of lamb's ears are memories that can last a lifetime.

Many botanical gardens are child friendly, so contact them about programs and gardens that can involve children.

Patented Plants

Labels with a "propagation prohibited" notice mean the plant is covered by a patent or by the Plant Variety Protection Act, which both seek to prevent reproduction of the plant for profit without permission.

Plant patents, granted since 1930, are given to cultivars and hybrids—plants that do not reproduce true to the parent from seed. All patented plants have to be reproduced asexually, for example, by grafting, cuttings, or layering.

In 1970, Congress passed the Plant Variety Protection Act, administered by the Department of Agriculture, to provide similar protection to new varieties reproduced from seed.

Patent and Plant Variety Protection Act numbers protect the plant breeder from competition, but individuals are allowed to collect seed from Plant Variety Protection Act plants or take cuttings from patented plants for their own use.

Organic and Inorganic

Every field has its own jargon, or inside language, frequently incomprehensible to outsiders. The special words are a kind of shorthand, a way of getting a precise meaning across quickly. Horticulture has its share of inside language, and it has a few words that are used inexactly and contribute only fuzzy meanings to insiders and outsiders alike.

Organic, inorganic, and *natural* are commonly misunderstood terms. Because these terms are used in reference to possibly dangerous substances, it is important that we understand them. We'll probably never all use them the same exact way, but we should at least stop and think when we see them on a product label or in an advertisement, or use them in conversation.

To a chemist, the difference between *organic* and *inorganic* is simple. Organic substances contain carbon and hydrogen atoms; inorganic substances don't. *Natural* simply means something that occurs in nature or is made from things that occur in nature.

Over the past few years, gardeners have added value judgments to these otherwise neutral definitions. *Inorganic* now reeks of heavy metals, diabolical poisons, and large, windowless factories owned by faceless international conglomerates. *Organic,* on the other hand, has come to mean pure, safe, and friendly, and *natural* adds a vision of being made by hand by gentle, clean-scrubbed, soft-spoken folk.

If these are your images, try to remember a few simple facts. Pure water is inorganic. Agent Orange was organic. And there is nothing more natural than the venom of a pit viper, capable of killing a cow without batting an eye.

Fall Gardens

Too often we are gardened out by fall. After rushing out too early in spring and then reveling in summer flowers, by fall we are reduced to haphazard weeding, tired of fighting pests and doing chores, and looking forward to quitting, going inside, sitting on the couch, and waiting quietly for the January seed catalog blitz.

Too bad, because the fall garden has plenty to teach those willing to look with a different attitude. Gardens should be molded variations of nature, not ham-handed remodeling jobs, and they look and feel best when they flow with, not against, the real thing. In spring and summer we fight nature, making the garden what we want it to be. But by fall, nature has outlasted us, and our tight color arrangements and distinct groupings are laid low by the weight of a bumblebee tumbling a tall, purple spike of *Salvia* 'Indigo Spires' into a magenta nicotiana.

The disorder of the fall garden brings new combinations among the late season's dark reds, purply-blues, bright or soft oranges, and full-throated yellows as lushly grown plants bob and weave among each other. New partnerships are created, as if the isolated couples in a stately waltz suddenly broke into a raucous square dance.

As the garden winds down in the fall, don't be in such a hurry to straighten up the messiness. Accept it for a while, and pay attention. As plants droop and drape, new combinations of color and texture form, even if only for a short time. You may find that what happens accidentally will become part of next year's plans.

Hopes for Next Year

I cannot prove that Alexander Pope was gazing out one November morning at his fig tree when he wrote, "Hope springs eternal in the human breast," but I wouldn't bet against it. This is the time that gardeners gently put reality aside and let selective memory propel their vision of next year. Failures fade, while the mental image of the garden last June is of roses, not black spot.

As I gather the twine, burlap, tarpaper, and oak leaves that I use for insulation, that everlasting hope sends me out again to wrap my last fig for another winter. One year I laid three of them near the fence, covered in leaves and each wrapped in an old rug, looking for all the world like the victims of a serial killer. Two died, and the survivor refused to bear fruit. Last year, I bound and stuffed it like a turkey. No figs this year either, but next year I just *know* I'll get figs.

The wisteria grew large enough to crush its wooden support, fall, and sprawl across the drive, but it never did flower. I keep hearing stories of grapefruit trees grown from seeds saved at breakfasts years ago. No matter what anyone says, the response is always the same: "It's sure to bloom next year."

I have certain orchids that haven't bloomed in so long I have forgotten what they looked like, but I keep them, and I'll probably build a sturdier support for the wisteria. Some ancient cultures hoped for a good harvest and made sacrifices to the gods if it failed. This I understand. Wrapping that fig once again is evidence of my hope. But if I don't get figs, that tree is headed for the nearest volcano next October.

Widening Plant Horizons

"That's nice, I think I'll get one too" is a natural reaction, but after years of home owners' saying this, most landscapes consist of very few plants, used over and over again. Gardeners should be open to using a wider variety of plants as they gain experience and confidence, but supply and demand—nurseries sell what they think customers want; home owners can buy only what nurseries stock—makes introducing new plants difficult.

Between 1976 and his untimely death in 1996, Dr. J. C. Raulston, the director of the North Carolina State University Arboretum, promoted diversity of superior landscape plants. The arboretum has tried 9,000 woody plants (trees, shrubs, and vines), watching for those that offer beauty, growing characteristics, and resistance to problems above and beyond plants typically used in our landscapes.

But Raulston was never satisfied simply to have better woody plants. He wanted them to be available to everyone. He served as a missionary to the horticultural industry, constantly traveling, speaking, and promoting the introduction of new plants to the trade, and he infected those around him with the same dedication and mission.

A book by Dr. Kim E. Tripp, formerly at the arboretum and now at the New York Botanical Garden, is illustrated with Raulston's photographs and her descriptions of 150 woody plants. *The Year in Trees: Superb Woody Plants for Four-Season Gardens* (Timber Press, 1995) is organized by the season when the trees and shrubs are most interesting. The arboretum in North Carolina tests plants all over the country, and many described in the book are winter-hardy in the Northeast.

Gardening Classes

Winter is the time to peruse not just seed catalogs but also the catalogs that can help grow your gardening skills and plant new ideas.

Whether you are a basic gardener looking for a morning full of help or a professional (or soon-to-be-professional) looking for certification, the New York area has what you want.

Interested in establishing a native wildflower garden? Have a desire to keep bees in the city? (Your neighbors will love it.) Suffer from fear of pruning? Want to know about grafting? (It's not a solution for pruning mistakes—better take both.) Have a garden near the ocean, one in shade, or one that came with your historic house and needs a little restoration? Want the chance to tour private or public gardens with someone who can answer your questions? All of these winter and spring offerings and more can be found at the centers listed here.

Renowned horticultural authors and professionals who practice what they teach are at your command for as little as a few hours or as much as six weeks. And everything they do is bound to make you and your garden smarter, prettier, and maybe even thinner.

Here is a list of some of the better-known organizations, each of which publishes a free catalog of its educational programs:

Brooklyn Botanic Garden, Adult Education, 1000 Washington Avenue, Brooklyn, NY 11225-1099, (718) 622-4433, ext. 223

Frelinghuysen Arboretum, 53 East Hanover, P.O. Box 1295R, Morris Township, NJ 07960, (973) 326-7600

Garden Education Center of Greenwich, P.O. Box 1600, Bible Street, Cos Cob, CT 06807, (203) 869-9242, ext. 20

Horticultural Society of New York, 128 West 58th Street, New York, NY 10019, (212) 757-0915

Institute of Ecosystem Studies, Education Office, Box R, Route 44A, Millbrook, NY 12545-0178, (914) 677-9643

New York Botanical Garden Continuing Education, 200th Street and Southern Boulevard, Bronx, NY 10458, (718) 817-8747

Planting Fields Arboretum State Historic Park, Oyster Bay, NY 11771-0058, (516) 922-9200, ext. 106

These are not the only places with educational programs. If you look around in your neighborhood, town, or county, you can find many more.

Plant Societies

The next best thing to gardening is being with gardeners. For someone who loves a particular kind of plant, the very best thing is a roomful of people on the same wavelength.

Nearly every kind of plant has its fans, and its national and local societies devoted to it. These societies all share some common traits. Each charges a minimal amount for annual dues, generally around $10 to $25, and meets once a month, with a break during the summer, when the members spend every waking hour fussing with their plants. All have educational aims, too, as well as promoting friendships, and offer lectures, workshops, demonstrations, or slide shows at each meeting. Most have monthly or bimonthly publications, and many organize trips to gardens or growers. All of them welcome beginners and visitors. From common to unusual, if it's green, there's probably a fan club.

Societies that meet in the New York area are easy to find since many meet at the Horticultural Society of New York, 128 West 58th Street, (212) 757-0915, which will relay telephone or mail inquiries to them. Among them are the New York City African Violet Society, the American Begonia Society, the New York Bromeliad Society, the New York Cactus and Succulent Society, the American Gloxinia and Gesneriad Society, the Indoor Gardening Society of America, and the Manhattan Orchid Society.

Others meet at area botanical gardens or colleges. The Bonsai Society of Greater New York has three chapters, with information available from the society office, 1243 Melville Road, Farmingdale, New York 11735. The American Fern Society, New York Chapter, meets at the New York Botanical Garden; information is available by calling (718) 817-8700.

Most societies have chapters around the country. A few years ago you had to know someone or hang around a nursery to find out about them. Today, they're all on the Internet, waiting for you to drop by.

Stretching Tulips

You know its nearly Valentine's Day when cut flowers pop up in lots of households that otherwise don't see them very often. For almost every bouquet, the life cycle will be routine. Over a few days most cut flowers start off as closed buds, drink some water, then open and start dropping petals as they change from flowers into trash. But some tulips are different. Somewhere between coming and going, they get longer, continuing to grow after being cut, like a 1950s B-movie monster, only prettier.

There are tulips (the Darwins cultivars and parrots, among others) that actually stretch. On the breakfast table, they sort of lean over to see what's in the bowl. It's a matter of genetics. Plant growth regulators (auxins) are produced in the female parts of the flower and are still there, trying to work, when the flowers are cut for market. Tulips are unusual in that their stem cells elongate just as if they were still in the ground.

To keep cut tulips going (and growing) as long as possible, remember that they are big drinkers, especially during the first twenty-four hours. Use plain, fresh water, without additives. Although you should cut the stems before putting them in a vase to make sure the conducting vessels are open, there is no need to cut them on an angle. The number of water-conducting vessels is what it is, and an angle cut doesn't increase the number and won't make any difference in the long (and getting longer) run.

Camellia Rx for Winter

When a blast of color is needed to counteract the winter gardening blues, the berries left on the hollies just don't do it. That may be why gardeners with cool, bright rooms love camellias. Any plant kind enough to bloom in January, February, or March is a friend indeed.

One cure for the winter blues can be found at Planting Fields Arboretum in Oyster Bay, Long Island. The arboretum's Camellia House was built between 1918 and 1919 and rebuilt after a fire in 1922. It contains one of the largest and oldest collections of camellias under glass in the Northeast. Planting Fields concentrates on cultivars of *Camellia japonica* (which blooms from December through April), *C. reticulata* (February through April), and *C. sasanqua* (November through January). It also contains other species, including *C. sinensis,* from which tea is made.

Planted directly in the ground, these hand-

Camellia

some evergreens with dark, glossy leaves have grown into large shrubs as tall as 15 feet. Since they bloom at slightly different times, with the end of February being the peak for the *C. japonica* hybrids, each visit is different. Throughout the winter, some of the shrubs will be covered with 2-inch to 5-inch flowers in red, pink, white, or streaked mixes; some will have just finished blooming and will be loaded with buds, hinting of the next display. With their showy flowers it's hard to remember that camellias are native to the Southeast Asian mountains, not the tropics.

Sources for camellias, including those that can be grown outdoors in the Northeast, are Camellia Forest Nursery, 9701 Carrie Rd., Chapel Hill, NC 27516, (919) 968-0504, catalog; Fairweather Gardens, P.O. Box 330, Greenwich, NJ 08323, (856) 451-6261, catalog; and Nuccio's Nurseries, 3555 Chaney Trail, Altadena, CA 91001, (626) 794-3383, catalog.

Nature and the City

Living in the city, even New York City, doesn't mean living without nature. But there certainly is a difference. Attention turns toward the inside of the home, where houseplants become the major green focus. But in every city, in more places than you might think, nature pops up—in parks and street trees, but also exotic fruit seeds suspended over water glasses and herbs planted on windowsills.

The most interesting thing about the relationship between city dwellers and nature is that the bond we share has not really broken, but sometimes it is bent. On one hand are people who no longer know one tree from another, for whom nature floats unnoticed below their urban radar until something unusual happens—the tree that blooms in the fall, the one that grows in a sidewalk crack, the gift of an unknown houseplant. But once awakened, they want to know everything about it.

On the other hand are the urbanites for whom every scrap of nature is of the utmost value. They will fight to preserve a common Norway maple or nurse back to health a discarded house-plant from someone else's trash. They want to start every seed that comes through the door and see no reason why they can't make a houseplant of everything. They guard their street trees, patrol the parks, and fight for everything green.

Cities would be a lot less interesting without both.

8

What Is It?
What Do I Do with It?

Something sparks a connection between a person and a plant, and the next step is adoption. I receive a lot of letters asking for an identification, and most of them go on to ask how to grow this mysterious plant—in an apartment or a city backyard. Anything green is fair game, from the smallest bulb to the biggest tree. The motto of the city gardener seems to be, "If there's a will, there's a way."

Cornelian Cherry

Just at the end of winter New Yorkers are startled to see here and there a small, low-branching tree loaded with small, yellow flowers. Sometimes they have several stems, like a large shrub, sometimes just a single trunk, but the flowers are a dead giveaway that they are the same. It always brings a smile.

The cornelian cherry dogwood, *Cornus mas*, always blooms in March before its leaves emerge, forcing winter to become spring.

Since it is often wider than it is tall, the mass of bright yellow-green flowers is positioned perfectly for admiring. Up close, each yellow puff is actually composed of many small flowers exploding from bracts that look like green popcorn kernels.

C. *mas* could be the perfect tree in many sites. It grows well in sun or shade and produces lustrous green leaves and, in late summer, small, shiny edible red fruit (accounting for the cherry part of the common name). Growing slowly to 15 feet, it is an ideal size for a small garden and is remarkably pest resistant and well adapted to city conditions. No one who has one can figure out why everyone doesn't have one.

Caladiums Indoors and Out

A sad story that might sound familiar: in July you buy a magnificent potted caladium; by September it is dead. It might be that it didn't want to be indoors and was following its natural outdoor destiny, or it might have been mortally traumatized by the sunshine that pervades every corner of your apartment from midday on. Or it might be something else altogether.

Sometimes a word makes all the difference. In this case it's the difference between *dies* and *dies back.* Caladiums lose their leaves in the fall as the tuber begins its rest period. Reduce watering when the process begins, and withhold it completely once the foliage has died. At that point you should unpot and clean the tubers, removing old leaves and roots, and store the tubers for the winter in dry sand or vermiculite at 60 to 65 degrees.

To get a jump on planting them outdoors, bring the rested tubers out of storage and pot up about four weeks before the ground is warm enough. Plan on putting them outdoors in mid- to late May, several weeks after the last frost date. The same calendar applies to caladiums grown indoors.

Your thumb isn't black, so for another attempt, caladium sources include Caladium World, Drawer 629, Sebring, FL 33871, (941) 385-7661, catalog; Fancy Plants Farms, P.O. Box 989, Lake Placid, FL 33862, (941) 699-1990, catalog.

Name That Tomato Yourself

Souvenir seeds brought back by friends visiting Europe are a great surprise, but they can lead to minor frustrations. Old-country tomatoes can look different (odd shapes, like bananas or hot peppers) and taste sweeter than the same old varieties available at the local garden center every spring. Saving seeds is one way to have those tomatoes year after year, but you may want to explore the world of heirloom vegetables in general.

Heirloom vegetables, with great taste and stories to match, are becoming of more interest to more people every year.

Home gardeners looking for remembered taste and researchers worried about the loss of genetic diversity in food crops have sparked groups of interested people to collect and sell or trade hand-me-down seeds, keeping older varieties alive. These small groups exist all over the country. Mostly they are the nonprofit love affairs of a few people, without fax machines, Web pages, or telephone-ordering capability.

One of them, the Maine Seed Saving Network (P.O. Box 126, Penobscot, ME 04476), lists seeds for a paste tomato with (at least) two common names. It is called 'Dad's Barber,' for the original source of the seeds that the Maine family has grown and saved, and now made available to the rest of us. The barber's family had grown it in southern Italy for generations. The size, shape, and history of the tomato give it its other common name: 'Italian Banana.'

Is it the same as the one you have? Can't tell, but does it really matter? Experimenting with heirloom vegetables is always rewarding, and if you find one you love, share the seeds and give it your own history.

Other preservation groups include the Garden State Heirloom Seed Society, P.O. Box 15, Delaware, NJ 07833, and the Eastern Native Seed Conservancy, S.R. 70, Box 131, Great Barrington, MA 01230.

Blooming at Long Last

New York apartment lobbies are home to some strange things. In more than one lobby corner I have seen a bedraggled old corn plant, often there longer than most of the residents. But once in a while that old plant will miraculously burst into bloom.

The real miracle will be if the night doorman agrees to stay in the lobby with it. Calling the scent very sweet is being kind. Once smelled, never forgotten. Out of respect for others, the flowers close during the day and open around dusk.

The *Dracaena massangeana,* or corn plant, has been patiently spending these years converting light, water, and nutrients into carbohydrates. Any extra it could make beyond the amount it needed to grow was kept in storage. Finally, it had enough stored energy to produce a flower. One look at the size of the plant and flower is enough to know that a lot was needed. It took so many years because lobbies aren't very bright. In a sunnier location, it should flower more often, although I'm not sure anyone would want it to.

Bright Spot in the Park

Take a walk through most major parks in early April and somewhere near the forsythia in bloom you'll probably find another shrub full of bright purple-pink, funnel-shaped flowers. If it wasn't for the fact that it doesn't have any leaves, you would swear it was a rhododendron.

This is one of the exceptions to the general rule that most rhododendrons are evergreen. *Rhododendron mucronulatum* (Korean rhododendron) is the earliest of the hardy rhododendrons to bloom in the Northeast, starting in late March or early April. Its showy rosy-purple flowers are out well before the leaves begin to grow. Cultivars are available with flowers in shades of pink and purple, from soft to glaring.

The Tree That Grows

The tree referred to in A Tree Grows in Brooklyn *sprouts in sidewalk cracks and empty lots everywhere. Untended and not formally planted, they grow happily wherever they can find a tiny break in the concrete and drive their roots into real soil, good or bad.*

Even in green-poor cities hardly anyone pays the slightest attention to it. Nine out of ten people couldn't even identify this miracle of nature.

Ailanthus altissima, or tree of heaven, is definitely a streetsmart tree. Nina Bassuk, director of the Institute of Urban Horticulture at Cornell University in Ithaca, New York, has studied ailanthus to find out just how this gangly tree, all leaves and few branches, manages to thrive in the cracks and crevices of New York and other cities.

Ailanthus comes into its own when the situation looks bleakest. The keys to its success lie in that scruffy look and keeping a low profile while it bides its time. For several years, it devotes nearly all its energy to growing long, vigorous, ropey roots, which are good at storing food and finding water over a much larger territory than the above-ground growth would seem to justify. When ready, it begins growing 3 to 5 feet a year, but prefers to grow large leaves for food production rather than investing energy in growing lots of branches.

A second strategy for success is the ability of the roots to send up another stem if the main stem is damaged. Combine that with prolific seed production, each fit with a wing to help the wind blow seeds to likely or unlikely spots, and a very high germination rate, along with drought and pollution tolerance, and you get the tree that grew not only in Brooklyn, but in practically every other city in the eastern and midwestern United States and Europe.

Prolific Paulownia

On a hike or in a park, or even along the highway, a tree grows that, at first glance, seems to be covered with wisteria in full bloom. Look again: the flowers are sitting upright, not hanging down.

The paulownia, or Chinese empress tree (*Paulownia tomentosa*), has its fans and its foes. Highly prolific, it is considered a weed tree by some and a lovely ornamental by others. It has naturalized widely in the eastern United States, but is generally not hardy north of the New York City area.

Its flowers have a lovely fragrance and have been called the most beautiful of all tree blossoms. Upright, pyramidal clusters of flowers 8 to 12 inches long appear before the leaves. Each flower is tubular, 2 inches long, and emerges velvety purple-blue from ocher suedelike caps, then fades to a pale lilac.

Young trees, or resprouting trees that were winter-killed back to the ground, produce huge leaves, 30 or more inches wide. Take this as a warning, like a puppy with large paws. Paulownias grow

10 feet or more a year when very young, eventually reaching 40 feet. Their heart-shaped 5- to 10-inch adult leaves cast a deep shade, but blacken and fall with the first hard frost. All of the leaves can fall overnight, hiding small plants and compact cars below.

Clematis Fences Make Good Neighbors

Sweet autumn clematis, one of the most beautiful vines, is surely one of the most vigorous. Planted against a fence, it will spread along the top and fill both yards with its flowers. But if your neighbors are unappreciative, keep the peace by pinching back the growing tips during the summer to control its size. The problem is not losing the fall's flowers.

Since this clematis doesn't set flower buds until summer, you can pinch it back until the end of June without losing too many flowers. However, a better idea might be to train the exuberant summer growth onto your side of the fence to keep as much of the display as possible where it will be appreciated.

But why worry about bud set on your neighbors' side? If they don't like the flowers, don't give them any. You can shear that growth back anytime to keep them happy.

Unwrap That Tree

Tree wrap, the stuff that turns a tree into a mummy, seems like an unnecessary improvement. After all, forests are full of healthy trees that have never been subjected to this indignity.

The typical reasons for wrapping the trunks of newly planted trees with paper, burlap, plastic, or other material sound sensible enough: protection from cracks in the bark due to rapidly changing temperatures in winter and physical protection from equipment or animals. But this practice is gradually succumbing to evidence that it is unnecessary and often unwise.

The evidence of protection is less than compelling. Wrapped and unwrapped trees next to one another seem to suffer equally from weather. Other touted benefits have proved equally elusive. Wrapping to prevent dehydration can trap too much moisture and can even conduct heat, causing bark and underlying wood to soften and deteriorate, providing entry for fungus diseases. Rather than preventing borers, wraps can protect them from predators. More important, wraps, and especially strings and wires used to tie them, can constrict and damage a tree as it grows, especially if they are not removed.

A summer planting in a narrow tree pit surrounded by streets and sidewalks may benefit from a wrapping until the summer is over to lessen the impact of reflected and absorbed heat, while the same tree planted on a grassy expanse would not need it. To wrap or not should be an individual, not blanket, decision.

Harmless Lichens

A second home in the mountains sounds ideal. But for a city person, there's a lot to learn about real nature. Some of the trees on the property probably have a lot of grayish mold or fungus growing on them. If the fungus is widespread and means they are dying, you probably should avoid buying that property, right?

Put your money on the table: those are lichens, and they are not dangerous. Actually, lichens are small co-ops. Algae and fungi combine to form partnerships, each doing its part. The algae create food by photosynthesis and provide some carbohydrates to the fungi. The fungi in turn provide shelter for the algae, keeping them from getting too much sun and drying out. Neither one bothers trees; lichens do just as well on rocks, fence posts, and dead trees as they do on live ones.

Lichens are slow growing and long-lived, and they hate pollution, which is one reason they are not common in cities. Use them as an indicator: if they die, put the place up for sale.

Plants in the Sick Room

Some old gardeners' tales are fun and some have enough of a kernel of truth to let them stand, but keeping plants out of a sick person's room because they will use up the oxygen is just too much.

If awards were given for longevity, this myth would be right up there. Since the eighteenth century, when it was discovered that plants use and produce both carbon dioxide and oxygen, two favorite conclusions for jumping to are that plants can dangerously deplete a room's supply of oxygen at night and that they should not be kept in the bedroom. As in many other myths, the small nuggets of truth are exaggerated, while the larger body of facts is ignored.

Yes, plants do use oxygen at night in a series of complicated chemical reactions that are part of making and using food. But remember that plants give off ten times as much oxygen during the day as they use at night. Over a very long time, green plants have been responsible for changing the composition of our atmosphere, reducing the amount of carbon dioxide and increasing the amount of oxygen.

But strong myths sometimes need a scientific stake driven through their hearts. In an hour, a pound of plant leaves (think of a big head of lettuce) uses about 0.1 liter of oxygen. By comparison, a 150-pound person resting quietly uses more than 71 liters of oxygen each hour. Thanks to André Jagendorf, professor of plant biology at Cornell University, who provided the respiration figures for the plants, and the reference department of the New York Public Library, which provided the figures for humans, maybe we can all sleep a little easier.

Chartreuse Viburnum

Sooner or later someone is going to give you a floral arrangement with a chartreuse pompon-like flower in it. When you finally decide you want to grow one for yourself, it's easy enough to find out that it is a viburnum. All the books or catalogs will offer you, however, are descriptions of viburnums with white or pink flowers and berries in the fall. No chartreuse.

There are several viburnums with blooms that begin chartreuse and eventually change to white, which is probably why you haven't found them listed. Most likely, the one you refer to is *Viburnum opulus* 'Roseum,' the European snowball, or guelderrose. A large shrub, it will grow to 10 feet high and wide in Zones 3 to 8, which includes the Northeast. Another possibility is *Viburnum plicatum* var. *plicatum,* the Japanese snowball. While it grows to 15 feet high and is covered in spring with clusters of bloom 2 to 3 inches in diameter, it is only marginally hardy in Zone 6, making it chancy for some areas in the Northeast.

Neither of these viburnums is likely to show up on anyone's Top 100 list. The European snowball is notorious for its appeal to aphids. On both, the flowers you see aren't true flowers, because they do not have sexual parts, just petals. They are sterile, so there won't be berries for you or the birds to admire, one of the best reasons to plant viburnums.

Slime Mold

Quietly working in the controlled environment of your garden, there are occasional glimpses of the much wider botannical world. You put a fine layer of mulch over the existing mulch in a flower bed and within a few hours a yellowish mound beings to appears. It starts off small, then it spreads to a mound. It almost looks as though it has a meringue consistency. You shovel it off the spot, but the next day it starts again in another spot in the bed.

Slime mold. One of the most perfectly named uninvited garden visitors, each yellow or orange mass is a single cell, slowly flowing across a wet area, engulfing bacteria and other microbes. If you had let it alone, you could have watched it glide along, moving as much as 2 feet in twelve hours. Clearly you had better things to do that day, and your approach, scooping it up with a shovel, is the best that you can do.

The slime came in with the new mulch, and it loves hot, humid weather. It will disappear when the mulch dries out or when they have eaten all that is available in it. In the meantime, slime mold does not harm the plants on which it grows and poses no known threats to people, except perhaps a faint level of disgust.

They'll Take New York

Walking a dog in New York or any big city takes you places and shows you things you might never see otherwise. For example, that funny plant that grows against a neighbor's house. It has flowers of various colors that are closed during the morning walk but open in the evening.

If a plant could be a New Yorker, this would be it. An immigrant with a story to tell, four-o'clocks (*Mirabilis jalapa*) were historically called the marvel-of-Peru. The name four-o'clocks refers to the flowers' habit of opening around 4 P.M. and closing in the early morning. It opens to greet people coming home from work, but it is closed when they are away.

Like many other New Yorkers, it left its distant rural surroundings, did some traveling, and feels right at home in the concrete city. The sixteenth-century conquistadors took it to Europe from Peru along with heliotrope. It came to North America with the colonists 100 years later.

The marvel or miracle referred to in the common and Latin names is that from early August until frost, tubular flowers 1 inch across and up to 2 inches long appear on the same plant in bright hues of magenta, yellow, and white, sometimes even striped or splashed a second color. As with most other evening bloomers, four-o'clocks depend on fragrance to attract pollinators to the 3-foot-tall densely growing plant.

It is not cold-hardy in the Northeast, and it is grown as an annual that reseeds itself. It forms large tubers that can be dug up in the fall and stored over the winter. But city dwellers have an advantage over suburbanites since they can plant the tubers near a foundation, wall, or other mass of concrete, and the winter sun on the concrete then provides enough transmitted warmth to let the tubers winter over in the ground, giving them a head start the following summer.

Prefers the city to the country; tolerates heat, humidity, and drought; opens late and works all night . . . sounds like a New Yorker to me.

Four-o'clocks are available from Johnny's Selected Seeds, 1 Foss Hill Road, RR1 Box 2580, Albion, ME 04910, (207) 437-4301, catalog. They are also sold by Select Seeds, 180 Stickney Road, Union, CT 06076; (860) 684-9310, catalog.

Russian versus French Tarragon

Tarragon comes in two choices: French and Russian. Herb books always advise using French for cooking and never even address uses for Russian.

While French tarragon (*Artemisia dracunculus* 'Sativa') adds its wonderful aroma and delicate anise-like flavor to chicken, sauces, and green beans, Russian tarragon (*Artemisia dracunculus*) smells more of leather and balsam and is charitably described as being unpalatable. It has an aroma that might be appropriate on men's faces, but it should stay out of their stomachs. Other than as a garden ornamental, it has no commercial uses.

While the chef may have a simple answer (if it tastes good, use it), poor gardeners face still more confusion. Dr. Arthur Tucker, research professor at Delaware State University in Dover, says French tarragon was originally a selection from Russian tarragon, found in southern Europe, probably in Italy, at least as long ago as 1189. It is called French instead of Italian tarragon because the French made the most extensive culinary use of it. Of course, it might just be an early example of clever marketing.

Unfortunately, the delicate flavor comes at a price: French tarragon is a weaker-growing plant, lax in habit, rarely taller than 18 inches, while Russian is more vigorous, growing to 3 to 4 feet, with strong, woody stems. More important, French tarragon seldom flowers and is sterile, while its Russian cousin is fertile.

Since it is sterile, French tarragon can be propagated only from cuttings, so it must be purchased as a plant. You may see seeds offered for French tarragon in catalogs. The seeds will grow up to be Russian tarragon, not French—a beauty in the garden but a waste in the kitchen.

A Weed by Any Other Name

There's nothing like being in a new environment for making you pay attention to things that, at home, you might walk right by. In England you'll see a flower, Himalayan impatiens (that is clearly related to our weedy, wild, yellow-orange touch-me-not (or jewel weed), but its blossom is much larger and of a different color. Coming home, you might be enthusiastic enough to try to find some to buy.

Buy them? Well, yes, you can occasionally find them at nurseries. I even bought one myself in Vermont once before I realized

Himalayan Impatiens

that they grow wild in the northeastern United States and Canada in moist, shady, and not-so-shady spots.

While *Impatiens glandulifera,* the Himalayan impatiens, is not native to the United States, it long ago used its high-powered springy seed capsules, like those of its smaller cousin, jewelweed, to spread itself around. Now fully naturalized, it has nearly lost any garden status it might once have had and become just another weed. I'm glad to hear that the English at least still appreciate the pink, rose-purple, or pinkish-white tubular flowers of this tall (up to 6 feet), fleshy annual. A reliable self-seeder, it will quickly cover an area it likes, but can be controlled because it pulls up easily.

Some of our own native wildflowers had to go to Europe before being appreciated, including monarda (bee balm), helenium (sneezeweed), and joe-pye weed. Echinacea (coneflower) didn't become popular here until European nurseries spent the time necessary to pick the best selections and then proceeded to send them back to us as desirable garden plants.

Himalayan impatiens seeds are available from J. L. Hudson, Seedsman, Star Route 2, Box 337, La Honda, CA 94020; no telephone listed, catalog. They need several months of cold to germinate, so plant in the fall or chill in the refrigerator.

Mystery Seeds

Kids, especially young school-age kids, bring strange things home from the street. You know that a stray dog can be a problem, but stray seeds? When your daughter brings home seeds from a tree near school, you will most likely tell her they won't grow, and she will most likely try anyway.

Once they sprout and she rigs up a mini-greenhouse for the apartment, and they grow through a few transplantings into larger pots, now you have a few 4-foot-high trees, possibly (because they are common in city plantings) with leaves that look like short branches, each with many small individual leaves. If you have a country home, you might plant them there.

Your honey locusts (a cultivar of *Gleditsia triacanthos*) should enjoy getting out to the country where the air is cleaner and the dogs are better behaved, but planting will have to wait until spring, when the ground is no longer wet. Their root systems are not yet ready to survive a winter outdoors.

In the meantime your daughter should try to provide them with the right conditions for winter dormancy. Place the trees outside, and wait for the leaves to drop. From then until next spring, the trees need to be kept in a place that is cool and light, but where the roots are protected against temperatures below 25 degrees. A well-lighted, well-insulated garage should work, but a cool, well-lighted room might have to do. Water just often enough to keep the soil slightly moist (that might be every three to four weeks, but every situation is different).

The trees may break dormancy and begin to put out leaves early because it isn't cool enough. They will probably be fine, although deciduous trees really need a dormant period of several months each year. That's one reason they make poor houseplants even before size becomes an issue.

Eating Juniper Berries

Dried juniper berries are called for in some recipes. You have ju-
nipers growing in your yard, and they are loaded with berries. You
are tempted to use these fresh berries in cooking but are not sure
whether they are safe. They seem to be as fragrant as the dried ones
and look exactly the same. All juniper berries are probably the
same, right?

"All" covers a lot of territory and a lot of different junipers.
The many species and varieties of junipers are found in many
parts of the world, and some have berries (botanically they are
fleshy cones, not true berries) used for flavoring in local dishes.
Some, on the other hand, taste just terrible. And taken in large
quantities, all can make you sick.

Juniperus communis, the source of commercial berries for culinary flavoring and, of course, gin, is an evergreen shrub that typically grows from 5 to 10 feet tall, with gray-green needle-like
leaves. It is commonly found in the Northeast. The cones, which
are green when young and about $1/3$ inch in diameter, turn blue-
black with a gray-white cast as they ripen during their third summer on the shrub.

The quality of flavor seems to be related to the altitude at
which the shrub is grown. Most commercial juniper cones are
grown in mountainous regions; those growing at lower altitudes
have a taste more reminiscent of turpentine.

Extracts of *J. communis* cones are listed as "generally recognized as safe" by the Food and Drug Administration when used in
very small quantities for flavoring. The rating is given for 50
parts per million of the extract, 95 parts per million for the essential oil, and up to 2,000 parts per million for the cones themselves.

You should be aware that juniper cones have medicinal as

well as flavoring effects. The cones have diuretic properties and can produce convulsions or kidney failure if taken in large doses. They should be avoided by pregnant women and people with kidney problems.

If your shrub is a species other than *J. communis,* the resins contained in the cones may be even more dangerous. At the least, they will probably taste awful.

If you ask me (and you did), I would leave them on the shrub.

Big Trees

Bigger must mean better, so the biggest must be the best, and the best is surely deserving of our support. At least that is the opinion of one Long Islander whose linden was described by his arborist as the biggest he had ever seen. The problem was that the tree needed extensive, expensive work, which the owner could not afford. He wondered if there was any organization that might help support his tree.

He thinks his tree is larger than the European linden (*Tilia europaea*) in nearby Glen Cove that measures 24 feet 2 inches around (at 4½ feet from the ground) with a crown that spreads 88 by 82 feet, it may be the largest one on Long Island. If so, an official designation in New York's Statewide Big Tree program may convince local officials to help preserve a new local landmark.

New York, New Jersey, and Connecticut have programs and will send an urban forester to check on possible champions. If you have a similar situation, provide as much information as you can: the tree name, its circumference at 4½ feet from the ground, the approximate spread of the crown. It's probably not a good idea to climb the tree to make these measurements.

Most state Departments of Environment keep records. New Yorkers with extraordinarily large trees should contact the Department of Environmental Conservation, Statewide Big Tree Program, Room 424, 50 Wolf Road, Albany, NY 12233-4253. New Jersey residents should contact the New Jersey Forest Service, New Jersey Big Trees, CN-404, Trenton, NJ 08625. In Connecticut, contact the Department of Environmental Protection, Division of Forestry, 79 Elm Street, Hartford, CT 06264.

Chrysanthemum Indoors

That supermarket potted chrysanthemum, with numerous blossoms and many more buds that promise even more, is a constant frustration. Not even the partially open buds ever open totally. Maybe the problem is having it on a sill indoors, even in a sunny window.

Put the plant outside where it belongs, and the buds will open. Garden chrysanthemums, whether from supermarkets or nurseries, are outdoor plants and need more sun to continue growing than your sunniest window can provide.

If you can't put it outside, give it the best environment you can. Since they are grown outside and are adapted to cool, moist conditions, they are likely to suffer moisture stress when brought inside because of the lack of humidity, lack of adequate light, and limited air circulation.

Find a window with a southern or southeastern exposure. Hardy chrysanthemums are beautiful, but they shouldn't be made into dining room table centerpieces.

Under very low light conditions in an overheated room, chrysanthemums can product ethylene gas. The gas is not dangerous to people, but it can cause chrysanthemums to stop their flower buds from opening and can even kill the plant.

A better idea for buying chrysanthemums for indoor display

is to buy the one with the most open blooms, and enjoy it while
it lasts.

Sweet Potato or Yam?

*No Thanksgiving ever seems to be complete without a family argu-
ment. This year it was about sweet potatoes and yams, and which is
which.*

It's doubly confusing because in this country *yam* and *sweet
potato* refer to the same plant (*Ipomoea batatas*), whether tapered or
not, yellow, orange, or white fleshed. But there are also true yams
(*Dioscorea* species) grown for food in tropical areas. True yams are
odd-shaped long tubers, sometimes as big as a leg, and the skin
can be scaly.

James Cannon, the resident director of the Sweet Potato Research Center in Chase, Louisiana, says that *yam* was a trade name
for southern Louisiana's moist and tender sweet potatoes in the
1930s and 1940s to differentiate them from drier, mealy, less
tasty varieties grown in other locations. Over time the trade name
has become a common name.

Sweet potatoes require a longer growing season than the one
in the Northeast. Cannon suggested gardeners in this area try
'Beauregard,' a variety that matures earlier than most others.

In some families the orange-fleshed ones are sweet potatoes
and the yellow or white ones are yams, and in other families the
names and preferences are reversed. But neither one is actually a
yam. The color difference is due to pigmentation; the shape,
which can range from nearly round to elongated, is due to the
combination of variety and soil type. Since the pigment is rich in
beta carotene, the orange varieties may be more healthful, but
that depends on one's opinion of beta carotene.

The sweet potato's distinctive sweetness results from an enzyme reaction that breaks starch down into sugar. Sweet potatoes freshly dug in September taste better if purchased two months later, because the sugar develops in six to eight weeks of storage as well as during long, slow cooking. The cold, dry air of a refrigerator can cause them to deteriorate quickly, so keep them in a cupboard or a closet at 50 to 60 degrees instead.

By the way, 'Beauregard' is orange.

Fall Flowering Trees

In the Brooklyn Borough Hall area there are four young trees that flower in mid-November, and everyone wants to know what they are

They are probably the ornamental flowering cherry *Prunus subhirtella* 'Autumnalis.' As you can tell by the name, they are notable for blooming in the autumn. Many of their buds open during warm fall periods into light pink, semidouble flowers that fade to white. The remaining buds open when spring comes.

Some people might object to having spring colors and flowering trees unexpectedly mixed among the fall colors and blowing leaves, but some fall days are just so beautiful that even trees want to celebrate.

Sources for this ornamental cherry include: Twombly Nurseries, 163 Barn Hill Road, Monroe, CT 06468, (203) 261-2133, catalog; and Greer Gardens, 1280 Good pasture Island Road, Eugene, OR 97401-1794, (800) 548-0111, catalog.

Winterberry

One often sees lovely bare branches covered with red berries at the florist. The florist will tell you that they are hollies, but hollies are supposed to be evergreen. Not only do you want to know what they are, but whether or not you could grow your own.

"Holly" always calls forth glossy, spiny, evergreen leaves with shiny red berries. The majority of native American hollies, however, are not evergreen. The branches of *Ilex verticillata,* or winterberry, that show up for Thanksgiving and Christmas are indeed hollies: deciduous natives that grow naturally throughout most of the eastern half of the country. Winterberry is hardy to Zone 4, where temperatures can go as low as minus 30 degrees.

However, native hollies, as well as many other plants, are protected on public lands in New York, New Jersey, Connecticut, and other states because they are classified as "exploitably vulnerable," the term used to refer to species that could become endangered if people continue to harvest them in the wild. So don't. On private land, permission of the owner is required, both by law and by good manners.

The best answer is to grow your own winterberry, save some branches for yourself, and divide the rest between your friends and the birds. Give the birds the largest portion.

There are a number of different cultivars and hybrids, varying in height (3 to 15 feet), berry color (dark reds to reddish-orange to yellow), and berry size ($1/4$ to $1/2$ inch). *I. verticillata* produces wonderful berries that are long lasting on cut branches in the house providing you don't put the branches in water. Outside, the berries persist as long as the birds allow.

The keys to growing *I. verticillata* are to remember that hollies are dioecious—a male is needed for the females to produce berries— and that the male and females have to bloom at the same time for pollination to occur. One of the best berry producers is a female cultivar, 'Winter Red,' with very long-lasting, intense

Winterberry

red berries. If all the plants you purchase are the same cultivar, all the plants will be the same sex. Be sure to get a compatible male that matches the blooming time of the females. 'Apollo' and 'Raritan Chief' are particularly good since they bloom long enough to pollinate many common cultivars.

Sources for *I. verticillata* and its offspring include Fairweather Gardens, P.O. Box 330, Greenwich, NJ 08323, (856) 451-6261, catalog.

Clementine, My Clementine

Christmas dinners always seem to involve conversations that lead to unanswered questions. This year they were about clementines. There were an awful lot of opinions about exactly what they are or how you can grow something if it doesn't have seeds.

Clementines, along with tangerines, are mutations of *Citrus reticulata,* the mandarin. The mandarin's most famous offspring is the mandarin orange, which seems to begin its life in a can and end it in desserts that wiggle.

The first clementine, found in Algeria at the turn of the twentieth century, was a naturally occurring cross between a mandarin and something unknown, but clearly from a good family. Now, according to Fred Gmitter, associate professor of horticulture at the University of Florida's Citrus Research Center in Lake Alfred, there are more than fifty different varieties of clementines, all from spontaneous mutations that happened over the years. They differ mainly in when their fruit matures (late September through February).

Most clementines cannot successfully pollinate themselves, so the fruit is seedless unless they are cross-pollinated by another type of citrus. The trees are propagated by grafting cuttings onto a root stock that is well adapted to that growing area.

Algeria and Spain still produce the most clementines, as the dry summers and cool winters of the Mediterranean are ideal for the best quality fruit. California, which seems to include every climate somewhere, is beginning to grow clementines commercially, and Florida growers are finding some varieties that do well in their climate.

Keeping Christmas Trees

Over the Thanksgiving weekend you drove by a cut-it-yourself Christmas tree farm and on an impulse stopped and bought a tree. Now what are you going to do with it? It is too early to bring it in the house.

The world seems to divide into those who buy their trees too early and those who buy them at the last minute. Early shoppers should take the advice of Jeff Bender at the National Christmas Tree Association in Milwaukee, Wisconsin: keeping the needles fresh takes water, and lots of it.

Even in the short time it takes to bring the tree home, sap flows from the wound and clogs the vessels that carry water upward. To make sure water can be absorbed, cut another ¼ inch from the bottom of the trunk before putting the tree in a bucket of water. Keep the tree outside, but protected from sun, wind, and freezing temperatures. Check the bucket every day, adding water when needed. It's probably a good thing your ride didn't take you past Rockefeller Center—it would be hard to find a bucket large enough for that tree.

Pass the Root Veggie

At a traditional New England holiday dinner you were served yellow turnips. They did indeed have yellow flesh, but they didn't taste like any turnips you remember. But they were good enough that you wanted to grow some, whatever they were.

It may depend on where in New England you were. Rob Johnston of Johnny's Selected Seeds in Albion, Maine, said "yellow turnip" is "Mainespeak" for rutabaga. There's plenty of room for confusion: turnips (*Brassica rapa*) and rutabagas (*Brassica napus*) are close relatives, and in fact, rutabagas are believed to be the result of a relatively recent (probably medieval) natural cross between a turnip and some kind of cabbage. Both have white-fleshed and yellow-fleshed varieties, although most turnips are white and most rutabagas are yellow.

Johnston said true turnips are best when they are just a little bigger than a golf ball and rutabagas are best when they are the size of a grapefruit. Rutabagas, grown for fall harvest, are less watery and store longer, while turnips are a summer vegetable. None of that helps identification when a dish of mashed something comes your way.

Both are available from Johnny's Selected Seeds, 1 Foss Hill Road, R.R. 1 Box 2580, Albion, ME 04910, (207) 437-4301, catalog.

What Kind of Cactus?

Whether something is a Christmas cactus or a Thanksgiving cactus seems to be a cause of confusion. One definition has it that a Christmas cactus's leaves have smooth-edged segments while those of a Thanksgiving cactus have jagged segments. Or maybe it's the other way around.

There used to be a real difference, but then again, Thanksgiving and Christmas used to be two distinct holidays and not merely the bookends to a shopping season.

Schlumbergera truncata, which blooms around Thanksgiving,

does have strongly toothed edges. In the 1800s it was crossed with *S. russelliana,* resulting in a hybrid *S.* X *buckleyi* with more scalloped edges and a later bloom period, closer to Christmas. But the 1800s was the last time the difference was so distinct. Hybridization has blurred the distinction, and there are now more than 200 named cultivars, with bloom times that slide around almost from Halloween to Superbowl Sunday, depending on their parents.

Holiday Cactus

You will, of course, find people who insist on a neat fit into one category or the other, but those of us with less aggressive tendencies simply refer to any and all as "holiday cacti."

Maybe the best idea is to have enough variety so that something is in bloom from Election Day to New Year's. If that compromise interests you, one source is Rainbow Gardens Nursery, 1444 East Taylor Street, Vista, CA 92084, (760) 758-4290. Its catalog lists more than forty varieties under the heading "Thanksgiving-Christmas Cacti." Very diplomatic.

9

Only a New Yorker Would Write

There is something very special about New York City and its people. The range of plants that New Yorkers want to know about, and usually want to grow in their apartments, is amazing. But I don't think it's just New Yorkers; I think they are representative of people in all huge cities, worldwide. New York is just a terrific example—the big city to the nth degree. One common thread that I think runs through all big-city people is a love of the little bit of greenery that they can call their own.

Face It, Christmas Is Over

Once the year-end holidays are over, many people would like some tips on year-round care for all those poinsettias they received.

Pink, red, white, yellow, marbled, or splotched, my postholiday advice for poinsettias is always the same: throw them out. By now many poinsettias have dropped their leaves, but retain just enough colored bracts to save themselves from the compost pile.

If you are intent on keeping them, do try, but poinsettias are persnickety, and failure is common. After you let them grow indoors, cut them back, grow them outdoors, pinch them back, and grow them indoors once again, they will be ready for the hard part. Poinsettias need temperatures around 65 degrees and fourteen-hour nights in the fall with absolutely no exposure to artificial light in order to color up. And poinsettias do not accept excuses or apologies.

Assuming they survive the usual whiteflies and spider mites, don't catch any interesting diseases, and have been protected from drafts both warm and cold, all one has to show for the effort is a poinsettia. At three for ten dollars, it hardly seems worth the trouble.

Nails in Trees

Apartment superintendents, kind souls that they are, sometimes nail signs onto one of the trees in front of their buildings. Communication is great, but the price is too high.

In general, putting nails in trees is a bad idea; save nails for posts, not live trees. Any wound is a potential site of invasion by insects or disease-causing organisms that can decay wood or living bark (the layer under the exterior bark). The exterior layers of bark provide a barrier between the dangers of the outside world and the living structure inside. Woody plants defend themselves by walling off the wounded tissue in a process called compartmentalization. Provided the tree can make the barrier quickly before harmful organisms can get past it, no significant damage will result. Trees growing in stressful conditions, like drought, produce this barrier more slowly, increasing the risk.

Wounds that continue to cause stress—like those from swing sets, clotheslines, and hammocks—are more serious. For example, swing sets should not be screwed into trees for support because the frequent push-pull or up-down action on the screws reopens the wound, enlarging the hole and making invasion easier.

Cats and Plants

City dwellers need both plants and animals to keep themselves in touch with nature, even a little. Cats are adorable, but some of them nibble on plants. There ought to be a list of plants that cats don't find attractive (but that humans do), or at least would not be dangerous if the cat should take a few bites.

It isn't quite that simple. First, any list of houseplants that are toxic to animals, even a long list is never complete because not all houseplants have been scientifically tested. Not being on a list is, therefore, no guarantee. And second, "toxic" can mean anything from all parts of the plant being highly poisonous, such as oleander, to minor irritation to mouth or stomach. The part of the plant, the amount eaten, and the individual cat are all parts of the equation. The old saying, "One man's meat is another's poison," also applies to animals.

Typically cats go for plants that call out to them. Drooping or fragile leaves or flowers that hang down in a handy location or move in a light breeze attract their attention and raise their hunting instinct. Keeping staid plants, and keeping them out of reach, is the first line of defense. Even if they are safe, who wants to look at nibbled leaves?

The ASPCA National Animal Poison Control Center offers a good list of plants in three categories: proven toxic, proven nontoxic, and those suspected of being dangerous but not yet scientifically tested. It is available by calling (888) 4ANI-HELP (426-4435) or (900) 680-0000. These lines are answered by veterinarians and veterinary toxicologists who can advise you or your veterinarian on animal poisoning emergencies for a fee.

On the other hand, you may want to provide some plants that are known to be safely edible and reasonably attractive in a cat-culinary sense for an indoor summer garden on a sunny windowsill. Catnip, of course, leads the list for most cats, although it does tend to get straggly if the cat is not conscientious about pruning. Kentucky bluegrass and fine fescues are also on the menu, along with parsley, dwarf marigolds, and dwarf zinnias. Grasses with finer textures are better choices than rough-bladed grasses, which can cause irritation and vomiting, a definite drawback indoors.

Giving any order of preference is impossible since any two cats will generally have three opinions between them, especially about eating. Texture seems to draw a cat's interest with many plants, rather than taste or smell. Have pots of parsley around, especially after a traditional tuna-in-sauce dinner—it may even alleviate some of that fish-breath that only a mother can love.

Ornamental Grass Woes

A cautionary tale of woe about planning: after moving into a new house the first thing you did was remove the "builder specials" from the front yard. In their place, you decide to install Japanese-inspired landscaping. Pebbles and rocks, a Japanese maple, and a few varieties of decorative grasses, as predicted, have been low maintenance, require little or no water, and work quite well with the house. But the grasses will not stop growing. Now, a few years later, they are almost 6 feet high and the clumps are almost double their original diameter. Without chopping off the tops or replacing them, you want to return everything to the original scale.

Enlarge the house.

Ants in the Peonies

Ants and peonies are not exactly bacon and eggs, but it seems you hardly ever see a bud without ants on it. There are, of course, many conflicting stories with few actual facts to back them up. Some people say that the ants kill the blooms while others say that the peony flower buds have a waxy coating and can't bloom until the ants eat it off. Or maybe the ants make absolutely no difference to the peonies.

None of the above. Ants are too busy to climb peonies just for the view, and certainly do not wish them harm. But there is a good reason, as there always is when you see effort exerted in nature.

Peonies have tiny nectaries—specialized tissue that secretes nectar—at the edges of their bud scales (delicate leaflike structures covering the bud). Nearly microscopic and amorphous in shape, the nectaries go unnoticed. Even looking carefully, you'll see the ants and the beads of nectar, but not the nectaries. The nectar is a highly nutritious blend of sugars, proteins, and amino acids and attracts the ants to the flower buds.

But peonies aren't Mother Teresa. In exchange for the nectar, the ants provide protection for the buds. Any bud-eating pest is attacked, beaten, robbed, and thrown off. Since some ants can bite from one end and spray caustic acid from the other, they make formidable foes. The ants may be just protecting their food supply, but the peonies are getting well-armed guards.

Don't spray the ants with poisons or water. The peonies know what they need better than you do.

Crocus That Blooms in Fall

Saffron is the most expensive spice in the grocery store. Since it comes from crocus, more than one person has wondered why they can't grow it themselves.

The same question has been asked for the more than 4,000 years that *Crocus sativus* has been in cultivation. And the answer is still the same: it takes a lot of crocus and a lot of work to make a little saffron. Unlike the bright and colorful crocus that bloom in the spring, *C. sativus* blooms in the fall and is not very showy.

Mostly used in rice dishes, saffron adds a delicate aroma and flavor and a beautiful yellow color. It is the world's most expensive spice, with a long history of use in medicine, dyes, perfumes, cooking, and even as a store of wealth. In medieval times a pound of saffron cost more than a horse and was a lot easier to hide.

Spain, Greece, and India provide the bulk of saffron today, but it has been grown in many regions, including England. Saffron is simply the dried, orange-red stigmas of the *C. sativus* bloom. It takes several thousand stigmas to make an ounce of saffron. Planted 6 inches apart, in rows 12 inches apart (you'll need room to step and bend, step and bend, at both planting and harvesting), a rather intense garden of 35 feet by 50 feet will contain 3,500 corms. After careful harvesting, separating of the stigmas from the flowers, drying, and storage, these will yield about an ounce of saffron—if everything goes well and your back doesn't give out first.

Another thing to look forward to is the fact that *C. sativus* can be difficult to grow. It requires full sun and very well-drained, deep soil that bakes dry during the summer. The corms have a tendency to migrate up or down as they grow daughter corms, and they won't bloom if they are too deep or too shallow or too crowded. Sometimes they peter out after a few years for no apparent reason.

Order for early September delivery, and plant them immediately. Sources for the bulbs include Charles H. Mueller Company, River Road Route Box 21, New Hope, PA 18938, (215) 862-2033, catalog; and French's Bulb Importers, Box 565, Pittsfield, VT 05762, 800-286-8198, catalog.

Arbor Day Advice

Arbor Day is an appropriate day to plant a new tree. But if you have a city backyard, there are things to do besides dig a hole.

Arbor Day trees are like Christmas puppies. They seem like a good idea when they are cute and small, but they sometimes grow up to be a bit less appealing. Rather than recommend a specific tree, I recommend planting only after thinking.

Robert Beyfuss, Cornell Cooperative Extension agent in Greene County, New York, suggests some questions to think about:

- Is the location good for a full-sized, mature tree? Overhead power and telephone lines don't mix well with tree branches, and pruning in this situation can be dangerous, expensive, and ugly. A small tree in a small yard looks perfect, but how will it look full grown? After all, the yard isn't going to get any bigger.

- Is the tree good for the location? Roadside sites are inappropriate for trees that are not tolerant of deicing salt, like white pine and sugar maple. And placing a mulberry near a wooden deck is asking for a future of permanent stains and bird droppings.

- How much maintenance does the tree need? If spraying, pruning, climbing, and frequently cleaning up sound like fun, then a high-maintenance tree, such as a fruit tree, is a good choice. Disease resistance and insect pests as well as messy fruit drop should be considered before purchase, not after.

As with art, trees should be for enjoyment, not investment. Planting a black walnut or other tree whose wood has commercial value makes very little sense. It may sound like easy money, but most carpenters prefer to buy their wood in a more convenient size than a whole tree.

Where's the Rain?

The same thing that makes a great summer for the beach makes a crummy one for the garden: no rain. After a dry spring and summer, water restrictions are often waiting in the wings should a drought watch in New York City change into a drought emergency.

Don't misunderstand the restrictions. Metro Hort, a professional horticulture organization, worked with city officials and drafted new rules in 1991 to take into consideration the value (in dollars and quality of life) of landscape plantings and the understanding that while lawns generally recover from drought stress, trees, shrubs, and other plants may suffer permanent damage or death.

Under the rules, in Stage 1, 2, or 3 of a declared drought emergency, trees, shrubs, other plants, and lawns may be watered only if you follow these guidelines:

- Use a handheld hose (with a maximum of 5 gallons a minute), drip irrigation, or watering can.
- Do not water between 11 A.M. and 7 P.M. In a Stage 1 Emergency, lawns may be watered only between 7 and 9 A.M.

and 7 and 9 P.M. every other day (using house numbers as a
guide, people with even numbers water on even days, odd
numbers on odd days).

- In a Stage 2 or Stage 3 Emergency, all lawn watering is
  prohibited, but trees and shrubs can be watered, following the
  same guidelines.

The rules are designed to make the most of water. Early
morning and evening temperatures are lower, causing less evaporation. Hand-held hoses, drip systems, and watering cans don't
throw water into the air, where some will evaporate or drift before
it lands.

Water well when you water. One inch each week provides
water at the right depth and quantity for most trees, shrubs, and
other plants. A quick sprinkle encourages roots to come to the
surface, where they can dry out.

Remember your street trees. If you think your apartment is
small, look at how *they* live. Restricted root space, underground
obstacles, and compacted soil near streets and sidewalks mean
they need your help.

People who live outside New York City should check with
their local water authorities to determine whether an emergency
has been declared and what, if any, rules are in effect.

Planting Peach Pits

*Truly great peaches are few and far between, so when you have a re-
ally delicious one, planting the pit to ensure a future full of the
same peaches seems a natural.*

It's true that peach stones, or pits, grow up to be peach trees,
but the peaches will have no loyalty to their mother. Like most

other fruit, your peach was the result of years of cross-breeding designed to meet the desires of a very demanding consumer. Dr. Gregory Reighard, associate professor of horticulture at Clemson University in South Carolina, says that breeders are looking for fruit with all the characteristics that both consumers and growers want. Consumers are interested in taste, skin color, size, stones that don't break when bitten into, firmness, minimum fuzz, roundness, flesh color, and consistency. Peach growers are also concerned about disease resistance, time of ripening, acid-to-sugar ratios, and the ability to ship without bruising.

These complicated hybrids have to be reproduced vegetatively from cuttings or by grafting to guarantee that new trees will be true to the parent. Peaches from your stone, however, will likely resemble some ancestor along the breeding route—maybe a good one, maybe not.

But if you are still game, plant the stone outside because it needs a winter cold period to sprout. It may not grow at all, or it may take several years to break though the stone and grow, so some people crack the stone slightly (often with vice grips) before planting. It can be transplanted during spring, but not until it has had a full year to grow. And since seedlings of hybrids are sure to lose some of their pest resistance, use this possibly very long period to familiarize yourself with brown rot, bacterial rot, peach scab, bacterial spot, thrips, red spotted mite, European mite, silver mite, plum curculio, oriental fruit moth, peach tree borer, and lesser peach tree borer. They are looking forward to your peaches too.

Reminders of Home

So many New Yorkers are originally from somewhere else, and they would like a piece of home to remind them. Coming from New Or-

leans, for example, where oleander trees flourished in gardens and parks, you might decide to try one. A nice, bright apartment with a southern exposure sounds perfect.

While oleander (*Nerium oleander*) grows wild in tropical and subtropical climates, the one problem you might face in growing one indoors is providing full sun and the right temperature in winter. Oleanders prefer a winter temperature of around 40 degrees; at normal room temperature they tend to get restless instead of resting, resulting in lanky growth. In summer, oleanders prefer to be outdoors where it is hot and sunny, but a sunny apartment should do.

If you can provide the cool, sunny winter and a hot, sunny summer, growing them should be a breeze. When they are actively growing, oleanders seem to be made for gardeners who typically kill though love. Feel like watering, or forget to water? *Frequent* and *copious* are its favorite adjectives, but oleanders tolerate drought when they have to. Forget to empty excess water from the saucers? They can handle it until you remember. Like to fertilize? Oleanders like to be fed every other week from the time growth begins until early August.

Oleanders are available with single or double flowers, in red, pink, white, salmon, and even yellow. But remember, as beautiful as they look, every part of the oleander is poisonous if eaten.

Oleanders are available in nurseries and by mail order from Louisiana Nursery, 5853 Highway 182, Opelousas, LA 70570, (318) 948-3696, catalog. Serious fans might want to join the International Oleander Society, P.O. Box 3431, Galveston, TX 77552-0431, (409) 762-9334.

Tree Girdling

Kids being kids, sooner or later one of them will strip a band of bark all the way around one of the neighborhood trees. We always think this will kill the tree, but things aren't always that simple.

It's going to depend on how aggressive the kids were. Most likely the bark split off from the tree at the cambium layer, a thin layer of cells whose job is to divide and become other tissues. Those cambium cells that are nearest the outside become phloem cells, part of the complex set of tissues we call bark, which carry the sugar and growth hormones manufactured by the leaves down to the rest of the tree. The cambium cells toward the inside of the tree become xylem cells, part of the sapwood, or living wood, of the tree. Some xylem cells carry water and nutrients up from the roots, while others store food.

If you didn't go blank during that anatomy lesson, you noticed that stripping the bark removes the cells that conduct food down from the leaves, making it sound as if the tree were certain to die. Fortunately, trees are sort of ambidextrous. Remaining cambium cells can move food down with one hand while they hurry to make new phloem with the other.

Generally, although it varies by species, the tree won't die if a narrow strip of bark is removed unless the wound goes beyond the bark into the sapwood. However, if the strip of bark removed is wide, say a foot, the cambium may not be able to make up for the loss in time for the tree to survive, and death is a real possibility in a year or two.

Ultraviolet Blocking Glass

Modern office buildiings typically have ultraviolet blocking glass in their windows. We have all heard that plants need ultraviolet light but we would still like to bring some houseplants to the office, but not if they will die.

It depends. To block ultraviolet (which causes colors to fade) and infrared (which heats the air), a special film is laminated to normal, clear glass. There are several brands, but it is generally called low-e glass ("e" for emissivity, the relative ability to reflect heat). Its function is to turn buildings into thermos bottles, preventing heat from moving inside during the summer and outside during the winter.

Plants use the blue part of the light spectrum, and a tiny bit of the neighboring ultraviolet, to regulate their enzyme and respiratory processes and encourage compact growth with dark green leaves. They skip the green portion, simply reflecting it from the leaf surface, making them appear green. Red light stimulates stem and leaf growth.

Untinted low-e glass blocks light outside the range of wavelengths that plants use, so plants can get along quite well behind it. In fact, the Missouri Botanical Garden's spectacular Climatron is made of low-e glass. As long as there is enough light (brightness and duration) and the temperature is right, growth rates are not noticeably affected.

Plants may suffer, however, when low-e glass is tinted. If gray is added, all light is reduced. Too much gray, and plants suffer as if they were in the shade. Bronze and green tinting are more serious. Bronze blocks blue light, and green blocks both blue and red. Under these conditions, you may want to raise silk flowers instead of spider plants.

New Guinea Impatiens

It's fall and your New Guinea impatiens still look good. You would like to dig them up, bring them inside for the winter just to have something in flower on the windowsill. And then in spring, they can go back outside.

If you bring your impatiens indoors in the fall and they somehow manage to survive, they will be straggly, depressed, and probably covered with spider mites by spring. You'll be sick of them, and they'll be too sick to go back into the garden.

Not to imply that you are not a good caregiver; it's just that not everything makes a good houseplant. New Guinea impatiens do poorly in low light, and the best windowsill in the winter is no substitute for a sunny garden in the summer. Spider mites, on the other hand, love both New Guinea impatiens and the hot, dry indoor life.

If you aren't totally discouraged, at least try to do it right. Cut the foliage back by half, and root prune about the same amount. Don't let the plants dry out, and be sure to use a well-drained potting medium. Keep a plastic bag over them for a week to help prevent moisture stress. When the bag comes off, find the sunniest windowsill, watch for spider mites, and hope for the best.

Oaks from, Yes, Acorns

Sometimes you want to take a piece of the city to the country. Acorns gathered in Central Park during the fall might be nice planted in the Catskills. But you might want to wait a bit before planting them.

No tree resonates within us like an oak. Symbolic of strength, beauty, and longevity, it is one tree that many people want to grow from seed.

Acorns fall from September through November, but it's better to gather them later rather than sooner, since those that fall in
September are often infested with weevils.

Northeastern oaks are divided into two groups: white oaks
and black (or red) oaks. Black oak leaf lobes end in small bristles,
and the inside of the acorn shell has a velvety coating.

To germinate, acorns require a cold period, and although they
can be planted outside in the fall, squirrels, deer, and low germination rates conspire against you. Ken Asmus, president of Oikos
Tree Crops, a Michigan nursery, suggests storing black oak acorns
in a refrigerator in sealed plastic bags with barely damp sphagnum moss. Open the bag occasionally to provide fresh air, and
look for weevil holes in the shells. If you find them, throw out the
acorn. White oak acorns send out roots in the fall, but do not
grow shoots until spring. They can be stored in the same way,
Asmus said, but check often for signs of mold once germination
begins.

In March, plant them an acorn deep in an 8- to 10-inch-tall
pot, to accommodate their long taproot. In a sunny window, they
should send up a shoot in about two weeks. After danger of
frost, move the pots outside until mid-October, when the
seedlings can be transplanted into a permanent sunny location.
Before choosing a spot, take a good look around and up—oaks
can be giants.

Oaks are available in a wide variety, as seedlings or as acorns.
Planting acorns lets you know the oak's birthday, but seed-
lings save you a couple of years. Seedlings are available from
Oikos Tree Crops, P.O. Box 19425, Kalamazoo, MI 49019-
0425, (616) 624-6233, catalog; and Arborvillage Farm Nursery,
P.O. Box 227, Holt, MO 64048, (816) 264-3911, catalog.
Acorns of nearly seventy oaks are available from Sheffield's
Seed Company, 269 Auburn Road, Route 34, Locke, NY 13092,

(315) 497-1058. The International Oak Society, 1093 Mill Road, Pen Argyl, PA 18072-9670, offers a seed exchange among its members.

Penthouse Grasshoppers

One of the strangest stories I have ever heard was about tomatoes growing on the twenty-second floor deck of a penthouse office. It seems each spring for about five years they become infested with grasshoppers, and then each summer they get whiteflies. Insects on the twenty-second floor surely takes the cake.

The whiteflies are easy to explain: they come in on the tomato transplants. Carefully examine next year's young seedlings before bringing them up. Penthouses are no place for whiteflies.

The general opinion of the entomologists I consulted, after they stopped laughing, was that the office occupant does not really have grasshoppers, although none would hazard a guess as to what he really does have or how they got there. Grasshoppers, after all, prefer grasses on open plains, not tomatoes high above Park Avenue. Since the tomatoes seem not to suffer, whatever they are, live and let live. Who knows, maybe they eat some of the whiteflies.

The uninvited guests probably overwinter as eggs laid in the soil of the containers. Fresh, sterile soil may put an end to this nature preserve, but I suspect that the ability to mention them at parties is worth more than any inconvenience they provide.

Of course, the real question here is, Why was he tending tomatoes, not working?

Street Tree Roots

Like most New Yorkers, I have mixed feelings about our street trees. Obviously, I love having them bring a touch of nature to the city, but at the same time I feel sorry for them. It must be torture to be trapped in a small pit. I wondered if anyone was doing anything that might help these trees live better, longer lives?

Something new may happen under New York's streets and sidewalks. There's no room for another subway, but research at Cornell University's Urban Horticulture Institute in Ithaca, New York, and successful experiments in downtown Ithaca have shown that tree roots and urban environments can coexist.

The most serious of the indignities suffered by street trees is their inability to spread roots beyond their too-small pits because of the highly compacted soil found under sidewalks. Compared to the 80 to 150 years these trees might live in the wild, a short life—typically 7 to 15 years—is the result of limited growing space.

Dr. Nina Bassuk, a professor of horticulture at Cornell and the director of the Urban Horticulture Institute, and Jason Grabosky, a graduate student at Cornell, developed a mixture to be used in large urban areas, like city blocks. The mixture is clay loam bonded to 1½-inch pieces of crushed stone with moistened hydrogels, a water-holding compound, serving as a glue to prevent the fine soil particles from settling out like raisins headed for the bottom of the bran flakes. The stone supports the sidewalk, and the soil and small spaces in between provide a pathway for roots. Vigorous roots can grow into the mixture rather than lifting sidewalks or being stymied within their pits. Testing in a 50-foot-wide plaza in Ithaca two years after installation showed that root growth was three times as good.

The new material can't simply replace the soil in a tree pit because that would not provide any additional growing room. Instead, it is used to fill block-long trenches 3 feet deep, which are then covered with paving, leaving openings for the trees. Bassuk said that the New York City Transportation Department, with the New York City Department of Parks and Recreation, will conduct two long-term evaluations of the material as financing and locations become available.

If the studies are successful, the streets of New York, the world's most root-unfriendly place, may soon be home to the spreading roots of healthier, taller, longer-lived trees.

Sprouting Chestnuts

Left alone, grocery store chestnuts can sprout. You have to wonder if you can take advantage of this to attempt to grow your own chestnut tree.

You can certainly try it, but don't count on chestnuts soon, if at all. Ken Asmus, the owner of Oikos Tree Crops in Michigan, said that European chestnuts, the variety most commonly found in grocery stores, may or may not survive in the Northeast. And if the tree does make it, expect to wait eight to twelve years before harvesting any chestnuts.

Instead, look for new hybrid seedling ('Douglas' or 'Sweethart') or grafted chestnuts ('Colossal' or 'Silver Leaf') that combine the chestnut-blight resistance of the Chinese chestnut with the nut size of the American chestnut. Many of these grafted hybrids are now being planted on the eastern seaboard as far south as North Carolina. In a few years, their nuts should be showing up in stores alongside the European ones. The seedlings are available from Oikos, P.O. Box 19425, Kalamazoo, MI 49019-0425, (616) 624-6233, catalog.

Index

Names of plants appear in **bold** type. Page numbers in *italics* refer to illustrations.